Jean-Luc Godard

WISCONSIN FILM STUDIES

Patrick McGilligan, series editor

Jean-Luc Godard

The Permanent Revolutionary

Bert Rebhandl

Translated by Edward Maltby

THE UNIVERSITY OF WISCONSIN PRESS

Publication of this book has been made possible, in part, through
support from the Anonymous Fund of the College of Letters and Science
at the University of Wisconsin–Madison.

The University of Wisconsin Press
728 State Street, Suite 443
Madison, Wisconsin 53706
uwpress.wisc.edu

Gray's Inn House, 127 Clerkenwell Road
London ECIR 5DB, United Kingdom
eurospanbookstore.com

Printed in the United States of America
This book may be available in a digital edition.

Library of Congress Cataloging-in-Publication Data

Names: Rebhandl, Bert, author. | Maltby, Edward (Translator), translator.
Title: Jean-Luc Godard : the permanent revolutionary / Bert Rebhandl ;
translated by Edward Maltby.
Other titles: Jean-Luc Godard. English | Wisconsin film studies.
Description: Madison, Wisconsin : The University of Wisconsin Press, 2023. |
Series: Wisconsin film studies | Originally published under the title Jean-Luc Godard:
De permanente Revolutionär, ©2020 by Paul Zsolnay Verlag Ges.m.b.H., Wien. |
Includes bibliographical references and index.
Identifiers: LCCN 2022028835 | ISBN 9780299341800 (hardcover)
Subjects: LCSH: Godard, Jean-Luc, 1930–2022. | Motion picture producers and directors—
France—Biography. | LCGFT: Biographies.
Classification: LCC PN1998.3.G63 R4313 2023 | DDC 791.4302/33292 [B]—
dc23/eng/20220822
LC record available at https://lccn.loc.gov/2022028835

Contents

Preface

Jean-Luc Godard made his thoughts on biographies clear in the title of one of his most famous films: *Two or Three Things I Know about Her*. This referred to Juliette Jeanson, a Parisian housewife and occasional prostitute played in the 1967 film by Marina Vlady. When it comes to people, whether real or fictional, we can only ever know a fraction of what they are. Of course, this is even more the case for an artist like Jean-Luc Godard, who disappeared ever more into his work over the course of his long life. Personal events became less and less important, as through the power of cinema he was transformed into a kind of world spirit, with a filmography running to more than one hundred titles.

JLG/JLG is the name of an autobiographical film from 1994. The formula is clear enough: Jean-Luc Godard only exists as and through JLG, the figure whom he is and represents, as a filmmaker and an outstanding intellectual of cinema. This book does not attempt to look behind this constellation. That is what the three biographies to date have done, at least to a certain extent—the British one by Colin MacCabe, the American one by Richard Brody, and finally, the most detailed and by far the most comprehensive French one by Antoine de Baecque—and they have certainly brought a great many things to light. Godard's life makes for a highly readable novel. And his life story shall be told in that style here, where appropriate, and not simply serve as scaffolding for a work mainly preoccupied with his films. But first and foremost, Godard must be understood, and pointedly interpreted, as the cipher of the century: JLG—an ambiguous figure teetering between biography and opus, between history and historiography, between subjectivity and politics, between modern art and the digital age. He was a key figure in cinema, and he is the key to many questions and issues of the twentieth and twenty-first centuries.

I have tried to do justice to each of the stations on Godard's path, as even-handedly as possible. The unknown—or at least oft-neglected—Godard of the years 1968 to 1980, when he was first making revolutionary cinema and then television against television, is dealt with just as seriously as the later Godard, whose work is often perceived as inaccessible or rambling.

Work on this book began twice. The initial impetus came in 2012 from Alexander Horwath, then director of the Austrian Film Museum. Personal circumstances then delayed progress until, with Godard's impending ninetieth birthday on December 3, 2020, a date came into view that offered sufficient incentive for me to complete the work after all. Finally, I have resisted the temptations of inconclusiveness that are inherent in an artist as radically open as Godard, and I have attempted to offer a compact interpretation.

Among the helpful friends and colleagues whom I shall thank personally, I would like to mention one publicly: Not only is Volker Pantenburg perhaps the best Godard connoisseur in the German-speaking world but he has also very generously shared his knowledge with me. Regina Schlagnitweit edited the book on behalf of the German publisher—I couldn't have wished for a better editor.

Chronology

1930—Jean-Luc Godard is born in Paris on December 3. His father is a Swiss doctor; his mother comes from an upper-class French family. He spends most of his youth on Lake Geneva.

1946—After the end of World War II, Godard returns to Paris. He becomes part of the cinephile culture that develops around the Cinémathèque française and various film clubs. Friendship with François Truffaut. Acquaintance with the film critic André Bazin and with Henri Langlois, the founder of the Cinémathèque.

1951—Founding of the film magazine *Cahiers du cinéma*, for which Godard writes articles and which develops into the most important journalistic organ of the emerging Nouvelle Vague.

1960—A year after *Les Quatre cents coups* (*The Four Hundred Blows*) by François Truffaut and after five short films, Godard debuts with *À bout de souffle* (*Breathless*). The film becomes a global artistic and commercial success. Extremely intense production follows until 1967, including *Le Mépris*, *Pierrot le fou*, *Alphaville*, *Two or Three Things I Know about Her*. Relationship with the actress Anna Karina.

1967—A new chapter begins with the film *La Chinoise*; the leading actress, Anne Wiazemsky, becomes Godard's new partner. Examination of the philosophy and politics of the student movement and May 1968. Conversation with Jean-Pierre Gorin. Founding of the collective Groupe Dziga Vertov, as a part of which Godard makes agitational and revolutionary films until 1972.

1970—Stay in Palestine at the invitation of the Palestinian organization Fatah.

1971 until 1975—Godard is critically injured in a motorbike accident in Paris. Beginning of the relationship with Anne-Marie Miéville. With *Tout va bien*, Godard and Gorin attempt a commercial revolutionary film starring Jane Fonda and Yves Montand. Godard begins working with video. Foundation of the product company Sonimage. Moves to Grenoble in 1973. Completion of *Ici et ailleurs*, the film that emerges from the failure of the Palestine project.

1975 until 1980—Experimental television works (two series: *Six fois deux* and *France, tour, détour, deux enfants*). Moves to Rolle, Switzerland, where Godard and Miéville lived until his death. National television project in Mozambique. Projects in the United States with Francis Ford Coppola's company American Zoetrope.

1980—With *Sauve qui peut (la vie)*, Godard returns to cinema. A new period of intense productivity follows with films such as *Passion, Je vous salue, Marie, Détective, King Lear, Nouvelle vague*. Collaboration with stars like Isabelle Huppert and Alain Delon.

1991—With *Allemagne neuf zéro*, Godard reacts to the end of communism in Eastern Europe and the fall of the Iron Curtain. His work increasingly takes on the form of essays.

1994—*JLG/JLG*, a "self portrait."

1998—Completion of *Histoire(s) du cinéma*, an eight-part (film) historical collage on which he had been working since 1988.

2001—*Éloge de l'amour* comes out. Depending on how it's counted, this is his third or fourth "first" film. The films that followed are characterized by an increasing interest in universal-historical and media-historical questions.

2006—Exhibition *Voyage(s) en utopie. Jean-Luc Godard, 1946–2006* at the Centre Pompidou in Paris.

2020—An interview Godard gives to a professor at the ECAL art school in Lausanne is streamed on Instagram and shared worldwide. He announces another film project in which he wants to deal with the pioneer of photography, Joseph Nicéphore Niépce.

2022—Godard dies on September 13 in Rolle, Switzerland, at age ninety-one.

Jean-Luc Godard

Introduction

Nothing but cinema may not be the whole cinema.

—JEAN-LUC GODARD, 1957

I am a legend.

—JEAN-LUC GODARD, 1991

In June 2013 a camera belonging to the data giant Google accidentally recorded two famous passers-by in a small town in Switzerland. Jean-Luc Godard and Anne-Marie Miéville, the former already over eighty, the latter fifteen years his junior, were perhaps out running some errands or just taking a walk on a sunny afternoon. The short clip, in which Godard and Miéville appear, did not go unnoticed in the vastness of the Internet and has since appeared on various timelines or been uploaded in various places again and again. Cinema nerds all over the world share and post this find like a precious trophy. The scraps of online folklore that have arisen around it are fitting for a filmmaker who was unceasingly productive for sixty years and who, in that time, experienced all the transformations in cinema, from the temples of the cult of celluloid to the latest digital possibilities.

For more than forty years, Godard lived in Rolle on Lake Geneva, as if in a refuge, withdrawn from the world. As an individual, he became increasingly anonymous. But as an embodiment of cinema, he became more expansive.[1] Godard was a media enthusiast, albeit a subversive one: he was consistently concerned with breaking the power of dominant images. If in recent years he shot films with a mobile phone or in 3D, if he was an early adopter, after 1968, of elements of video technology that were still exotic, he did these things above all in a quest for independence. He wanted to make cinema the way the early-modern Montaigne had written his *Essais*, that is,

3

entirely on his own or within his working partnership with his wife Anne-Marie Miéville, with whom he shared a secluded life beginning in 1977.

In a surprising step taken shortly before his ninetieth birthday, he made his hermitage public. It became possible to visit Godard's workshop in Milan. The Fondazione Prada has displayed the Rolle studio as if it were a permanent installation: two rooms have been reconstructed as exhibition spaces, with all the equipment he used to create his later films and the bits and pieces with which media artists surround themselves. A large picture of Hannah Arendt made one reporter uneasy: Godard, who faced repeated accusations of antisemitism, could now be accused of trying to enlist the author of *Eichmann in Jerusalem* in support of an interpretation of history that is hostile to the state of Israel. "We are straight into controversy and enigma. Godard would not have it any other way," wrote the *Financial Times* correspondent.[2]

In France in 1960, when Jean-Luc Godard made his debut as a director of feature films with *À bout de souffle* (*Breathless*), he changed the grammar of cinema from the ground up. There followed, in rapid succession, a series of works whose names to this day remain linked to Godard's own—many of which have become rather like household names, such as *Deux ou trois choses que je sais d'elle* (*Two or Three Things I Know about Her*) or *The Children of Marx and Coca-Cola* (the subtitle of *Masculin féminin*). This early Godard is still received as a pop star today, for example by Quentin Tarantino, who named his production company "A Band Apart" after Godard's film *Bande à part*, in which three young people run through the Louvre at record speed.

But by 1967 Godard was already tiring of this role, and no filmmaker of the French Nouvelle Vague engaged more radically with the revolutionary experiences of 1968 than he did. He no longer wanted to simply make films: he wanted to make cinema. It was not enough for him to supply an industry with content: he wanted to possess the means of production and become an industry in his own right. In this way, he thought to lend a future to his art, about which he repeatedly raised methodological doubts.

IL CINEMA È UNA INVENZIONE SENZA AVVENIRE. This sentence is written in stark capitals underneath the screen of a projection room in the Roman film studios Cinecittà, where in *Le Mépris* (*Contempt*, 1963), the

American producer Jerry Prokosch has gathered a few people to watch a screen test for a film version of Homer's *Odyssey*. Cinema is an invention without a future. Louis Lumière, one of the two French inventors of cinema, is credited with this dictum, which has proven to be wrong in its time, and yet perhaps true over the longer term. Of course, measured against the dignity of the ancient epic, one of the oldest European texts, this is an argument over trifles; alongside the history of the *Odyssey*'s impact, cinema has so far been a mere episode. But the passing emphasis with which Godard inserts the sentence into the picture is characteristic of his entire opus. More than any other filmmaker, Godard has not simply understood and developed cinema as a series of individual achievements but has also made his work an ongoing commentary on the medium with which he began. "Le cinéma," as they say in France, has a much more pronounced emphasis on cultural weight than does "das Kino" in German.

Godard, as a filmmaker, is the permanent revolutionary of cinema, and of the methods he deploys, the slogan, the quotation, the insert, and the aperçu are among the most important. The sentence "Cinema is an invention without a future" is all those things—a slogan that in 1964 was already pointing ahead to the revolutionary rupture of 1968; a quotation that, with its originator Louis Lumière, qualified cinema as being already obsolete from its outset; and an aperçu that hangs in space, inconsequential because it does not entail any consequence. Godard claims no authority for the phrase. He merely assigns it a certain position in a polyvocal discourse that unfolds through the images and sounds of *Le Mépris* and also—tangentially, yet centrally—addresses the future of cinema within a technical context and an industrial system dominated by producers and determined by financial interests.

Godard has gradually migrated away from this system over the course of a career that has lasted for more than six decades. He has dismantled the form of the feature film, a form that he has been playing with from the very beginning—"like a child investigating a toy with a hammer."[3] Apparently a hipster *avant la lettre* in 1960, he has become a hermit, whom today's YouTube generation has to track down using surveillance images. In the subsystems of the democratic public sphere in his two countries of reference, Switzerland and France, he no longer really belongs anywhere. In his adopted spiritual home of Germany, he was awarded the Adorno Prize in 1995 in an attempt to build a bridge between Godard the philosopher of images and Godard the philosopher *tout court*.

Almost all his films have premièred in Cannes in recent years (*Film Socialisme* was released simultaneously as video-on-demand in 2010, an innovative approach at the time), and there was even a theatrical release for his great recent film *Le Livre d'image* (*The Image Book*, 2018), which for now stands as the final, universal poetic summation of his work. But all the same, box office receipts make it clear: Godard no longer belongs to cinema. But he does not belong to the visual arts either, although he made an attempt in this direction in 2006 with an exhibition in Paris, and the Fondazione Prada is preparing his afterlife in the museums with the installation in Milan. Nor does he belong to the literary world or the sphere of the public intellectual, although he has strong, if reluctant, affinities with both. Volker Pantenburg wrote with some justification that one could "interpret his entire work as the compensatory gesture of a failed writer,"[4] and designations such as "multimedia poet" (Michael Witt) or "filmic writer" ("cinéaste-ecrivain," Raymond Bellour) hit on something essential. But the Nobel Prize, which he would deserve as much as Elias Canetti, Octavio Paz, or Peter Handke, an admirer of his early films at least, has thus far eluded him, because a literature and a philosophy composed of images and sounds simply does not fit anywhere. In the absence of alternative classifications, then, Godard can still be said to belong to cinema, having appropriated its history in a dual way: that is, he began to write the history of the art (in filmic form) while he himself was still revising it, and with a much sharper awareness of aspects of form, epoch, and technology than almost any of his colleagues. The *Histoire(s) du cinéma* (1988–98) are the potentially infinite, later pictorial texts that Godard wrote as a historical summary of the medium at the very moment when the technical medium of cinema—celluloid—began to disappear. With the possibilities of video, the image once again became "writable" in a different way than Godard and his contemporaries had thought in the era immediately after World War II.

At that time, they were still oriented toward the painter's brushstroke and the writer's penmanship, in other words, toward a debate about the respective potentials of the arts, which after the war was being conducted with reference to cinema. Godard never let this debate die away, although at times he had to carry it on almost single-handedly. His later works run the gamut from painting to the technical impressionism that can be obtained from the algorithmic camera optics of modern devices. And so, in the words of the great French film critic André Bazin, we might understand Godard's work—and his interpretation—as being oriented toward the future: "Cinema has not yet been invented!"[5]

CHAPTER 1

Modern Times

1950 to 1959

In 1950 Godard made two débuts into the world of cinema. He played the lead role in Jacques Rivette's short film *Le Quadrille*. The money for the production, he would later claim, "was stolen from an uncle." A contemporary account comes from the English critic Tom Milne.

> One evening late in 1950, at a ciné-club in the Rue Danton in Paris, I happened to attend one of those purgatorial programmes of 16 mm experimental shorts which are sent to try the cineaste. One film, however, had something: a certain hypnotic, obsessional quality as, for some forty minutes, it attempted to show what happens when nothing happens by observing, in strict objectivity, behavior in a dentist's waiting-room. No plot, no dialogue; simply the play of silence, covert glances, magazines nervously skimmed, cigarettes furtively lit, as strangers casually thrown together try to come to terms with each other with nothing to come to terms about. Called *Quadrille*, the film achieved a minor *succès de scandale* when the half of the audience still present at the end almost came to blows in passionate disagreement. It wasn't until years later that light dawned as to the name of the director and leading actor: respectively, Jacques Rivette and Jean-Luc Godard.[1]

In June of the same year, the *Gazette du cinéma* published an article about the American director Joseph Mankiewicz, whom Godard, then making his debut as a critic, considered so extraordinarily brilliant that he chose a comparison that was not immediately obvious: "I am not afraid to give him as important a place as Alberto Moravia occupies in European literature."[2] Here, with the greatest matter-of-factness (and with the presumption of the genial know-it-all), Godard brings together two areas that have almost nothing in common. There can be hardly any comparison between the American studio system of film production and the European literary public, except precisely in terms of the sensibility of a postwar generation that was confronted with new impressions on all fronts and did not shy away from fierce debates about how to order these impressions.

That there were many impressions, right after the war, is made clear by another testimony from that time: François Truffaut was a very young critic for the magazine *Travail et Culture*. He met the eighteen-year-old Godard for the first time in 1948.

> What struck me most about him was the way he absorbed books. When we were at friends' houses in the evening, he would easily open up to forty books and he always read the first and last pages. He was always very nervous and impatient. He liked cinema as much as any of us, but he was capable of going to see fifteen minutes each of five different films in the same afternoon. . . . After having told us well for months that he was going off to Jamaica, he left one day with his father. When he returned, we hoped for a long, detailed description of his trip. Nothing. From that moment on, he no longer spoke.[3]

This memory dates from the year 1970. It tells of an encounter between adolescents in an era of upheaval. The sensitive Truffaut meets the restless Godard. Films and books pointed the way to a new era, but was there enough time to read everything, to see everything? Godard was fifteen years old when France was liberated. Intellectually, he was a child of the *libération*. By nationality, however, he was Swiss, the son of a doctor who ran a hospital for wealthy patients on Lake Geneva and married Odile Monod, a daughter of an upper-class Parisian family from the eighth arrondissement. Godard later cast the succession of generations in terms of mythical imagery: "It was like a Greek myth, my grandparents were gods, my parents were demigods, and I, the child, was merely a man."[4] This interpretation echoes the "brief transfiguration" that the narrator witnesses in Proust's *In Search of Lost Time* when he sees the Guermantes family in the theater: "And when I turned my eyes to their box, far more than on the ceiling of the theatre, painted with cold and lifeless allegories, it was as though I had seen, thanks to a miraculous rendering of the clouds that ordinarily veiled it, the Assembly of the Gods in the act of contemplating the spectacle of mankind, beneath a crimson canopy, in a clear lighted space, between two pillars of Heaven." Godard's Combray lay on Lake Geneva. In the small town of Anthy, where his father worked, he experienced an idyllic childhood,[5] but his relationship with his Parisian relatives was strained. Among the Monods there were strict Pétainists, supporters of the regime that collaborated with Germany, while his parents in Switzerland had a pacifist attitude. His father was committed to the Red Cross, while the son followed the fates of the armies of the great powers like football teams, maintaining a sportsmanlike neutrality. He experienced Rommel's defeat at El Alamein as a personal defeat for himself, as a fan.

In 1946 Godard left Switzerland and returned to Paris, where he had spent the first four years of his life. He moved into a room in the Rue d'Assas near the Jardin du Luxembourg. From here he began to explore a new landscape. The many offerings of the *ciné-clubs* and the Cinémathèque française, at that time in the Avenue de Messine, became for him an alternative kind of educational institution from 1947. "I discovered cinema when I was seventeen, reading the *Revue du cinéma*, which opened up a new world for me, an artistic continent I had never heard of before and which I was now able to survey myself thanks to the researchers who described it."[6]

But just as he was about to launch himself into this new world, there was a serious setback. He provoked a break with the Monod family with an act that, considering their divine status, was almost Promethean: he stole signed first editions by Paul Valéry, who was revered by the family and Monod's personal friend, from a specially reserved "Valerianum" in the flat on the Boulevard Raspail. He sold them, was caught, and was forced to return to Switzerland for a while in 1947. His childhood, which he later looked back on as resembling "a Paradise," was over. In a piece of writing reported by his biographer Antoine de Baecque, Godard struck out against the Monods with a quote from Bismarck: "In my nature I am not born to be a spy, but I believe we deserve your thanks if we condescend to follow malignant reptiles into their cave to observe their actions."[7]

There is a concept that clarifies the contentious element of his younger years (and contextualizes it within an idiosyncratic historical picture): together with Francois Truffaut, around 1950 Godard was one of the "Young Turks" of a film criticism that aspired to more than just carrying on conventional arguments, although without falling into the other extreme of being dominated by politico-ideological jargon. The historical Young Turks of the Ottoman Empire, to which radical groups of the French left also explicitly referred in the 1930s, took the name as a way of declaring themselves passionate modernizers. Even if the young critics only adopted the term playfully, it nevertheless reveals a lot. The allusion to a historically powerful reform movement from the early twentieth century could only have been regarded as a multiple provocation in France immediately after liberation. Above all it would have been received as a criticism of that society as being outdated, even though French society was apparently in a mood for change.

Godard's most important criticism in the years in which he entered the field was also one of the most voluble and most dazzling: He found Roger Vadim's *Sait-on jamais* to be "resolutely modern"—indeed, this was his view of the medium as a whole: "As a matter of fact, the cinema is in any case too resolutely modern for there to be any question of it following any path other than an open one, a perpetual aesthetic inauguration."[8] But just what modernity meant in France around 1950 was not at all clear, and indeed Godard's own writings testify to a characteristic openness in this respect. From today's perspective, many theorists and intellectuals of cinema identify the beginning of modernity with the moment of liberation from fascist systems. Three films by Roberto Rossellini are prototypical of this new beginning: *Roma, città aperta*; *Paisà*; and *Germania, anno zero* are founding documents of neorealism, the first substantial movement of renewal in cinema of the postwar period. The critic Serge Daney, born in 1944, alluding to a term roughly equivalent to the German "economic miracle," has called the era then beginning "the 'thirty glorious years' of modern cinema."[9] As a starting point, Daney expressly names the film *Roma, città aperta*, which tells of the Roman resistance against the Germans in 1943. For the most important critic of the era, André Bazin, neorealism became the most important example of a principled redefinition of cinema, based on photographic technique: "The guiding myth, then, inspiring the invention of cinema, is the accomplishment of . . . an integral realism, a recreation of the world in its own image, an image unburdened by the freedom of interpretation of the artist or the irreversibility of time."[10]

André Bazin was the decisive figure in the culture of cinephilia,[11] which the young Godard encountered in Paris. He was a critic, curator, and mediator. In the numerous *ciné-clubs* that existed during these years, the "holy trinity" of presentation, projection, and discussion was considered mandatory. During the German occupation, Paris had been largely cut off from American cinematic releases, but now it was making up for lost time. This culture of cinephilia found its most important outlet in the film magazine *Cahiers du cinéma*, which was founded in 1951. But even before that, and alongside it, there were a multitude of publications in which the "Young Turks" could try their hand and in which Bazin developed his theory of open cinema in a series of programmatic texts published in quick succession. He was also interested in offering an interpretation of commercial cinema as potentially avant-garde. The whole approach of Objectif49, the film club that Bazin cofounded, was based on this idea of a "popular vocation of cinema" and was intended to further it.[12] During these years, Objectif49 would organize *ciné-club* screenings of new films by honorary member Orson Welles, William Wyler, Preston Sturges, and also by Jean Renoir (who deliberately undermined his status as a classicist with his postwar works and posed a major puzzle for the critics), Robert Bresson, and Roberto Rossellini.

Modernity had necessarily become a flexible criterion, given that around 1950, the main oppositional school of criticism promoted a principally political understanding of the term. For the communist critic Geoges Sadoul, cinema had been most truly realized in the Soviet Union. In his opinion, no fewer than three "golden ages" had followed one after another in a short period of time; and *Padenie Berlina* (1949) sent him into raptures: "[The director] Mikhail Ğiaureli has recovered the simplicity of Giotto and his pupils, as displayed in the frescoes of Padua or Assisi. Stalin, in his presence among the people is this brother, this true comrade."[13] The scene with Stalin soaring in an airplane, which in its propagandistic naivety might have been taken as an imposition, inspires Sadoul to make an art-historical comparison of a sort that suggests that Godard read this text. In his 1950 essay *Towards a Political Cinema*, the latter adopts a similarly liturgical tone:

"The actor infallibly becomes what he once was, the priest. *The Fall of Berlin* and *The Battle of Stalingrad* are Masses for a coronation. In relation to history, the Soviet actor interprets his role (his social character) in two ways: as saint, or as hero." Godard speaks of the "spontaneous and passionate poetry of the event" and concludes: "No doubt only Russia feels at this moment that the images moving across its screens are those of its own destiny."[14]

The more systematic text on the subject of political cinema was written at almost exactly the same time by André Bazin. In *Le cinéma soviétique et le mythe de Staline*, he addresses the question of why in Western films there is a reluctance to portray important people during their lifetimes, as was readily done in the Soviet Union in the case of Stalin. Bazin finds his answer in a reflection on the historicity of individuals. Stalin can appear as a character in the propaganda films because he is not judged by the "human measure" that is usually applied to characters and their behavior. He does not appear in a psychological light but rather in a theological one. The form of his representation as an infallible and omniscient leader is mythic. He is cinematically embalmed: in his lifetime he incarnates the end of a history (specifically, that of the Great Patriotic War, but generalizable beyond that) that he has victoriously steered.

The differences between Godard's article and the one by Bazin, who was then at the height of his creative powers despite serious illness, are telling. The young critic, searching for his criteria, even plays with the linguistic registers of religion to lend a film he admires the appropriate aura. Bazin, on the other hand, personally a devout Catholic until his premature death, also sees through the political religion of communism, because his theory of film requires him to undertake a mental demythologization: in the film images of Stalin, he sees the mummy that propaganda has turned him into.

The juxtaposition of these two pieces, one by a novice, the other by an authority, finds further poignancy in Godard's final sentence. Whereas Bazin moves onto the ontology of cinema, Godard ends with a provocative appeal: "Unhappy film-makers of France who lack scenarios, how is it that you have not yet made films about the tax system?"[15] Here, with a mixture of chutzpah and sarcasm, Godard is almost intuitively picking up on a debate that was just beginning when this article was written and would preoccupy film criticism intensely for more than a decade. The key term is *sujet*. In reaction to this concept, the central category of cinephile criticism of the fifties was developed: *mise-en-scène*, that is, the process of staging a work in all its aspects, including camera work, lighting, color, setting, and costumes. The *Gazette du cinéma*, in which Godard's article on political cinema appeared, served as the short-lived organ of a pioneering regrouping within the circles of Parisian film enthusiasts. For the central figures of this magazine, the film club CCQL (Ciné-Club du Quartier Latin) was the most important meeting place. The publication set itself apart from the authoritative Objectif49, whose president was Jean Cocteau and which provided Bazin with his most important forum. The *Gazette*, on the other hand, published the young cinephiles who would be found occupying the front row (and the floor in front of it) at the Cinémathèque française, where they were acquiring an education in film: Godard, Jacques Rivette, Jean Douchet, Jean Gruault, Charles Bitsch, Suzanne Schiffman (née Klochendler). Maurice Schérer, who was several years older and who used the pseudonym Éric Rohmer for his later film criticism writings (and then for his films), was the authoritative figure in this group, which defined itself against the existing authorities. In the first three issues of the *Gazette*, Alexandre Astruc and Schérer, who both also wrote for *Les Temps modernes*—the newspaper of the followers of Jean-Paul Sartre and Simone de Beauvoir—helped carry out a journalistic coup. Sartre published his text *The Cinema Is Not a Bad School* (*Le cinéma n'est pas une mauvaise école*) in installments. This was a transcript of a speech that Sartre had given as a young teacher in 1931. This was around the time of the introduction of sound in film, an innovation that Sartre expected would be short lived: "I believe that film has bought itself the right to fall silent." But the contemporary interest that made publication worthwhile after twenty years lay in the reflections on the place of cinema in comparison with the other arts, namely theater and music. Compared with theater, Sartre emphasized cinema's clearly greater aesthetic of impact: "For this art will penetrate you more thoroughly than any other, and it will gradually make you love beauty in all its forms." On the other hand, film had something in common with music, which Sartre calls "thematic unity." As in composition, in which several musical themes are taken "to their most perfect unfolding," film is also able to create a "cinematographic polyphony" through the thematic connection of motifs or themes, an "ambiguous, meaning-laden concatenation," whose possible significances Sartre illustrates with examples from G. W. Pabst's *Die freudlose Gasse* (1925).[16] Godard carried out intensive experimentation in the *Gazette du cinéma*. He also used the pseudonym Hans Lucas, a translation of his two first names—an indication of a deeper inclination toward the German linguistic and intellectual world, which shines through at many points in these writings, for example, in references to the National Socialist propaganda films that were being shown in Paris at the time, of which he acquired a detailed knowledge.

From April 1951, the newly founded film magazine *Cahiers du cinéma* became the forum for this generation. The young critics were now no longer writing for short-lived, hectographed, hand-distributed media but in a professional publication that they would henceforth use as a platform. Within the editorial team, they were perceived as a group named after their oldest representative: the "Schérer gang" came over like "dogs playing at bowling" (which is how Alexandre Astruc described the vivid impression left by the young cinephiles. He added, however, that this group would give the *Cahiers* "a dimension of its own" in the years to come. A "new cinema" was announcing itself here, for the time being, through critical articles.[17] The Nouvelle Vague had basically already formed, and its individual representatives were busy positioning themselves. Maurice Schérer, using his *nom de plume* Éric Rohmer for the first time, provided important themes and contributed to his "school." He was regarded as the right wing of the *Cahiers*, especially by leftists like Pierre Kast, who belonged to Schérer's generation and had been a member of the Resistance. The two editors in chief, Jacques Doniol-Valcroze and Bazin, had to do plenty of mediation, but ultimately they sided with the "Young Turks." A young man arose from this group to become its most important figure alongside Schérer (and Godard would be measured against him again and again over the following two decades): François Truffaut, André Bazin's "foster son." Truffaut grew up as a half orphan under much less idyllic circumstances than Godard did. But there were significant parallels in each man's rebellions: both were guilty of theft and both were temporarily confined in psychiatric hospitals. Truffaut was sent to prison for embezzlement and made a serious mistake when he enlisted in the military. To avoid being sent to Indochina, he deserted, and it took several interventions from Bazin and other friends to finally have him declared unfit for service. While Godard commuted between Paris and Switzerland during these years and also undertook a major trip to Latin America at the end of 1950 (he accompanied his father, who was considering opening a clinic in the Caribbean, then continued on his own via Peru to Brazil), Truffaut struggled to make ends meet in Paris. Even then, they shared a restless appetite for books and films; articles emerged almost out of daily conversation, or so it seemed.

In 1952 Jean-Luc Godard's first article appeared in *Cahiers du cinéma*. It was a short text, only two pages long, and the film it addressed was hardly worth talking about. *No Sad Songs for Me* (1950) by Rudolph Maté tells the story of a woman who suffers from cancer but keeps this secret from her husband and even provides him with a new companion for when she dies. Godard takes the film as a jumping-off point for several reflections on fundamentals. For him, the "classically constructed script" here goes hand in hand with "considerable psychological force," a force that is evident in the close-ups of Margaret Sullavan, whose "heart" is revealed in the "oddity of her modesty." "The cinema makes reality specific. It would be useless for it to try to make more of the instant than the instant itself contains."[18]

Shortly afterward, with an article on Alfred Hitchcock, Godard made his first intervention in one of the crucial controversies of those years. The title of his review of *Strangers on a Train* (1951) is programmatic: "Suprématie du sujet" (Supremacy of the subject). Two lines of argument cross in this piece. One concerns the assessment of Hitchcock (and of American cinema as a whole), the other the question of what makes good material for cinema. Many of the young critics' insights crystallized around their assessments of Hitchcock. A large part of the intellectual landscape in France after World War II was openly anti-American. This is especially true of the communist Georges Sadoul, who rejected most Hollywood output for ideological reasons. The *sujet*, the subject matter of a film, became a fertile field of contention, to which the debates over formalism in the socialist countries provided a constant background presence. Sadoul often judged the importance of films in terms of whether they were constructed around a worthwhile theme. Conservative critics had contrary ideas about content: they tended to think in terms of literary classics, whereas Sadoul had his eye on the progress of socialism. But in both cases, the value of films was measured by their content. With Hitchcock (and implicitly with many Hollywood genre and B movies), the center of gravity shifted. For him, it was the execution that counted above all, or what is described by the term *mise-en-scène*, which was already in common use at the time. It was thus a double provocation for Godard to title his article about *Strangers on a Train* (published under the name Hans Lucas) as "Supremacy of the Subject." The depiction of the content gave Godard an opportunity to reflect on modernity. "I know no other recent film, in fact, which better conveys the condition of modern man, who must escape his fate without the help of the gods. Probably, too, the cinema is particularly suited to record the drama, to make the best not so much of the myth of the death of God . . . as the baleful quality it suggests." The example that he goes on to offer is audacious. For Godard, the murderer's adventure is the important one here, and Hitchcock, in his opinion, underlines this through his staging, namely by showing "the Promethean image of his [the killer's] murderous little hand, his terror in face of the unbearable brilliance of the fire it steals."[19]

This formulation reveals an overemphasis on the concept of *mise-en-scène* that would remain a feature of the Young Turks' reception of Hitchcock throughout. To see a Promethean act in a shameful murder at a fairground testifies to the pathos through which Godard and his friends were transforming elements taken from pop culture into a new mythology. Speaking of *Strangers on a Train*, Godard concluded: "The point is simply that all the freshness and invention of American films springs from the fact that they make the subject the motive of the *mise-en-scène*."[20]

At the same time, Truffaut was brooding over an essay on the subject of the *sujet*, which would not appear until two years later and which would have far-reaching consequences: *A Certain Tendency of the French Cinema* takes the concept of the *sujet* so literally that Truffaut even had the writing pair Jean Aurenche and Pierre Bost send him an unpublished script, which he then took apart with great relish. The text is a polemic against the conventional French cinema of those years, for which the term *cinéma de qualité* (cinema of quality) had been in use for some time. *A Certain Tendency* eventually appeared in the *Cahiers* at the beginning of 1954, after Bazin had demanded repeated improvements and for certain things to be toned down. But even in its final, published version, it is difficult today to comprehend from where it drew its power. The effect of the piece probably lay above all in a new concept: filmmakers could now also be *auteurs*. Truffaut distinguishes psychological realism from a *cinéma d'auteurs*, still defined above all by the fact that directors "often write their own dialogue and in some cases make up the stories they bring to the big screen."[21] In other words, their aim is to make films autonomous, to free them from their dependence on literature. In a significant passage, Gustave Flaubert is called as a chief witness in this connection, for like the young critics of cinephilia, the author of *Madame Bovary* was skeptical of the significance of the *sujet*. "For the first time in French literature, the author of that novel, Gustave Flaubert, adopted a distanced, external attitude to his subject matter, which thus became like an insect under an entomologist's microscope," Truffaut wrote. The optical metaphor is no accident here: in this conception, Flaubert becomes a literary cameraman, an author who wants to overhaul the technical apparatus using language. His novels do not attempt to "embellish" stories with "subtleties" but, on the contrary, aim to arrive at a substantial characterization of the novel form in abstraction from these embellishments. The *cinéma d'auteurs* was also in search of a genuine cinema that does not allow itself to be tied down by the subject, by the story.

It is characteristic of Godard that he eschewed the detail of these debates by making his concept of *sujet* so expansive that it basically encompasses all the possible models of the photographic medium of film. He operated with an arsenal of terms whose meaning he kept suspended in limbo. His possible real meaning is concealed behind multiple different approaches. In the interpersonal dispute itself, however, Godard took a clear position: he was in favor of Hitchcock and thus on the side of the critical minority that saw itself as an avant-garde and put its pioneering role at the service of defending a new classicism that it represents as authentically modern. In his second major text of 1952, Godard chose his title as an act of renewed and deliberate provocation. "Defence and Illustration of Classical Construction" cannot but be understood as taking aim at André Bazin,[22] who in his essay *The Evolution of the Language of Cinema* had described the stylistic device of depth of focus, used most notably in Orson Welles's *Citizen Kane*, as a substantial achievement in terms of *mise-en-scène*. As is so often the case, it becomes apparent here that Godard's contribution was not aimed at conceptual clarification. Rather, he made use of aesthetic and filmic oppositions such as depth of field versus shot/countershot or *"plan-séquence"* versus "classic construction" as an opportunity to find contrary observations with which to feed his appetite for provocation.

∼

On October 1, 1952, another short article appeared in *Les Amis du cinéma* in which Godard describes an evening's encounter with Éric Rohmer that develops into a dialogue. In it, essential motifs of the current discourse are recapitulated in a play. Rohmer talks about a film project. He wants to adapt *Les Petites Filles modèles* by the Comtesse de Ségur very faithfully. Godard is surprised by the choice of material from popular women's literature of the nineteenth century: "I was astonished. What! The scriptwriter . . . object of admiration in the postwar avant-garde circles—was this man to make his début in the professional format with the rosiest story in the Bibliotheque Rose?"[23] Rohmer defends himself: "There are, of course, more cruel stories, but quite apart from the fact that I shall have little difficulty in proving that the adventures of Sophie Fichini of Fleurville can rival the most epic of Westerns, I don't think this is a problem. . . . I believe the cinema more capable than anybody of glorifying a conception of man which is that of both Racine and Goethe." Godard suspects, with good reason, that with this project Rohmer might appear reactionary, but the latter tackles this "conventional" project in such a way that it could be seen as connected to neorealism, according to which films would be shot "as if commanded by God." "Rohmer lit a Chesterfield and blew the smoke thoughtfully to the sky." Godard only reports this conversation in broad outline, but he seems to have sensed that there was more at stake here than merely the transition from critique to practice. At that time, the first films of the later Nouvelle Vague were beginning to take shape, but for the time being only in the form of ideas that haunted conversations. For Godard, however, this description of a city scene was also a form of farewell. He stole money from the cash register of the *Cahiers du cinéma* and thus made himself persona non grata for some time in the circles that dominated his Parisian life. He returned to Switzerland and stayed there for four years.

His first film was made during this period. *Opération "Béton"* (1954) is a short documentary film about the construction of a dam in the Swiss Alps. The Grande Dixence dam is a monument of modernity, and Godard explicitly compares it to the Eiffel Tower (whose height the dam nearly rivals) in the inserts with which the film begins. The work has the character of a military undertaking. *Opération "Béton"* is clearly a commissioned work, an industrial film about mastering nature set to classical music, in which the main aim is to present the project in a positive light. Functional metaphors are used both in the off-screen commentary (which Godard himself edited and then recorded) and in his visual elements (shots of conveyor belts and gears). Godard speaks at one point of "marvelous machinery," and the technical details that explain and justify the construction of a power plant like Grande Dixence also characterize the style of his explanations.

The pragmatism with which he approached *Opération "Béton"* proved profitable. The company bought the film, Godard received what was by his standards a considerable fee, thereby winning himself a measure of personal and artistic freedom for a time. This he used to make his first short film, *Une femme coquette* (*A Flirtatious Woman*, 1955), shot in Geneva. The story is based on a novel by Guy de Maupassant, *Le Signe*, in which a woman makes a gesture to a man, signaling that she is inviting him to a tryst. In a frivolous experiment with mimicry, another woman watches her from across the street: "I got out my opera glasses to take a closer look at her method. Oh, it was very simple: first a quick look, then a smile, then a nod of the head that meant: 'Are you coming up?' But it was so subtle, so slight, so discreet, that you had to be pretty smart to do it as well as she did. I began to wonder if I could do it as well, that little movement of the head, up and down, bold and subtle. It really was very subtle, her little sign. I went to try it in front of the mirror." Godard moves the action outdoors, and he himself plays the suitor who reacts to a signal from a coquette and seeks her out. A young woman named Agnes observes the scene and reenacts it in a park. A man looks up from reading his newspaper, and things get too hot for Agnes: he chases her by car right up to the door of her flat. Helpless now, Agnes takes the fifty francs that the man matter-of-factly thrusts upon her, and she gives herself up to him. The incident has a classical framing: Agnes writes everything down in a letter to a friend, seeking to exculpate herself. Godard turns these ten minutes into an homage to the cinema of the silent film era: the gestures are a little exaggerated, the chase is a concession to the same element in slapstick films. A central motif of his later films is already established here: authenticity and alienation combine in the phenomenon of love for sale. At the same time, he makes good on what

Rohmer had cast as one of his goals in their discussion prior to Godard's temporary departure from Paris: that is, rendering a conventional story personal. However, he does this in an ambivalent way, appearing in three different roles: "Jean-Luc Godard presents" a film "staged by Hans Lucas." And the actor? This is the Godard of those years, a slender young man with a cigarette, a duster, and the glasses of an intellectual.

~

In 1956 Godard was back in Paris. He was ambitious and measured himself against Orson Welles, who had made *Citizen Kane* at the age of 25. A substantial screenplay based on Goethe's *Die Wahlverwandtschaften* (*Elective Affinities*) bears the title *Odile*, which could easily refer to Ottilie but also to Godard's mother, Odile Monod, who died in a traffic accident in Paris in 1954. In the meantime, the "Young Turks" were almost exclusively preoccupied with their own film projects, although the flow of articles never let up. In the *Cahiers du cinéma*, Godard continued working on the themes that had exercised him since 1952. In an essay on Hitchcock's *The Man Who Knew Too Much* (1956), he once again spells out the tension between modernity and classicism in the seemingly exaggerated mechanics of Hitchcock's suspenseful dramaturgy: "People say that Hitchcock lets the wires show too often. But because he shows them, they are no longer wires. They are the pillars of a marvelous architectural design made to withstand our scrutiny."[24] Godard takes up an *aperçu* by Paul Valéry about puppets and spins it out further: the classical impression given by Hitchcock's cinematic puppet show arises precisely from the fact that its artificiality is made so plain.

A few weeks later, in a text on montage, "Montage, My Fine Care," Godard returned to his defense of the classical construction. He does not revise anything but takes additional, decisive steps. He emphasizes that "montage is above all an integral part of *mise-en-scène*." The *mise-en-scène* is not intended to make montage superfluous (through the spatial and continuous development of a scene), which was the view Bazin tended toward, but rather, it finds its highest expression in accentuating development through cleverly placed cuts. For Godard, the beauty of a work is virtually doubled when "a film brilliantly edited gives the impression of having suppressed all direction."[25] For Godard, the editor does not belong exclusively in the editing room but should also be present on the set, because that is where it becomes apparent what cuts are required. For Godard, it is not simply a matter of "cutting on movement" but also of what he tentatively describes as "cutting a scene just as it was going to become interesting. In so doing, the editor would be taking his first steps in direction." Godard, who was in fact editing for the producer Pierre Braunberger at the time, was anticipating his transition into practice but also implicitly already writing about the approach to montage that would shape his own cinematic work: an organization of cinematic transitions that would exchange "cutting on movement" for more interesting, contrary transitions.

Between 1956 and 1959 Godard was involved in the film business in many different ways. He wrote press releases for Fox in France; he wrote dialogue for a film by Pierre Schoendoerffer and Jacques Dupont about the Afghan war in the nineteenth century (*La Passe du diable*); and he continued to write film reviews in the *Cahiers du cinéma* and in *Arts* magazine, at which Truffaut had resigned his position. In his major pieces on Nicholas Ray, Mizoguchi Kenji, Ingmar Bergman, or Anthony Mann, it is striking that Godard pursues a special variant of the *politique des auteurs* ("auteur politics" or "politics of authorship"). His aim is to describe these directors set against the background of the entire history of art and culture. This often leads him to make passionate, unguarded statements, for example, that Anthony Mann is "the most Virgilian of filmmakers" or that Nicholas Ray's *Bitter Victory* is "the most Goethian of films" (a statement that he immediately qualifies as having little meaning). Godard is not interested in defining certain characteristics of directors and tracing their artistic development. Rather, he accentuates their features in a way that could be described as momentary essentializations. In one case, he goes so far as to say: "And the cinema is Nicholas Ray." About Mizoguchi, who passed away in 1956, he writes: "When he re-creates old Japan, he goes beyond tinsel and anecdote to give us the unvarnished truth with a mastery equaled only by a Francesco, Giullare di Dio. Never have we seen with our own eyes the Middle Ages exist with such intensity of atmosphere."[26] The article on Anthony Mann's *Man of the West* appeared in February 1959 in the *Cahiers du cinéma*, a few months before the Nouvelle Vague found its breakthrough at the Cannes Festival with *Les Quatre cents coups* by Francois Truffaut.

Jean-Luc Godard (*left*) visiting with François Truffaut during the filming of
Fahrenheit 451, 1966 (ANGLO ENTERPRISES / Ronald Grant Archive / Mary
Evans, image no. 0103151003)

In May 1959 Godard brought to Paris his third short film (filmed in
1957) belonging to the Nouvelle Vague: *Tous les garçons s'appellent Patrick
(Charlotte et Véronique)* (*All the Boys Are Called Patrick*). This film is based
on a screenplay by Éric Rohmer and tells the story of two female students
who each, independently of the other, meet a young man. Jean-Claude
Brialy plays this rather uncouth Casanova, who looks to Charlotte "like that
American actor, Anthony" (Perkins, she can't recall his last name), whereas
Véronique thinks he resembles Cary Grant. The two share a flat in which
Godard has hung two pictures: Pablo Picasso and James Dean are the cultural markers here. Piano music in the style of a *divertissement* shows how
seriously the twenty minutes are to be taken—that is, not very! The first
few minutes, in which Charlotte and Véronique are still alone, one busy
with cosmetics, the other laying aside Hegel's aesthetics, her ear pressed to
the radio, from which the word "Casanova" can be heard, form an early

iteration of those complex sound-image montages that will later form a
pillar of Godard's style. It is a scene in which intimacy is broken by media
noise and into which the demands of fashion also intrude from outside,
for that morning Véronique is already reciting what she wants to buy for
herself that day: a tartan skirt, a coat, a beret. In the café to which Charlotte goes with Patrick after she has given in to his advances, a man sits in
the background reading *Arts* magazine, where Godard succeeded Truffaut
as film critic.

"Le cinéma français crève sous ses fausses légendes [French Cinema Is
Dying Under False Legends]," reads the headline. This is the title of a
famous article by Truffaut, written in May 1957, the year in which *Tous les
garçons s'appellent Patrick (Charlotte et Véronique)* was written. Truffaut's piece
ends on a similarly elevated note: "The film of tomorrow shall be an act of
love."[27] What is meant here is a love other than that which was being exper-
imented with between the sexes during these years. The point of Godard's
short film is anticipated by the title: the women don't take their discovery
that they have fallen for the same man too hard. They see him get into a
taxi with a new woman, shoot him a look that makes him self-conscious
for a second, and then go their separate ways. Love is, at least to the then-
young men Godard and Rohmer, nothing dramatic. At any rate, a line
delivered when Charlotte and Véronique can already guess at what their
Patricks are up to hints at a new order of love: "We could all go to the cinema together." That would be the other love, the one Truffaut wrote about.

~

In the spring of 1958, the Paris region was hit by widespread flooding. Truffaut seized the opportunity and shot a film in the unusual landscape: a
romantic comedy that he did not finish. The material lay around for a while
until Godard edited it into the twelve-minute film *Une histoire d'eau (A
Story of Water)*. The allusions (in the original French) to the erotic classic
Story of O by Anne Desclos, published in 1954, are limited to the title and
a few kisses in the bushes, so like the whole film, they represent nothing
more than a gag. A young woman (Caroline Dim) leaves the house in the
morning and needs help on the landing. She must go to Paris, but the interspersed aerial shots show that this will be no easy feat. Dancing acrobati-
cally over a board, in rubber boots and on a boat, she reaches a road where

she is given a lift by a young man (Jean-Claude Brialy) in a car. The drive ends bogged down in mud; the pair wind up on an "island." *Une histoire d'eau* is a playful study of digression, which finally concludes at the story's objective: Paris, the Eiffel Tower, a love story. In terms of editing, Godard took inspiration from early cinema. He dedicated the film to the father of Hollywood slapstick, Mack Sennett, but it is at the level of language that he really runs wild here. Anne Colette recorded a soundtrack together with Godard, in which she gave a wonderfully self-deprecating narration of the adventure. Literary references abound (for example, to Edgar Allan Poe's famous castaway Arthur Gordon Pym but also to the comic book heroes *Les Pieds nickelés*, who will appear again in Godard's *Pierrot le fou*, 1965), and her character, which Truffaut had conceived as a classical love object, becomes a fleeting apparition, made up entirely of imaginings and insinuations. The man, too, appears to be simpleminded rather than a seducer. With his pride in the German Ford Taunus, he is simply too stuffy for a young woman who knows all the American car brands by heart. *Une histoire d'eau* anticipates the constellation of *À bout de souffle* (*Breathless*): Godard takes a basically conventional template by Truffaut and turns it into something completely different, in this case a slapstick film in which it is not the bodies but the words that slip, slam into boards, and perform somersaults.

In an article on Ingmar Bergman in 1958, Godard once again summed up what he demanded of cinema under the intertitle *The Last Great Romantic*: "The cinema is not a craft. It is an art. It does not mean teamwork. One is always alone, on the set as before the blank page. And for Bergman, to be alone means to ask questions. And to make films means to answer them. Nothing could be more classically romantic."[28] He was to live up to this programmatic aspiration more radically than he himself could have imagined at the time.

CHAPTER 2

Pop Art

1959 to 1967

For the twenty years of its existence between 1931 and 1953, the American film studio Monogram Pictures was known as one of Hollywood's "Poverty Row" production companies. The films made in this poor man's dream factory cost comparatively little money, were often formulaic or unsophisticated, featured second-rate stars, and were considered lowbrow at any rate. For the young directors of the Nouvelle Vague, however, Monogram embodied something in American cinema that they considered exemplary, and which hardly anyone in their homeland had noticed. The critic Manny Farber described a comparable preference in his essay *Underground Films* (1957). By underground, he did not mean the underground cinema of the sexual and artistic avant-garde associated with names like Jack Smith, Jonas Mekas, Stan Brakhage, and Andy Warhol but rather a certain type of commercial Hollywood film bereft of any glamour and whose directors withdraw deliberately into obscurity. Such underground films are shown in cheap cinemas where hygiene is not a priority, and they are made under conditions about which the inhabitants of the studio's management offices appear unconcerned. "In each case, the director is taking a great chance with clichés and forcing them into a hard natural shape."[1]

The names that Farber associated with underground film were more or less the same as those revered by cinephiles in Paris: Howard Hawks, Raoul Walsh, Anthony Mann. Godard made a particularly clear reference to these models in his first full-length feature film, *À bout de souffle* (*Breathless*, 1960). The dedication *Dédier à Monogram Pictures* precedes the first image of Jean-Paul Belmondo, who, in a gesture borrowed from Humphrey Bogart, runs his thumb over his lips after looking up from a tabloid called *Paris-Flirt* because a girl has made a gesture at him. The scene takes place on the pier at Marseille. An American couple gets out of the car; Michel Poiccard (Belmondo) hot-wires the engine and is ready for a drive to Paris. He does not take his accomplice with him. On the way, he shoots a policeman with a gun he found in the glove compartment. This turns a petty criminal into a murderer, who from now is on the run. He only goes to Paris because someone there still owes him money and because he wants to see a woman again—Patricia Franchini, an American in Paris, an aspiring journalist, a newspaper columnist on the Champs-Élysées—whom he hopes to persuade to flee with him to Italy. The plot of *À bout de souffle* is in many ways made up of clichés, but you have only to see the dirt under Jean-Paul Belmondo's fingernails to realize that Godard is presenting precisely that which Manny Farber termed "the unheralded ripple of physical experience": physical details that break up the clean surfaces of high-quality cinema.

When Godard started shooting *À bout de souffle* in August 1959, he was late. The Nouvelle Vague had already been firmly established by this point and might have had sufficient momentum as an innovative movement in French cinema even without him. But if one looks at the early films of this generation in context, it is astonishing to note the extent to which the Nouvelle Vague became modern only with the release of *À bout de souffle*. Strictly speaking, one should add a fifth to the four founding films that preceded *À bout de souffle*, because in addition to *Le Beau Serge* (Claude Chabrol, 1958), *Le Signe du lion* (Éric Rohmer, completed in 1959, undistributed until 1962), *Les Quatre cents coups* (François Truffaut, 1959), and *Paris nous appartient* (Jacques Rivette, 1959, undistributed until 1961), Jean Rouch's *Moi, un noir* (1957) is also considered an important point of reference for this young generation's efforts at authenticity. Especially when one looks at some of the stylistic devices that Godard was promoting, it seems imperative to take a fresh look at those competitors who, in a decision whose ramifications can still be felt today, were judged not to form part of the Nouvelle Vague (or even did not want to be thought as part of it): the *rive gauche* group around Louis Malle, Chris Marker, Alain Resnais, Agnès Varda. From today's perspective, it is clear that the aesthetic differences within the Nouvelle Vague are in part much greater than the distances between Malle and Chabrol or even Godard and Resnais, who presented a milestone of modern cinema with *Hiroshima, mon amour* in 1959.

Godard was still a critic when his colleagues' first films were presented to the public. Claude Chabrol fired the starting pistol. He filmed *Le Beau Serge* in the village setting of Sardent in the Creuse department of central France, drawing on his own experiences. François Bayon (Jean-Claude Brialy), who returns to Sardent after years of absence (during which he was able to mostly recover from a lung illness), is clearly the young director's alter ego, while Gérard Blain plays a wild, desperate alcoholic who reflects all the unhappiness of deepest provincial France, a part of the country that was not being borne along into the glorious future by the years of recovery after World War II. For Chabrol's second film, *Les Cousins*, Godard wrote a shooting report, or perhaps an announcement, in which he said that it was easy to distinguish a "Chabrolesque" film from a Marcel Carné film: Chabrol tells the truth, conveyed through lies. A central motif for Godard's entire oeuvre emerges here. For him, fiction is not an invention but a path into reality. And he used a rhetorical device that would stay with him: inversion—a dialectical form that had not yet received much attention.

Finally, at least as autobiographical as *Le Beau Serge* was the film that would become a foundational document for the Nouvelle Vague: *Les Quatre cents coups* by François Truffaut, which premiered in Cannes in 1959. In it, student Antoine Doinel experiences a series of events in Paris, most of which can be related to events in Truffaut's youth. The theft of a typewriter, visits to the cinema during school hours, a difficult relationship with his mother, who lives with a man who is not his father—all this leads Antoine Doinel on a path out of society, toward that famous freeze frame: the still on the beach with which Truffaut gives his film an open ending. It was Godard who set the tone for interpretations of this work with his proclamation in *Arts* magazine on April 22, 1959: "The face of French cinema has changed."[2]

For Godard, *Les Quatre cents coups* represented a cultural change of national political proportions, in support of which observation he called the culture minister, intellectual and filmmaker André Malraux, to the witness stand. With his "But yes, but yes!," this latter rather confirmed that Truffaut's film should be shown at Cannes "in the name of France." In terms of content, Godard saw the work as being doubly innovative: Truffaut stands for "attaching more importance to what is in front of the camera than to the camera itself. . . . Content, in other words, precedes the form, conditions it. If the former is false, the latter will logically be false too: it will be awkward." This is entirely in the spirit of Bazin, but it also opens all the possibilities of experimental forms, which Truffaut himself by no means fundamentally exhausts.

In Jacques Rivette's *Paris nous appartient*, Godard makes a brief appearance as a newspaper reader in a café, flirting with a woman at the next table, while giving evasive answers to the young Anne Goupil, who pesters him with questions about the circumstances of the death of the mysterious Spaniard Juan. His persona is already complete (the impenetrable glasses, the half-smoked cigarette), and the word that was to become so important in *À bout de souffle* is also dropped in: "dégueulasse," which functions here as a derogatory term for the woman at the next table, in essence calling her a slut. In the context of the early films of the Nouvelle Vague, *Paris nous appartient* is the one that most clearly refers to that era. Paris is the setting for a great conspiracy pushing for the return of a world-wide, right-wing dictatorship, this time definitive. An international milieu of scattered bohemians tries to preserve its autonomy, and a theatrical production of Shakespeare's *Pericles* becomes a rehearsal for their powerful but also destructive ideals. Anne Goupil traverses this milieu with a stern insistence on authenticity. She wants to know the truth about Juan, and she wants to find this tape on which he recorded a piece of opera music for the theatrical performance. His disappearance becomes a cipher for the slippery meaning of *Paris nous appartient*. Rivette comes closest to the existentialist mood that prevailed in those years among the directors of the Nouvelle Vague.

But it is Godard who, with *À bout de souffle*, best summed up the style and the vital feeling of the movement, while at the same time finding an explicitly modern (and according to some later interpreters, even postmodern[3]) approach. The first reviews already drew comparisons with *Citizen Kane*, Orson Welles's debut from 1941, with which he brought classic Hollywood cinema into modernity. Like so many other canonical works of cultural history, *À bout de souffle* is characterized by a meditation on contrasts. It is a film that is essentially about cinema and yet perfectly captures a societal mood in France at the end of the 1950s, a film that is almost a documentary in many respects, shot in a neorealist manner with a small crew on the streets, in cafés, and hotel rooms. It owes its final form to a sophisticated postproduction in terms of both montage and sound, so that for all its authenticity one must speak of a highly artificial work, an inter-cultural love story in which a young woman from America and a young man from France do not come together because Godard combines their respective mythologies in such a way that only collage, and no story, can result.

The template for *À bout de souffle* was created by François Truffaut, who gave Godard an elaborate screenplay that took up a sensational criminal case from 1952: Michel Portail, who had been deported from the United States following a robbery, enjoyed the good life with his American girl-friend (among other characters) on the Cote d'Azur for a summer, before he committed a car theft, murdered a policeman, and was betrayed by his lover. Godard took over many elements from Truffaut's script, but when he started shooting, he was working more or less from scratch. He took every day as it came and waited to see what it brought him. The filming of *À bout de souffle* is surrounded by a mythology of genius: a young direc-tor who escapes the structures of the film business and creates everything directly and spontaneously himself, running risks in doing so. One of the things that made this possible was that he found a perfect cameraman in Raoul Coutard—no routinist with studio experience but rather a reporter who had worked in Indo-China and filmed with Pierre Schoendoerffer in Afghanistan. Coutard willingly went along with all of Godard's ideas; he was flexible and would film in a tiny hotel room, where a long and cen-tral scene was shot, just as well as on high window ledges or hidden in a three-wheeled mail van on the Champs-Élysées. Godard and Coutard used unusual material: highly sensitive, so-called slow films that were actually intended for photography, such as Geva 36. "Everyone thinks it stinks. I find it extraordinary. It's the first time that we asked the film to give its all, making it do what it's not made for. It's as if the film itself is suffer-ing from being used to the extreme limits of its possibilities." Godard went on, more pointedly: "Even the film, you see, is getting breathless."[4] This was an unusual experience offering a great deal of freedom for Jean-Paul Belmondo and Jean Seberg, who made up the professional cast, as most of the other roles were cast among friends. The film was shot without direct sound, and it was clear to everyone from the start that the dialogue would only be worked in postsynchronization. Jean Seberg, whose short haircut was at least as sensational as Ingrid Bergman's in her Hollywood debut *For Whom the Bell Tolls* (1943), had already made a similar appearance in Otto Preminger's film version of *Bonjour Tristesse*. Seberg played a seventeen-year-old teenager under the influence of her father, a seducer whose ephemeral relationships worked a melancholy influence on her own romantic experiences from an early age.

One might imagine that the Patricia of *À bout de souffle*, who sells the *Herald Tribune*, remembers these experiences from *Bonjour Tristesse*, and that her indecisiveness may also stem from them. Godard saw it that way himself. "I could have taken the last shot of Preminger's film and started after dissolving to a title: 'Three years later.'"[5] At the same time, however, he sets up clear signs of difference. *Bonjour Tristesse* is ultimately pulp fiction, "a conventional story" that serves as the starting point for an ambitious undertaking. Godard wanted to revise ("*refaire*") the "whole of cinema" that had already been made by then.[6] This formulation, which Godard had used in 1962 to situate his film in the history of cinema, highlights what is decisive about *À bout de souffle*: a zero point is marked out here, which simultaneously concludes one story and opens it back up in new ways, in the form of a "remake."

And what, essentially, is new about *À bout de souffle*? The argument that this is the point where cinema begins to talk about itself is based principally on a social observation. With the triumph of American-influenced popular culture after World War II, idols like Humphrey Bogart also became widely known in Europe. Michel Poiccard is not at all unique in understanding a poster as a mirror, in front of which he corrects the image he perceives of himself. The trademark gesture that Bogart first displayed in *The Maltese Falcon*, of running his thumb along his lower lip, also becomes a moment of transition in *À bout de souffle* as Michel stands in front of a poster for *The Harder They Fall*, a boxing film starring Bogart in the last role he would play before his death. His role has thus fallen vacant, and at this moment Belmondo is expressing Michel's desire to become a second Bogart, as least as much as he is Michel's doubt that this desire will amount to anything more than a borrowing or a pose. *À bout de souffle* reveals, more than any other film of the Nouvelle Vague, that cinema has become a component of mass media society. All the elements of this society are already present in Godard's film: art prints on the walls of Patricia's hotel

Jean Seberg and Jean-Paul Belmondo, the main actors in *Breathless*, 1959 (Jacques Boissay / akg-images, image no. AKG4802295)

room; the interview (actually a small press conference where the reporters shout their questions over one another) with the famous writer Parvulesco (played by Jean-Pierre Melville), at such a nonplace as Paris Orly airport; the neon signs in urban spaces announcing that the net is tightening around Poiccard; the pieces of music, from Haydn to *chansons*; the many car brands named in the film, along with their implied mythologies.[7]

À bout de souffle grasps, with vehement clarity, that under these conditions, identities can no longer be constructed according to the model of the bourgeois realist novel or the rules of continuity of classic Hollywood cinema. Michel and Patricia, for all the immediacy of their portrayal, are artificial characters; they are creatures of signs in whose design there converge many elements of what had interested Godard from the start of his career. That is why Truffaut is thought to have been touching on tradition when he later said of his friend and colleague: "He needed to film death."[8] Whether Poiccard could get away with his crimes or not (about which Godard was allegedly still unclear during filming) has less to do with a positive or negative disposition on the part of the artist than with the tradition of the gangster film genre, and it is part of the rules of the latter that the authorities must prevail. Patricia's betrayal is not so much an expression of submission to these authorities as it is a form of displacement activity that arises from the incompatibility of the logics of the genre film and the overt work of art. The scene in the hotel room with its extended temporality is also a formal indicator for the opening up of the genre formula to that calculated indeterminacy through which modern art systematically operates. Godard returned to this problem a few years later in *Bande à part* (*Band of Outsiders*), in which he found a different, more conventional solution.

~

The soundtrack and the montage form the innovative part of this film. Here, we see what Godard means by *refaire*—a freedom in dealing with cinematic syntax that results in an experimental text. With the many jump cuts in *À bout de souffle*, Godard invents an artistic device (or renders it acceptable for use in feature films)—one comparable to syncopation in jazz. In contemporary reviews, *À bout de souffle* was already being described as a cinematic counterpart to jazz, without this comparison being reflected upon in any detail. Jump cuts depart from the fluidity of standard montage, creating a stuttering effect. Two examples are to be found in the scene in which Godard himself can be seen pointing out Poiccard when he recognizes his image from the newspaper. Patricia, meanwhile, steps out of the *Herald Tribune* offices and into the street, and her walk to her car is interrupted twice by a cut that introduces a small, barely noticeable jump into the movement. The unorthodox cuts in the scene in which Poiccard shoots the policeman are clearer examples and also more relevant in terms of content. Godard resolves the confrontation in a way that is anything but clear;

he almost completely omits the policeman from the construction of the scene and opts for three images in abrupt sequence, in which first Poiccard, then the revolver, and finally the gun's magazine can be seen in close-up. Only then is there a countershot, in which the policeman clearly falls into the bushes.

There is extensive debate about the moral implications of this representation against the backdrop of Luc Moullet's then-well-known dictum that morality in cinema is a matter of camera movements. Godard himself had turned this dictum around in his 1959 review of *Hiroshima, mon amour*: "Traveling shots are a question of morality."[9] Behind this statement lies the pathos of the fact that morality and aesthetics cannot be separated. The question is whether Godard intended to convey a moral characterization of Poiccard through this daring sequence of cuts or whether he simply wanted to express his unpredictability. The older colleague Claude Autant-Lara, who was certainly not fond of Godard, described the new cut of *À bout de souffle* as destructive: in his opinion, Godard had turned on the producer, who would have demanded a commercial film. Georges de Beauregard, a relatively nondescript figure among producers in France at the time, chose Godard precisely because he felt that he was the most contrary and daring of the former "Young Turks." A conservative like Autant-Lara perceived only meaningless ellipsis, but he had to realize that jump cuts were coming into fashion. Beauregard's decision to gamble on Godard was also successful in that he got more than just a good film: *À bout de souffle* represented the start of something completely new. Godard himself later remarked of the innovative montage that when he was faced with the task of shortening the original version by almost an hour, he was concerned not so much by questions of content but by rhythm. This is the most plausible explanation.[10] Godard transformed the "invisible" montage, as was common in the standard Hollywood model, into an obtrusively visible, in some places downright irritating cut.

The complexity of this montage, which incorporates sound, is particularly striking in the scene in which Michel and Patricia take refuge in a cinema showing Budd Boetticher's *Westbound*. The Napoléon is one of the most important places for postwar Parisian cinephilia, along with the Mac-Mahon, which is also featured in *À bout de souffle* (a splinter group among Parisian cinephiles who were keen on American cinema were also dubbed

MacMahonists). Through her successful efforts to lose the police, Patricia becomes an accomplice. She and Michel are now on the run together. The cinema offers them a place of sanctuary,[11] where they can kiss and kill time until their evening rendezvous in Montmartre. In this scene, Godard shows how willing he is to manipulate the connection between image and sound. Not only can dialogue from *Westbound* be heard offstage but so also can a meta-dialogue into which Godard has incorporated passages from poems by Apollinaire (*Cors de chasse*) and Aragon (*Elsa je t'aime*). A male voice (Godard's own) says: "Take care, Jessica. On the kiss's beveled edge, the years pass too quickly. Avoid, avoid, avoid broken memories." And a woman replies: "You are mistaken, Sheriff. Our story is noble and tragic, like a tyrant's mask. No hazardous or magic drama, no indifferent detail, makes our love pathetic." Pathos and irony are close together here.

The care with which Godard preserves the original tone of the Boetticher film (and its French dubbing) also sheds light on his own, particular cinephilia. American cinema is not important to him in terms of its authenticity; he is not at all concerned with bringing Michel and Patricia into direct contact with the revered American role models. Instead, the Westerns and gangster films that he brings into play throughout the film serve as material for further editing, in which we can recognize Godard the consumer of films in a very personal moment, in a "poetic" exaggeration of his love for American genre cinema, which represents concretely a highly modernist editing of the original text. Godard turns an indirect film quotation (we only actually see the poster of *Westbound* on the way out of the cinema) into a collage. He opens up cinephilia to culture in the broader sense and introduces an element of counterfeiting into the quotation.

This then also applies to *À bout de souffle* as a whole. As a palimpsest of a classic gangster film, it is at the same time its counterfeit, whose aim is to draw from this distinction a concept of art, as opposed to mere entertainment. *À bout de souffle* was a resounding success, and Godard was now the face of the Nouvelle Vague alongside Truffaut, who followed up in the same year with *Tirez sur le pianiste*.

～

The second feature film, *Le Petit Soldat* (*The Little Soldier*, 1960/63), followed on the heels of *À bout de souffle*, and it was true to Godard's motto:

before the release of a film, the next one should already have been negotiated with the producer, which means that the budget may be lower, but the most important thing is that continuity of work is guaranteed. In this case, however, it became apparent that many obstacles may lie between production and evaluation. *Le Petit Soldat*, expressly conceived as a response to the accusation that the Nouvelle Vague was apolitical, ran into troubles with French censors because of explicit scenes of torture. This meant that it was not released in cinemas until early 1963. The delay created confusion in this rapid phase of Godard's work and deprived the film of much of its immediate explosive charge, as in 1962 the Evian Accords officially ended the Algerian War with a ceasefire. To this day, the film is seen as a poor relation.

Le Petit Soldat begins with a border crossing into Switzerland and a striking sentence: "For me, the time for action is over. I have grown older. Now begins the time of reflection." It is spoken by a young man named Bruno Forestier (Michel Subor), who acts as the retrospective narrator of his own story, set in the espionage milieu of Geneva and against the backdrop of the Algerian war. Two images contradict each other in time. First, we see Forestier reading a newspaper report of new terrorist attacks. The paper is dated April 7, 1960, which would place it late in the process of filming, at a moment that coincided with the preparations for the cinema release of *À bout de souffle*. A little later, the time of the action is given an explicit date: May 13, 1958—a historically significant day when the French military in Algeria staged a coup against its own government. Subsequently, General Charles de Gaulle, who had resigned in 1953, returned to politics, had himself appointed prime minister, and was finally elected president of the Republic in December of the same year. On May 13, 1958, then, the Fifth Republic began to take shape in France, an event alluded to in *Le Petit Soldat* in the form of de Gaulle's occasional radio speeches, which speak of an "arrêt du système," a collapse of the political system.

Bruno Forestier, who says of himself that he is a "man without ideals," becomes a pawn in the conflicts that characterized French colonial policy at the time. It is characteristic of Godard that he has not chosen a figure of the anticolonialist left as his protagonist but a man of the right who is ambivalent, because disloyal, and ready to jump ship, a member of an antiterrorist group financed by a man who is expelled as a collaborator in the Vichy regime and a supporter of the antimodern, antisemitic protest movement of the Poujadists. On behalf of his group, Forestier will kill a journalist named Palivoda, who is responsible for a program titled *A Neutral Speaks*. The boundaries between terrorism and secret service activities become blurred, especially since Forestier disguises himself as a journalist. Most of the statements in his off-screen narration, however, attempt to retain a principled distance: Everyone is "completely crazy"; the "secret war increasingly confused people and ideas."

Godard gave Forestier an additional quality with which to emphasize his distance: he made him a photographer. Through a friend, the disillusioned agent, ready to desert to Brazil, meets Veronica Dreyer, who comes from Russia and whom he meets for recordings in her flat. There is a sentence that has become one of Godard's best-known catchphrases. "Cinema is truth, twenty-four times a second."[12] The context makes this statement more understandable. Forestier precedes it with another sentence: "Photography, that is truth." Specifically, he refers here to a particularly fast Agfacolor film that allows photography without additional light. Godard thus once again explicitly alludes to the positions of Bazin, who became one of the most influential theorists of realism with his analyses of the ontology of the photographic image (1945). Godard, however, is not interested in the implications for his own cinematic work; he is not concerned with securing the status of *Le Petit Soldat*, for example, as an authentic testimony of the times in terms of materialist theory. He transforms theory into a *bon mot* and assembles a world from fragments of cultural knowledge and understanding that is not characterized by rigid references or deeper understanding but in which culture remains a surface phenomenon, something that one picks up without delving deeper into it. As in *À bout de souffle*, books, records, pictures, and media are omnipresent in *Le Petit Soldat*. An agent with whom Forestier gets into a car is reading Cocteau's *Thomas l'imposteur*; Veronica Dreyer plays a Haydn record after Forestier had found Bach and Beethoven unsuitable for morning listening; and finally he himself quotes *Reiters Morgenlied* by Wilhelm Hauff in German: "Morgenrot, Morgenrot, leuchtest mir zum frühen Tod? [Morning sky so red, do you herald my early death?]" (another early example of Godard's knowledge of German culture, and a text that will run through his work as an underlying leitmotif).

The absentmindedness that characterized the long bedroom scene between Belmondo and Jean Seberg in *À bout de souffle*, the short attention span, is also at work here in the scenes between Forestier and Veronica. They play around each other with associations and remarks, the principle of photographic truth being accentuated by a second principle, one of narrative collage. Godard assembles figures from incidental signs, and here we are also looking at an event in retrospect: Forestier narrates from the start, so he is already outside and elsewhere, and so fundamentally unaffected by the dramatic developments. He finally turns "the French and the Arabs" against him, is taken by supporters of the Algerian Liberation Front (FLN) into a flat where numerous leftist texts (Stalin, Lenin, Mao) are lying around, and is tortured there. He saves himself by jumping out the window, quoting the Resistance fighter Pierre Brossolette: "A complex situation suddenly became very simple." The price he pays for his freedom is enormous. Veronica (of whom a French secret agent says, "A girl who lives alone is either a prostitute or an informer") turns out to be a supporter of the FLN and is tortured and killed (which we only learn in passing at the end), while Forestier finally goes through with the murder of Palivoda after all. His final sentence is both cynical and melancholic: "I was just glad I had so much time ahead of me."

Twenty years later, Godard looked back on the controversies that accompanied this film after its delayed release. He was accused of taking the wrong side in the Algerian conflict. Even then, he was concerned with positioning himself between all the different camps.

> And in that sense, today I certainly admit that *Le Petit Soldat* is a fascist film, but what matters is that you can detach yourself from it, more easily than from the famous speeches, the speeches of Himmler and Hitler, which, by the way, have neither really been looked at nor analyzed. The real history—like the real history of the Jewish people—is never told, even by the Jews. It is extremely interesting, but it really needs to be said. But if they really said it out loud, their whole house of cards would collapse. Then they would have to change their lives. And for that you are least willing to change your life, to look for another place.[13]

In Agnès Varda's feature film *Cléo de 5 à 7* (1962), there is a scene in which the protagonist, who must get through two hours of a midweek afternoon while waiting for a possibly devastating diagnosis, goes with her friend to the projection booth of a cinema. The projectionist is just putting in a film, a burlesque before the main feature. In it, Godard can be seen as a young man in a white suit saying goodbye to his lover Anna. She walks down a staircase to the Seine; he puts on the black sunglasses that have long been a Godard trademark. He sees Anna killed by a jet of water, a man (Death) carrying her away. He runs after the car in vain, finally buying a wreath on which is written "À ma poupée d'amour" (For my beloved little doll). Only when he takes off his glasses does he realize that he has fallen for an optical illusion. He has seen everything in black, but it is now all taking place as a cheerful event. "Maudites lunettes noires!" (Damn sunglasses!)—that's the lesson of the three minutes that end with a circle fade (another silent film motif) and a kiss.

Through this episode, Agnès Varda, who belongs to the *rive gauche* group, meaning that she was not in fact a part of the Nouvelle Vague, paid ironic tribute to a new star couple in French cinema. Godard and Anna Karina, who had played Veronica Dreyer in *Le Petit Soldat*, were conducting a love affair that was being closely observed by the media. This was the first of several relationships Godard was to have with women he discovered as actresses. Anna Karina, born in Denmark in 1940, lived as a model in Paris. She came to Godard's attention when he saw a soap commercial in which she was sitting in a bathtub. He offered her a supporting role in *À bout de souffle* that expressly called for a nude scene. She canceled but let it be known that she wanted to try her hand as an actress. Godard came back to her when he was looking for a leading actress for *Le Petit Soldat*. The frivolous spirit of the casting call is expressed in an advertisement that the producer Georges de Beauregard placed in the magazine *La Cinématographie française*: "Jean-Luc Godard . . . is looking for a young woman between 18 and 27 to be his actress and his soul mate [*âme sœur*]." A number of facets of the later relationship are implied in the term *âme soeur*: the woman is idealized and she is supposed to be a muse, rather than the lover that Anna Karina became on the set of *Le Petit Soldat*. The film is also a coded declaration of love. The wedding was reported all over the world, and it was in keeping with Godard's status at the time, immediately after his triumph with *À bout de souffle*, that the couple was featured on the front pages of the big magazines. For *Paris Match*, Godard and Anna

Jean-Luc Godard with his first wife, Anna Karina, 1960 (Photo 12 / Alamy Stock Photo, image no. B85N2Y)

Karina were a couple with comparable glamour to John F. Kennedy and Jacqueline Bouvier.

But to follow the story of their relationship, the paparazzi would only have needed to go to the cinema. From the very beginning, the relationship was a tense mix of romance and eroticism, with the childlike appearance of Anna Karina in Agnès Varda's miniature strongly accentuated by the use of the term "doll." For Godard, even though he has an intimate relationship with them and undoubtedly desires them sexually, female stars are first and foremost objects in his elaborate arrangement of desire. This becomes clear in *Une femme est une femme* (*A Woman Is a Woman*, 1961), the second film he made with Anna Karina, which, however, had its theatrical release before *Le Petit Soldat* did. For the actress, this was a breakthrough in what was ostensibly a musical, for which Godard had rather loftier intentions than a mere homage to American films with Cyd Charisse (who is explicitly alluded to).

At the center of a love triangle is Angela, who lives with Émile Récamier (Jean-Claude Brialy). She hires herself out as a dancer in a nightclub. The strip tease routines are comically overproduced. They are only shown in fragments, but their inventive *mise-en-scène* with often-elaborate costumes is out of proportion to the staid atmosphere in the club, where men sit alone at tables with red-and-white checked tablecloths and drink beer. At one point, Angela is seen inserting the tape for her act herself. The whole operation has a distinctly unglamorous charm, and its patina is thoroughly artificial. Godard shot *Une femme est une femme* in a studio, thus abandoning, in his third feature-length film, a principle of the Nouvelle Vague (the immediacy of shooting on the street) without completely replacing it with an invented world. He created an idealized Paris of street corners and kiosks, small cafés and stairwells, where people pass the telephone from flat to flat because they lack connections of their own. Angela wants to have a child, but Émile won't give her one. Godard at best hints at her expectations—there is a suggestion of a reaction to Patricia's fickleness in *À bout de souffle*, who is pregnant by Michel and yet betrays him. Angela surely wants to stabilize her relationship with Émile, but he is more interested in the radio broadcast of a game between Real Madrid and Barcelona than in happiness at home with his girl. He sees her as a modern woman, while Angela resorts to a melodramatic register: "Girls who don't cry are stupid." Godard gives no hints as to whether Angela is merely in need of protection (she crosses herself at important moments) or whether she is more or less consciously turning against the concept of emancipation that was under discussion in Paris around 1960 and was an essential aspect of the social Nouvelle Vague from which the cinematic movement of the same name arose.[14] The fact that Émile brings his girlfriend the magazine *Marie Claire* in the evening, a central organ of the new femininity that embraced independence, consumer culture, and a certain ideal of a partner, is an indication that with Angela, Godard is addressing a kind of nonconformism that hardly differs from older ideals of femininity. For Angela is first and foremost a loyal, true-hearted girl who is not taken in by the flirtatious song she sings at one point: "Je ne suis pas sage, je suis très cruelle, mais aucun homme n'enrage, parce que je suis très belle." Because of her beauty, men forgive her for being less than wise and, on occasion, being cruel.

As complex as this female role is, and as pointedly as Godard develops it, it is also clear that in *Une femme est une femme*, he is concerned with a more fundamental ambiguity. This is addressed by the question that is raised about the difference between comedy and tragedy. It is answered several times, and at an almost conceptual level. The most explicit approach to the question is represented by the elements of slapstick. Godard takes a certain idea of cinema as his model for a form of romantic farce ("Beziehungsburleske") in which Angela and Émile carry a floor lamp across the flat when they are searching into the night for a book and in which Angela throws a fried egg out of the pan into the air to turn it and then runs to the neighbor to take a call before catching the egg again.

These elements of the light entertainment genre are exaggerated by two distinctly modernist gestures. One refers to the musical, which Godard radically defamiliarizes. The soundtrack by Michel Legrand, who, at nearly the same time as making it, helped create an ideal postclassical musical sound for Jacques Demy's *Lola* (1961), shows that *Une femme est une femme* could also have contained captivating melodies and unforgettable songs. But in Godard's work, the soundtrack becomes a collage, whose rhythmic, atonal, unwieldy contours are used to choreograph the movements of the figures and the montage of images. The detail of what was structured in each case is not important; what is essential is that *Une femme est une femme* operates using techniques of fragmentation (almost sampling), all of which counteract a simple, even nostalgic reading. In addition, as a second modernist gesture, there are graphic elements that would become much more important in Godard's later work: inserts comment on the action; the title and end credits are not merely informative, but also offer visual poetry (IL ETAIT / UNE FOIS / EASTMAN COLOR—Once upon a time there was Eastmancolor).

The difference between comedy and tragedy is also emphasized in the final scene, in which comedy has the upper hand. Angela, who comes home with a guilty conscience after sleeping with Émile's rival and friend Alfred, admits to herself that although she still loves Émile, she desperately wants to have a child. The couple is thus faced with the decision to part at this point (which would not be a tragic end, but a dramatic one). But at just that moment Émile, obviously inspired by seeing Angela lying in bed next to him, jumps over his shadow and falls for a "very simple idea": if they slept together now, the pregnancy would also be theirs together, the paternity would be an open question, and their relationship could remain intact. The "Ouf" with which Anna Karina emphasizes her relief when she comes back into the picture after an insert representing sexual intercourse (LA CHOSE FAITE—the thing is done) is a wonderful moment of comic relief, which she underlines with a pun: now she is no longer "infame" (infamous) but once again "une femme." The film ends with a wink to the audience, which is not the only thing that sets it apart from the genre to which it refers, that is, tales of fallen girls that were popular in postwar French culture. Angela is rehabilitated after finding an illegitimate way to satisfy a desire that the relationship with her lover could not fulfill legitimately.

In the next film, *Vivre sa vie* (*My Life to Live*, 1962), there is no room for a playful solution to the relationship problem. In it, Godard tells of a girl who is lost—and also clearly addresses the looming failure of his own relationship with Anna Karina. Nana is a young woman who works in a record shop. The film begins with Anna Karina looking head-on into the camera: a close-up of a face lying in the dark, only the eyes shining, because Nana is crying. *Vivre sa vie* is divided into twelve tableaux, with explanatory intertitles that refer to Brecht's epic theater technique. In a conversation at a bar that is filmed in a striking way, Nana breaks up with her boyfriend— the actors are turned away from the camera throughout. This is one of many striking stylistic maneuvers in the film, in which Godard and Raoul Coutard experiment heavily with unusual perspectives.

The real prelude to Nana's journey is a visit to the cinema, where she sees *La Passion de Jeanne d'Arc* by Carl Theodor Dreyer and the scene in which Maria Falconetti accepts her martyrdom in expressive close-ups, which Nana also faces in another, postreligious form. Nana wants to become an actress, and she is willing to sleep with men to do it, like the photographer who she wants to do her portfolio. In the fourth tableau, the police take her personal details after she tries to steal a thousand-franc note from a woman who has accidentally dropped it on the floor: Nana Kleinfrankenheim from Flexbourg in Alsace, "*sans domicil*," without a fixed abode. Her way out, itself a dead end, is prostitution, which interests Godard here as a contemporary phenomenon, a commercial strategy for women in an age of sexual liberation and improved medical care. He also takes as his starting point a contemporary best seller, Marcel Sacotte's study *Où en est la prostitution*, which he quotes at length in the eighth tableau. This sociological perspective is set against Nana as a girl, who possesses "much goodness" ("beaucoup de bonneté": this terminology refers once again to Joan of Arc) and who, with existentialist pathos, does not want to live her own existence inauthentically: "Je suis I" (I am responsible), she insists at one point.

In the eleventh tableau, she meets the philosopher Brice Parain and proves to be a reflective being who is both the object of a narrative and a relationship. "In *Vivre sa vie* I have attempted to film a mind in action, the interior of someone seen from outside," Godard said in 1962. In the twelfth tableau, this person is radically objectified in a double way: Godard refers off-screen to the story *The Oval Portrait* by Edgar Allan Poe, which is about a painter who goes mad in his attempt to create an ideal portrait of his wife, while the subject herself dies. Shortly afterward, Nana actually dies, in a scene in which she first becomes an object of exchange between pimps and finally the victim of a male feud. Nana lies shot in the street like Michel Poiccard in *À bout de souffle*, but no one bends over her here; she is not worthy of any gesture or nod to the history of film (apart from her Joan-of-Arc idealization); no one speaks a swear word that could also be a declaration of love. Nana's abrupt and senseless death corresponds with another gun battle that takes place outside a café in the sixth tableau and from which Nana only just manages to escape. The scene is later identified as being political, in an offhand manner. For contemporaries, the context was clear: In October 1961 and February 1962, there were massacres in Paris of supporters of Algerian independence, and what Godard was showing in *Vivre sa vie* was the tail end of one of these police actions—a man who was chased into a small alley and shot down.

~

If the audience's reaction is anything to go by, the momentum of the Nouvelle Vague had petered out two years after *À bout de souffle*. Godard might well have been regarded as a one-hit wonder. He was maintaining his hectic pace of production because he accepted several commissions for so-called omnibus films, to which different directors each contribute shorter chapters. For *The Seven Deadly Sins* (*Les Sept Péchés Capitaux*, 1962), Godard chose sloth (*La Paresse*). Outside the studios in Boulogne-Billancourt, southwest of Paris, a young actress (Nicole Mirel) waits for Eddie Constantine, best known for playing the secret agent Lemmy Caution from 1953. She gets into his open-topped car to drive back to the city with him. Her sexual advances toward him are clear, and she soon reveals her ulterior motive: she is hoping that he can land her a role. But Constantine is not in the mood, and what is more, he is very tired. Godard makes no effort to define the character of this exhaustion in detail (although the clues point more in the direction of existential ennui than just a lack of sleep). But Constantine does accept the invitation to the young woman's flat, nestled away on the top floor, where there are also two servants who are sworn to secrecy. No tryst in fact takes place: inertia wins out (Constantine imagines how he would have to get back into his clothes after sex, and the very thought seems unbearable to him). This is how Godard arrives at the important punchline: "Who dares to say that sloth is the mother of all sin? We have just seen, on the contrary, a sloth so strong that it overwhelms the other sins." "La Paresse" is no more than a caprice, a deliberate subversion of the theme, for laziness here becomes an obstacle to a competing "mortal sin," lust, or rather to its instrumentalization for career reasons.

~

The thematic task for the directors of the omnibus film *RoGoPaG* (1963) —Roberto Rossellini, Jean-Luc Godard, Pier Paolo Pasolini, and Ugo Gregoretti—was to tell of the "beginnings of the end of the world." Godard took the assignment literally and titled his contribution *Il nuovo mondo* (*The New World*). In it, he combined motifs of contemporary atomic apocalyptics with a study of a couple living it up. It remains unclear whether this is not simply a psychological study of a man (Jean-Marc Bory) who has a paranoid reaction to the way his girlfriend Alessandra (Alexandra Stewart) draws away from him. "Io ti ex-amo," she says to him, declaring her love to him through a play on words. The man wants to know what is going on. He reads in a newspaper about a super-nuclear explosion at 120,000 meters above Paris. The headline changes his view of the city, he now sees signs of a strange hysteria everywhere, and he also finds a key for Alessandra's phrase. She may be "contaminated."

Through some of its various motifs, *Il nuovo mondo* gives a foretaste of some of Godard's later films, especially *Le Mépris* (*Contempt*, 1963), in which Michel Piccoli and Brigitte Bardot play a couple in a comparable state of lethargic, mistrustful estrangement. The dagger that Alessandra fixes to the side of her bikini bottom plays with the motif of terrorist savagery, of an armed Eve in the swimming pool (Godard uses the scene for one of his characteristic puns: CINE becomes PISCINE with a slight pan of the camera) who throws herself at a strange man, going for the throat. But the most striking element of *Il nuovo mondo* remains the construction of a female figure who takes refuge in mysteriousness to escape a man's obsessive attention. The man gets the last word: he writes a "last testimony from a world of freedom," but this narrative is deceptive, interwoven as it is with fear: a fear whose external cause is the contemporary context of the Cuban Missile Crisis.

~

The next feature film project saw the Italian forerunner of the Nouvelle Vague, Roberto Rossellini, work with Godard. Godard had published one of his fictional interviews on April 1, 1959, in which this sentence is put into Rossellini's mouth: "But falsehood presupposes truth. And when I got to India I understood. Masks are very nice and I am in favor of them; but I am in favor of them in so far as they must be removed. It's like the sailors from the *Potemkin* who are about to shoot their mutinous comrades. It is because their heads are covered by tarpaulin that they realize these men are their brothers."[15] The neorealist Rossellini had made a documentary in India and was already on his way to his experimental later work, which essentially amounted to educational television. Godard took up Rossellini's suggestion and made *Les Carabiniers* (*The Carabineers*, 1963), which was based on a play by Beniamino Joppolo. The result is a film about war: not about a specific war but about the events of wars in the twentieth century in general. Two men, Ulysse and Michel-Ange, live with two women "in a desolate wasteland reminiscent of the scenes of Beckett plays."[16] One day, two policemen show up. They hold a letter from the king. Ulysse and Michel-Ange are being called up, and they are to depart on that very day. The two policemen combine coercion with temptation. War means enrichment in every respect. One can discover new countries and bring home their spoils. The two women, Venus and Cleopatra, immediately start dreaming of bikinis and velour dresses, and the naive Michel-Ange's imagination runs rather wilder: can you "burn women" in war, "massacre innocent people," and "leave restaurants without paying"? All of this is war, and Godard shows it in the following three-quarters of an hour as a grotesque, shocking journey around the world, interrupted by inserts in which passages from the letters that Ulysse and Michel-Ange send home can be read. This is not a war of the military technologies invented in the twentieth century. Rather, this is the war that lies behind the technology, waged by foot soldiers who invade homes, attack women, commit shootings, harass civilians (when cannons and bombs are on screen, Godard uses documentary material, effectively propaganda films, including some made by fascist countries in World War II). Michel-Ange in particular becomes a negative identification figure because he plays the role of Simplicissimus in this odyssey, the locations of whose episodes Godard often identifies only through the postcards. Michel-Ange is obviously unaware of the moral implications of his actions, which is made particularly clear in an ambiguous scene in which he forces a woman to undress in front of him. He is distracted by a print hanging on the wall: a self-portrait by Rembrandt. Michel-Ange responds with a greeting: "Un soldat salut un artiste"—a soldier salutes an artist.

There is an irreconcilable difference between art and war, which Michel-Ange negates through his absolute guilelessness. He was empowered by the king (who never appears on screen) to make his fortune by appropriating goods. He rationalizes his actions in terms of need, but Godard exposes the short-circuit in Michel-Ange's logic in a scene in which he visits a cinema for the first time in his life. His reaction is the same as that commonly reported from the first demonstrations of the new medium in the late nineteenth century. Faced with a shot of a train seemingly about to roll out from the screen, he throws his arms up to guard his face, but when a woman is then seen in the bathroom, he tries to enter the picture, only to tear the screen from the rough wall that is visible behind it. This is a slapstick scene invented by Godard, but it neatly captures the nature of Joppolo's play.[17] It is a farce, absurd theater in a broader sense, in which a slow-witted rural population is confronted with an abstract king, in other words, a principle of unpredictable sovereignty represented by his henchmen, the carabinieri. The war in the actual sense is largely left out in Joppolo's work. His two soldiers never get into a position where they might recognize the consequences of their actions. Godard clearly named this unconsciousness: "It all takes place at the level of the animal, and, moreover, this animal is filmed from a point of view that is vegetal, unless it is mineral, which is to say, Brechtian."[18]

~

"A commissioned film interested me," Godard said in 1977 about *Le Mépris* (*Contempt*, 1963), based on the novel *Il disprezzo* by Alberto Moravia. The commission was from Carlo Ponti, one of the most important European producers at the time, who in addition to his successes also kept the tabloids busy thanks to his relationship with Sophia Loren. Ponti was the first of many producers who wanted Godard in their cabinet like a trophy. The Moravia adaptation gave him an opportunity to reflect on his position in the cinema of the sixties and at the same time to create a mythology of cinema. Most important was the fact that Godard landed the Austrian-German-American director Fritz Lang for the role of the old master, who in Moravia's book is called Rheingold and is hired to work on a film version of Homer's *Odyssey*. The other relevant characters are the screenwriter Paul Javal (Michel Piccoli), the American producer Prokosch (Jack Palance), his assistant Francesca Vanini (Giorgia Moll), and last but not least, Javal's wife, Camille, played by Brigitte Bardot, the biggest French star of the day. The power relations of Western postwar culture are inscribed into this constellation, as are the various modern and countermodern movements in European cinema after the war.

In the 1954 novel, Battista, the producer, spells out an essential demarcation: "Everything is pushing toward a new formula. As for neorealism, to give just one example, more or less everyone is already a little tired of it."[19] Battista represents a commercial trend that overcame neorealism with "sandal films," basically B movies featuring mythological stories with billowing costumes, cheap tricks, and legendary heroics. In *Le Mépris*, Godard mentions a contemporary title, *Totò contro Maciste*, in which the legendary comedian Totò meets the muscleman Maciste (Samson Burke). A cheap, serial cinema spectacular thus replaces neorealism—along with other tendencies—but Godard does not content himself with merely tracing this change in Italian postwar cinema. He expands the constellation both systematically and historically. At one point in *Le Mépris*, the producer signs a check on his female assistant's back, almost on her backside, and in a play on an infamous phrase: "When I hear the word 'culture,' I take out my checkbook." It is Fritz Lang, who went into exile in 1933, who provides the original line: "When I hear the word 'culture,' I take the safety off my revolver"—a dictum by Joseph Goebbels that was itself a quotation from the *völkisch* play *Schlageter*. In 1933 the National Socialist minister of propaganda, who was also in charge of film, had offered Lang the position of Reich director of film, but the director of *Die Nibelungen*, *Metropolis*, and *M* had preferred to go to the United States (via Paris) and work in Hollywood.

In Godard's work, the figure of the producer stands for a further change in film history, namely, for the decadence of the American studio system, which had taken in countless filmmakers from Europe in the 1930s and provided them with work and an artistic home, and whose representatives were now going around Europe with checkbooks (throwing around roles in films). The *Odyssey*, as the oldest material of European narrative art and as the original text for the relationship drama of *Le Mépris*, interests Godard not in a psychological sense but as a source for his technique of citation. Brigitte Bardot rounds out Godard's cast, drawn from a family of historic film figures. She embodies the contradictions of postwar French cinema and the time's new cultural freedoms, which were brought together so perfectly in the final scene of *Et Dieu créa la femme* by Roger Vadim in 1956. There, Bardot played the orphan Juliette in Saint-Tropez, a sensual, unruly, newly married and soon "fallen" woman who prefers to go barefoot; in the back room of a prostitutes' bar, she meets a black jazz band to whose wild music she dances, before Vadim resolves the sequence with good cheer, as Bardot is brought home by the domesticating hand of her husband. The fact that Godard worked with Bardot in *Le Mépris* could be seen as a triumph of the Nouvelle Vague, a document of its prestige and its access to the established star system. But Godard used Bardot like an object and fulfilled his commission in such a way that his contempt for the system to which he himself now belonged was unmistakable.

～

The film begins with the shooting and staging of a dolly shot. We see a young woman with a book in her hand walking down a sloping street. Parallel to her path run rails on which a camera is moving, and behind the woman a sound engineer is walking, carrying a microphone boom. Godard himself reads the credits for the film from off-screen: once again the camera-work was done by Raoul Coutard, and the music is by Georges Delerue (it will become even more famous than the film). Even the place where the film material was developed is given an express mention. The shot ends with a look into the lens of the camera that was in the picture: recording meets recording, and the cinema regards itself as an apparatus. A quotation leads into the narrative: "The cinema, said Andre Bazin, substitutes for our gaze a world more in harmony with our desires. *Contempt* is the story of this world."

In Moravia's work, the story is told from the perspective of the screen-writer Molteni, who watches impotently as his wife slips away from him. He registers "Emilia's infidelity, which, I felt, was somehow related to the venality of my work, which made me dependent." The *Odyssey* is also read psychologically by Moravia's characters, especially Rheingold, who under-stands Odysseus's late return home to Ithaca as "the story of marital revul-sion." The ideal marriage, which proves itself in Penelope's long wait and on Odysseus's long journey home, was already in crisis before the Trojan War, according to Rheingold.

In *Le Mépris*, on the other hand, Godard is hardly interested in these aspects of the literary model. In every respect, he turns the adaptation of the novel into a film about cinema. Here, neorealism becomes an explicit point of reference. Rossellini's *Viaggio in Italia*, published at the same time as Moravia's novel, tells the story of an English couple who, during a holi-day in Italy, become powerfully alienated from each other and eventually experience a rapprochement in the landscape of the Bay of Naples, with a happy ending that plays with elements of the miraculous. The couple gets lost in the crowds of a Catholic festival procession before finding each other again. This solution is inconceivable for Paul and Camille, because in Godard's work they are not driven apart by the fatigue of a prolonged relationship but by circumstances that cannot be explained at the level of character psychology.

The couple in *Le Mépris* are assailed by genuinely cinematic elements: CinemaScope and Technicolor. A detailed analysis of the *mise-en-scène* reveals that in the central scene in Paul and Camille's flat, Godard uses the widescreen format to transform spaces of togetherness (for the sake of which Paul takes on the degrading wage labor for the producer in the first place) into an architecture of separation. Brigitte Bardot and Michel Piccoli move through this flat in a way that always leaves something between them; they are only in the picture together and close to each other for individual moments before moving apart again. Here Godard radicalizes the volatility that characterized the corresponding scene with Belmondo and Seberg in the hotel room in *À bout de souffle* and makes it a quality of the picture format about which Fritz Lang had previously dropped a contemptuous bon mot: "A format for snakes—and funerals." CinemaScope, the format that gave cinema a new legitimacy as a form of spectacle in competition with television, is precisely not the format in which psychological dramas can be filmed. The same is true of Technicolor, which Godard clearly emphasizes in such a way that it catches the eye as an artifact.[20] At one point, he even has Fritz Lang explicitly compliment the film's "beautiful yellow color" in the manner in which one might speak of a "beautiful yellow bathrobe."

But the film's visual appeal, which is the aspect most strikingly over-emphasized in *Le Mépris*, is not a technical one but a human one. Brigitte Bardot's nudity is shown throughout the film as an ironic concession to a producer's interest, betrayed by his childish grin when he finally cheers up at the sight of mermaids at the screening of Fritz Lang's initial samples for the *Odyssey* film, which mostly consisted of shots of statues against a blue sky. Unlike Anna Karina, whom he had filmed, exhibited, and reflected on as his own love object, Godard clearly understood Brigitte Bardot as a counterpart belonging to the system: she lies in the sphere of interest of the producer Carlo Ponti. Her objectification goes so far that she could be said to belong to that field of sculptures to which Fritz Lang initially seems to reduce his *Odyssey*. The excerpts that can be seen show an almost abstract film about antiquity,[21] in which the characters are represented by classical statues and the action is represented by poses against monochrome backgrounds.

The politics of color gains an additional dimension in that Fritz Lang had ceased making films of his own by the time he was hired by Godard for *Le Mépris. The Tiger of Eschnapur* and *The Indian Tomb* became test cases for advocates of *politique des auteurs*, requiring some artful arguments to justify the naive storytelling and anachronistic colonial politics of these remakes of classics from the 1920s. Technical aspects played a role here. Technicolor made this essentially commercial notion of India appear as something artistic and experimental.

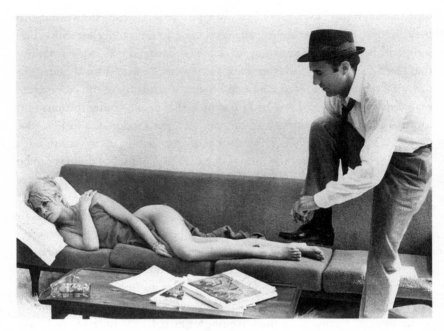

Brigitte Bardot and Michel Piccoli in *Die Verachtung*, 1963 (Everett Collection, image no. 0097549261)

In November 1964, Godard and Lang shot a slideshow for the television series *Cinéastes de notre temps* by André Labarthe and Janine Bazin, which was not broadcast until 1967. *Le Dinosaure et le bébé* stages the encounter between an old filmmaker and a young one. Godard asked the question: "What is a *metteur en scène*?" The answer cannot be given directly. Rather, it develops out of a meandering conversation about work and art, in which Lang, who speaks good French, deprecates his art. Films, to him, are like "petits pains" (bread rolls). *Le Dinosaure et le bébé* becomes particularly interesting where it deals with the aspects to which the title refers: two different eras of cinema. Lang describes himself as a dinosaur and jokingly calls Godard a baby, to which Godard replies, "Children are always punished," perhaps a reflexive reference to his juvenile misdeeds.

The argument that emerges from this is significant, even if it is not spelled out. Godard asks how to deal with censorship (also meaning commercial censorship by producers, who always want mere entertainment). "Should we want to smash everything like children or should we go around the censors?" Lang has to admit that in two or three films he had to sacrifice the very scenes that had originally inspired the whole work. Godard gave an example of how to deal with censorship with *Le Mépris*. What is a *metteur en scène*? The question is answered with the help of examples: scenes from *M* by Fritz Lang and *Le Mépris* by Godard. Lang is the man with the pencil who immediately makes a sketch. Godard is the man with the cigarette, who relies on improvisation. He is interested in "ensembles," not details. Both name "the documentary" as the vanishing point of their work. Both hazard a look at the future. Lang would like to make another film. It would be called *Death of a Career Girl* and would show a woman who is alive and yet already dead ("un mort vivant"). Godard wants to make a film about students, along the lines of *On the Waterfront*, in which Marlon Brando plays a dockworker who develops an awareness of his situation. It was to be another three years before he was able to realize this idea with *La Chinoise*.

~

The next film, *Bande à part* (*Band of Outsiders*, 1964), is based on the crime novel *Fool's Gold* by Dolores Hitchens. In the German translation, the novel is titled *Flucht nach Las Vegas*; it is a piece of "pulp fiction" of the sort that Quentin Tarantino made canonical outside the United States with his 1994 film of the same name. *Bande à part* is the title Tarantino explicitly quoted when he named his production company "A Band Apart" in 1995. With Godard and in the francophone world, there is another term that applies to the genre: *série B*. As always, several other texts are at play in the work on *Bande à part*, most notably Raymond Queneau's *Odile*, a key novel on French surrealism in which André Breton can be recognized behind a character called Anglarès. Godard brings together two kinds of literature: high and low, experimental and commercial, and from this, together with many allusions to the traditions of cinema, he makes a film that he quite rightly calls "*mon histoire*" (my story)—he speaks as an off-screen narrator, albeit in the manner of an interrupted chorus. When he first reveals himself, the film has already been running for a while, and Godard himself admits at this moment that his intervention is actually unnecessary and that the images are meaningful enough. Later, however, he does become more engaged, and close listening reveals that he introduces the tone of a different sort of novel into the pulp fiction of the original, a classically realist tone, which he subtly and ironically breaks ("The Austerlitz sun rose over the Bastille"; "The Seine looked like it was from a painting by Corot").

Bande à part tells the story of three young people in Paris who get to know each other at a language school. Odile (Anna Karina), Arthur (Claude Brasseur), and Franz (Sami Frey) want to learn English. The teacher takes Shakespeare's *Romeo and Juliet* as her starting point—a pedagogical choice that she justifies with an equation on the blackboard: "classique = moderne." Here Godard's central aesthetic theorem emerges once again, in a logical form that allows him to maneuver between these major categories in both directions. The modernity of *Bande à part* is open and clear: The film is hardly interested in resolving everything through some "coup." Godard paints the three protagonists as dawdling layabouts, who have happened upon one another by chance and are held in suspension by their three-way dynamic. A constellation made up of one girl between two boys creates numerous possibilities for leaving matters unresolved. At the same time, this is a classical arrangement, comparable to that of Truffaut's *Jules et Jim* (1962) but also that of many criminal cases. The romantic saga is determined by the offence.

The Seine is the connecting line in *Bande à part*, along which the film's scenes are strung. Odile lives with an aunt in Joinville-le-Pont, in an area in the southeast of Paris where the city blends into nature, with detached houses, garden allotments, and garages. The large cable reels that can be seen again and again indicate that this part of the city is being connected to infrastructure, but it remains an undeveloped, enchanted area in which separate residential communities like that of Odile's Aunt Victoria's seem to be quite normal. Under her roof lives a Monsieur Stolz, who hoards a large pile of cash that he is hiding from the taxman, so it seems almost justified to relieve this man of his wealth. When Arthur and Franz drive out to Joinville-le-Pont for the first time in their open-topped Simca, they act out a Western scene on the road: Pat Garrett shoots the bandit Billy the Kid. This scene has no further significance, but it immediately makes it clear that Godard, as in *À bout de souffle*, is at work in the echo chambers of an Americanized postwar culture.

Bande à part is "his" story not in the sense that he is the one pushing the narrative forward but rather in that he is searching, by way of aesthetic digressions, for alternative motifs for his film noir paraphrase. Odile is not a femme fatale but "a romantic girl" who is quizzed and teased by both men, by the rude Arthur in particular. Anna Karina plays her as if Odile is just discovering her own erotic appeal. In a casual scene, we see how she undoes her hair, which she had initially tied into two side buns and had let down in English class in front of Arthur's covetous gaze, in front of a mirror so that she can see whether it would cover her breasts—she is reacting to the fact that she feels that Arthur, and probably also by Franz, have undressed her in their minds.

The fact that the film is not under any time pressure to produce a plot is emphasized by Godard in two scenes that have become famous. In a café, Odile, Arthur, and Franz playact at holding a minute's silence, but it is Godard who cuts the sound while the protagonists obviously continue talking. John Cage's *4'33"* was created in 1952, and Godard's digression here could be understood as a variation on it: with Cage, it is a matter of musical instruments that are not being played for the duration of the piece; with Godard, it is one of the instruments of cinema, the soundtrack, that is suspended for the duration of this intervention.

Later, Odile, Arthur, and Franz pass the time until the robbery, which is to take place at night "out of respect for the laws of *série B*," walking through the Louvre. They want to beat the alleged record of a man called Jimmy Johnson and cross the museum, which Odile had not been familiar with, in nine minutes and forty-three seconds—two seconds faster than the "record." It is not an iconoclastic scene but rather a moment of isolation for the protagonists, who here, as in the language school, become recognizable as not belonging anywhere (culturally, socially). They live in a world of sporadic references ("You'll never win Indianapolis," Franz says to Arthur as he races the Simca through the mud), but they do not belong to any milieu, and certainly not to a bourgeois one familiar with the Louvre; they are scattered individuals in a landscape whose confusion Godard specifically emphasizes in a long, comic sequence. Odile runs out of the house to her waiting friends. She must cross a canal, throws a steak to a tiger on the way, and finally arrives breathlessly at her destination. Here, motifs of surrealism (the arbitrary juxtaposition of things that do not belong together) are combined with the wild chases of slapstick films. At the same time, this scene, which is superfluous to the narrative, serves the specific development of a landscape and its romantic exaggeration within the odyssey of an out-of-place girl.

The particular crime that Arthur is driving at, under the pressure of a petty-bourgeois kinship, ends grotesquely but also "tragically and *méfiantly*," in a manner full of mistrust. It is Arthur who betrays his increasingly unwilling accomplices, who finds most of the money in the doghouse and wants to keep it for himself, and who is confronted and shot by his uncle. Godard has the gunfight drag on excessively, so that even Arthur can fire a fatal shot before he dramatically staggers out of existence; all the "criminals" are dead, no one else has been badly hurt, and yet Odile is disgusted by the whole thing. She drives off with Franz, and after using a counting rhyme to make their decision, they opt to head south. The last picture shows them at a pier overlooking the sea (which is hidden out of shot). Love is a possibility; breasts and legs, the things you admire (from a heterosexual man's perspective) in the opposite sex, is reality. JEANLUC CINÉMA GODARD (this is how the director declares himself the author of the work at the beginning with one of his typical graphic credit sequences) has the last word: "My story ends here like a dime novel. At a superb moment, when everything is going right. Our next episode, this time in Cinemascope and Technicolor: Odile and Franz in the tropics."

~

In this hectic year 1964, Godard completed another film that he had promised to the director of the Venice Festival. For *Une femme mariée* (*A Married Woman*) there was also an immediate, personal connection. Anna Karina had begun a relationship with the actor Maurice Ronet, so she was now married (to Godard) and having a relationship with another man. *Une femme mariée* also tells of a love triangle: Charlotte (Macha Méril) is caught between her pilot husband, Pierre (Philippe Leroy), and the actor Robert (Bernard Noël). What Anna Karina says at the end of *Bande à part* about love, which she understands as a reduction to female body parts (breasts and thighs . . .), Godard takes over into the next film: He begins with a woman's hand in front of the white surface of a sheet, clearly wearing a wedding ring.[22] Shortly afterward, a second hand appears in the shot: a man's hand, as can be seen from the hairy forearm, reaching out to the woman's hand. This sequence makes clear in abstract form what the film will be about: tension between a tender gesture and a possessive touch.

A strong argument can be made to the effect that *Une femme mariée* is Godard's first truly avant-garde film.[23] The subtitle, which works on a crucial category of modernist aesthetics, gives a hint: *Fragments of a Film Made in 1964*. The fragmentation in question is, first, that of the bodies in the image and, second, that of the narrative. Godard only shows a conventional, semi-close-up view of Charlotte and her lover after a while—before that we see body parts, erotically charged zones, and the hooks and eyes of underwear, whose fashion and advertising is an important strand of the film. Even the dialogue is about parts of the body when Robert imagines that Charlotte could leave her armpits unshaven "like in those Italian films" (he might be thinking of Anna Magnani, an icon of neorealism); she, on the other hand, prefers the epilated female image from fashion magazines.

The fragmentation continues at the level of content, because Charlotte's life breaks down into parts between which she undertakes complicated maneuvers of transition (she never just takes a taxi from one man to another but instead changes vehicles in between, as if she were an agent who has to shake off pursuers—and Pierre does indeed at one point send a private detective after her). Her life is never settled in such a way that she can be at peace with herself, with a man, with everything. But that is her true ideal: to be completely at one with herself. Godard intensifies this underlying sense of alienation through a series of further cinematic interventions.

He stages an evening for three, when Pierre and Charlotte receive a guest for dinner. They do not communicate through conversation, but in the form of three consecutive monologues, each of which is given a title. Pierre, who has returned from a trip to the Auschwitz trials in Germany, has hung a photograph of a man in an SS uniform on the wall of his bedroom, for reasons that are not entirely clear. He talks about "mémoire" (remembrance) and talks about a parade in Paris, a "défilé de déportés": dressed in the outfits of that time, former concentration camp prisoners recalled their suffering, but now that they were better fed, they made a strange impression. Pierre refers to Rossellini, who is said to have observed this procession, and speaks of a "faux mémoire" (false memory).[24]

Charlotte's monologue is anchored in the present. She speaks longingly about what it would be like to be simply at one with herself, without reflective distance—a state that "keeps slipping through my fingers." The guest—the (Jewish) critic and colleague Roger Leenhardt, a thinker who led the way with many critical ideas of the "Young Turks"—gives a short lecture on intellectual prudence.

The evening ends with a comic chase between Charlotte and Pierre, involving the terrace of their apartment in a new housing development as well as a record titled *Music to Make Marriages Merrier*, another find from modern life that Godard exposes in all its latent absurdity.

Charlotte sleeps with Pierre that evening. The act is ironically described by him as a rape. The next day, which is marked by an existential dilemma ("To be or not to be," Charlotte murmurs in bed in the morning), she visits a doctor, whereupon the married woman finds out that she is pregnant. She asks some questions, behind which the moral discussions of the time can be discerned: "What do you think about contraception?"—"Is there a difference between lust and love?"

Since there are two possible fathers for the child she is carrying, she looks for evidence of biological paternity. Could the lust she felt for only one of the two men be a clue? In *Une femme est une femme*, double fatherhood was the playful solution to a dilemma created by Angela's desire to have children. In *Une femme mariée*, the determining adjective "married" replaces the self-conscious statement of identity of the woman "who is a woman" from the earlier film. The originally preferred title *"La Femme Mariée"* (*The Married Woman*), which would have identified Charlotte as more than an individual married woman but as typical of married women, was rejected by the censors, who suspected that adultery would thereby be generally asserted as a characteristic of married women in general. The dilemma is only superficially a matter of choosing between two men. Between them, the thespian and the pilot leave Charlotte no room to be herself.

But even in her femininity she is not with herself, as is made particularly clear in a scene in which she overhears the conversation of two girls who are just having their first experiences with boys. Godard sets off this teenage chatter against pictures from magazines advertising underwear. The brassiere and corset models have names like "Éloquence," and here what has already become clear throughout the film in brief flashes is condensed once again:

that modern life is beset by messages, that subjectivity is constantly being expressed in the form of words, which Godard defamiliarizes by emphasizing individual words, parts of sentences, and sometimes single letters.

At the end of the film, Charlotte and Robert meet again at Paris Orly airport, where there is a cinema in which they see *Nuit et brouillard* by Alain Resnais, the film about the concentration camps in which the perspective of the French deportees was so important. When the word "Auschwitz" is mentioned for the first time in *Une femme mariée*, Charlotte reacts with a Freudian slip. She is talking about thalidomide, the drug that caused the deformities that were uncovered in the thalidomide scandal in 1961/62. Roger Leenhardt corrects her: she does not respond. Charlotte's definition of the "present" thus also becomes a definition of consumer modernity—it is the present, excluding yesterday and tomorrow, and is thus opposed to coming to terms with the past, which is given different accents by the three men in the film. Robert is associated with Molière and Racine, Pierre with Auschwitz and computers (whose memories represent a special form of "mémoire"), Leenhardt with Auschwitz and Vichy. Charlotte does not react to *Nuit et brouillard* either, and so the affair with Robert leads back to her starting point. A hand grasps a hand—and pushes it away. "Oui, c'est fini." What is finished? An attempt to recover the present through a love affair.

~

In *Alphaville* (1965), Paris becomes fully a city of the future, but not a desirable one. Godard turns against the optimism of the early sixties and tells of the advent of a technocratic regime that forces the last people to flee. *Alphaville* is a science fiction film that does without special effects. All the technical processes are those of the medium of film; the artistic process is one of defamiliarization. The Paris of *À bout de souffle* is also the Paris of *Alphaville*—and yet it looks very different. This has to do with the locations (the film was shot mainly in La Défense, the district in the west of Paris where the business world had created new architectures) and with one of the leitmotifs in *Alphaville*, which is evident from the first shot: a spotlight breaks the blackness of the image. The hero who ventures into this dangerous world comes from outside, from the "pays extérieurs." He is a secret agent whom the audience knows very well. Eddie Constantine once again plays Lemmy Caution in *Alphaville*, a role that he had been reprising, with great success, since the early fifties. For these films, based on a series of books by Peter Cheyney, there was a formula: "Five fistfights and three girls" per installment. As in *Le Mépris*, Godard redeems the formula in his own way. He devises two seductresses to distract Lemmy Caution, who is posing as a journalist. These are no more than placeholders for the third girl—Natacha von Braun (Anna Karina), whose liberation from Alphaville is the ultimate focus of this story.

Producer André Michelin brought the idea for *Alphaville* to Godard's attention when he was negotiating with the two American authors, Robert Benton and David Newman, about some exciting material: *Bonnie and Clyde*. Truffaut, to whom the proposal went first, had declined and sent it on to Godard, who was immediately enthusiastic. Moreover, Benton and Newman, fans of French cinema, saw Godard as the better option: "Compared to Truffaut, Godard is the real revolutionary."[25] Negotiations fell through and *Bonnie and Clyde* was finally made only when actor Warren Beatty stepped in and Arthur Penn took over as director. This was the source of the greatest success of the early New Hollywood school of cinema. It was undoubtedly one of the most important turning points, and not only for Godard, whose career and political commitment would have been different if he had gained a foothold in America in the mid-1960s.[26] The experiences of his trans-Atlantic travels fed into *Alphaville*. The pop-culture energy of *À bout de souffle* can be felt once again here, in a film that successfully straddles the line between dystopia and thriller, driven by Paul Misraki's music and with all of Godard's experimental concerns at its core. For him, *Alphaville* was above all a "film about light."

~

Pierrot le fou (1965), one of Godard's most popular films from the sixties, is essentially the story of a husband who runs off with a babysitter. Ferdinand Griffon (Jean-Paul Belmondo) lives in Paris with his rich Italian wife and daughter. He brings this young woman home one evening and then never returns to his former life. He has a history with her: four and a half years ago, "no, five years ago, in October," they had met and had a love affair. The timing is suggestive, a reference to *À bout de souffle*, in which Belmondo also played a man on the run. In *Pierrot le fou*, Godard recapitulates many motifs from these intense five years, weaving them into a dense filmic text with which he expands upon his artistic strategies, going far beyond the previous categories. The fact that an American crime novel once again forms the starting point (*Obsession* by Lionel White, published in France under the title *Le Démon d'onze heures*) becomes almost a minor point in view of the sheer multitude of quotations from, and allusions to, the field of canonical French literature (Rimbaud, Queneau, Balzac) that abound in this work. In addition, Ferdinand takes certain guidebooks with him on his attempted abscondment: a comic book, *Les Pieds nickelés* and—a central reference text—the standard work on art history by Élie Faure, *L'Art moderne*, whose second volume Ferdinand reads at the beginning of the film while lying in the bathtub and smoking. His wife responds by imputing to him the attribute that makes up one half of the title: "T'es fou" (You're crazy). Over the course of this road movie, Ferdinand Griffon becomes the mad Pierrot. A man who says of himself that he is many ("plusieurs") is ultimately no one ("personne") at all.

The world that Ferdinand leaves is, in many ways, that of *Une femme mariée*, as is made clear in an aside by his wife, who is wearing an invisible bodice called a "Scandale," lingerie that keeps up with the latest fashions. Ferdinand reluctantly attends a party organized by his parents-in-law, where he also meets an American filmmaker, Samuel Fuller, one of the heroes of the *politique des auteurs*. Godard had written one of his most passionate texts about Fuller's *Forty Guns*,[27] but it was above all the young critic and later filmmaker Luc Moullet who recognized Fuller as the consummate director of the *politique des auteurs*.[28] The correspondence that Fuller began with Moullet in 1959 eventually resulted in the contacts that led to his cameo appearance in *Pierrot le fou*.

Here, Fuller takes on a role similar to that played by Fritz Lang in *Le Mépris*: a Hollywood veteran preparing to film a classic text in Europe, in this case *Les Fleurs du mal* by Baudelaire. The irony in this case is even greater than with the *Odyssey* in *Le Mépris*. Homer's work has an epic dimension and a designated hero, while Baudelaire's poetry cycle can only refer to a lyrical "I," hardly promising subject matter for a male American director. Fuller is asked about the nature of film, in a typical party conversation. He answers with a series of terms, each of which is translated by a woman from English into French: "A film is like a battleground. There is love. Hate.

Action. Violence. Death. In one word: Emotions." Film as a battlefield of emotions. This is a definition that Godard poignantly proves true in *Pierrot le fou*. This film is not so much about the feelings of the two protagonists, that is, the fate of a fugitive love, but rather about an attempt to decompose film as a medium of emotion into its component parts and put them together anew—in an open process in which Godard emphasizes the "happening," to use a term from art theory.

These components are the objective correspondences of the senses, which Rimbaud wanted to bring together in his poetry: to that end, he associated vowels with certain colors. Godard alludes to this with the credit sequence, which makes the title elements appear alphabetically against a black background, letter by letter, first all As, then all Bs, the Fs finally blue, while all the other letters are red: *Voyelles* (Vowels) was the name of the corresponding poem by Rimbaud that Godard quotes and transcribes here. The work on colors that goes into the *mise-en-scène* of *Pierrot le fou* is, on the one hand, an homage to comics, which are set on an equal footing with high literature. On the other hand, it pays tribute to cinema—which, in this latter medium's competition with television, has by now adopted an exaggerated, artificial look for which the Technicolor process has become a byword—and which Godard playfully places in historical context through reference to Élie Faure's book, which is shown over and over again.

~

The girl with whom Ferdinand takes off is named Marianne Renoir. The two write a story together, but they can never agree on it, because the underlying principle of *Pierrot le fou* is a constant revision of "words and things." (A year later, Michel Foucault published *Les mots et les choses*, a book that would publicize this formulation, which crops up haphazardly in Godard's work. On the other hand, Foucault's 1961 book, *Madness and Society*, was perhaps one of Godard's sources of inspiration for the "fou" Pierrot). The words in question here are the numerous statements by Ferdinand and Marianne about themselves, which are often quotations from others, that is, attempts to relate themselves to a culture that Marianne (whose name stands for France as a whole) is much less interested in than Ferdinand. The things, meanwhile, are the objective realities that the film must deal with: the landscape of the Midi with the port of Toulon as the vanishing point, the Mediterranean as the horizon with its waterside landscapes, summer-time France as experienced by (American) tourists, petrol stations. Along-side these things, it remains unclear to the couple whether they are now in an adventure film or a romance or whether it might be a good idea for them to switch from a Jules Verne novel to a crime novel, as Marianne suggests at one point, in the hope that there may still be escape routes to be found there.

From the beginning, she is involved in a story that Ferdinand finds laby-rinthine, as he makes clear through an anagrammatic game that he enters in his diary: Marianne—Ariane—mer—ame—amer—arme. The girl, who is supposed to lay an Ariadne's thread for him through a tale involving arms dealers, does not make him happy, but bitter. And it makes him lose his soul, because that's what it means to be crazy. Ferdinand is no cleverer with Marianne than Michel Poiccard is with Patricia in *À bout de souffle*. In both cases, a man who believed himself to be in a commanding position (Poiccard as a gangster, Ferdinand as an intellectual) is betrayed by a girl who ultimately refuses to engage with his genre.

Marianne's inscrutability, however, is more constructed than that of Patricia, whose character still bore some reference to national and gender stereotypes and to the spirit of the age. Marianne is a composite: a roman-tic object, a *femme fatale* who likes to dream of herself as being in musi-cals (again a reference to her own work, for Anna Karina had also become known as a singer with *Une femme est une femme*), an international "woman of mystery" who follows a trail of death (she kills two men while still in Paris)—and yet understands where, for Ferdinand, love might lie. After they have lost each other in the turmoil of an encounter with the arms dealers, she brings him his diary, which he had lost on a beach. She thus reassembles what makes him a character: theoretical or literary subjectivity, a self-understanding that does not insist on identity but is fulfilled through wordplay, through constant crossings-out. The only thing Ferdinand per-sists in rejecting is his own name, which Marianne considers not properly literary, which is why she makes him a Pierrot. For them, the name is a character from a nursery rhyme, but for the audience it is much more: a Punchinello figure, played by one of the manliest film stars of the sixties.

∿

The male hero of *Masculin féminin* (*The Children of Marx and Coca-Cola*, 1966) is "no Pierrot le fou," one of the girls in the film exclaims at one point. That is to say: he is not a daredevil who steals a car to make off with his mistress. He's more of a procrastinator, a little clumsy, occasionally quick tempered: one can make neither head nor tail of him. This Paul is played by Jean-Pierre Léaud, who provided the Nouvelle Vague with its first public face in 1959. That was the face of Antoine Doinel in Truffaut's *Les Quatre cents coups*, a boy from an unstable family who ends up in a home. Truffaut made a total of five films between 1959 and 1978 about this figure, in whom a whole generation saw itself. *Masculin féminin* belongs to this series to a certain extent, even if the protagonist here is called Paul and Godard is clearly less interested in comprehensible character psychology. His narrative model is that of sociological research, which he simultaneously demonstrates, methodically reflects on, and reduces to absurdity by insisting on contingency, the fundamental indeterminacy of human life experiences. Godard thus follows on from *Vivre sa vie*, whose nod toward factography is again reinforced by a subtitle: "Fifteen specific facts" are declared about the life of young people in Paris in the mid-sixties. Consumer culture meets political unrest, which gives rise to the film's second subtitle, *The Children of Marx and Coca-Cola*. This label refers to two particular young men and three young women. Paul is with Madeleine, who is just starting out as a singer (she is ranked number 6 in Japan). She has two friends with whom she shares a seemingly untroubled life that takes place mainly in cafés, office washrooms, and public places.

The critic Adrian Martin is right when he writes that *Masculin féminin* is the last film by Godard in which conventional characters appear, that is, people who can be seen as psychologically legible subjects. Later, he is more concerned with positions, but here he gives himself away, like the character Paul, as a sociologist or as an artist who listens to society. The acoustics of *Masculin féminin* are very important, as something from the environment is constantly intruding into the story. Important passages in the film have the immediate character of interview, including the famous scene in which Paul interviews a Miss 19—a prototypical contemporary whom Godard introduces in an insert as "un produit de consommation," a consumer product and also a product of consumer society. She seems somewhat uncertain about contraception, but then she also knows all about the pill and the diaphragm. As for Paul, on the other hand, we learn in passing that he relies on coitus interruptus.

The Vietnam War is already clearly present in Paris in 1965, and Paul also campaigns against it. Presidential elections are taking place in France this year, which Godard addresses with an audio document: De Gaulle's voice is heard in an excerpt from a speech in which he speaks of "these immense shadows" that "made Europe dance," a reference to the continent's wartime past.

～

With the fast-moving *Made in U.S.A.* (1966), Godard pursued three goals: "to do a favor for a friend, to highlight the Americanization of French life, and to make use of one of the episodes in the Ben Barka affair." The friend was the producer Georges de Beauregard, who had made a lot of money with *À bout de souffle* but faced ruin in the mid-1960s when French censors refused to give clearance to Jacques Rivette's *La Religieuse*, a film adaptation of Diderot's novella *The Nun*. Godard had personally campaigned for this project and now saw himself as responsible for it. He also wrote a letter to the minister of culture, André Malraux, who was responsible for the ban. In it, Godard expresses a remarkably self-confident assessment of his cultural position: "Because we are intellectuals, you, Diderot and I, that should surely provide a common basis for understanding."[29] In *Made in U.S.A.*, the Ben Barka affair is only mentioned insofar as a war in Morocco is alluded to several times. The central, invisible figure of Richard P—(the surname is lost in the noise of an airplane or another sound every time it is pronounced) can, however, be understood as an allusion to the Moroccan politician and left-wing activist who left his country in 1960 and was subsequently sentenced to death in absentia. In 1965 he was kidnapped (allegedly on his way to a meeting with the filmmaker Georges Franju, with whom he wanted to discuss a documentary film) on the Boulevard Saint-Germain by two agents of the French secret service SDECE and killed in Fontenay-le-Vicomte.

Made in U.S.A. is nominally set in America's Atlantic City, without Godard going to great lengths to make the filming locations in Paris unrecognizable as such. Americanization shows itself more through alienation: in a certain way of handling weapons or showing oneself unmoved

by violence and threats. At several points, *Made in U.S.A.* defines itself
as a Walt Disney film with blood, in other words, as a summation and
cross-sample of American cinema, which is much-cited, alongside numerous names—almost as secret allies taken from American politics (characters
are named Widmark, Nixon, Siegel, McNamara, or Aldrich; one street is
named after Otto Preminger), or as a combination of Disney and Humphrey
Bogart.

The allusions to film noir, and especially to the impenetrable plot of *The
Big Sleep* (1946), are particularly pointed. Anna Karina plays the lead role—
it is her last major role for Godard, and she characteristically takes the
place not only of Humphrey Bogart but also of Jean-Paul Belmondo. The
game of identification and translation, which has characterized Godard's
cinema from the beginning, continues as if on a casting merry-go-round,
which is also a kind of admission: "They had lost their desire for each other;
including the desire to work exclusively with each other and no one else.
So only habit remained."[30]

Anna Karina is Paula Nelson, who is in Atlantic City looking for her
former lover Richard Widmark, who is officially said to have died of a heart
attack. With a Larousse dictionary in which she has hidden her pistol (an
essential Godard image), she undertakes an investigation in which she is
also under suspicion from the beginning. On several occasions, Godard
allows the dialogue, and whole scenes, to collapse into surreal meapingless-
ness, especially in a café where barstool conversations trail off inconclu-
sively. The blonde woman who finally sings *As Tears Go By* by the Rolling
Stones is Marianne Faithfull, a guest appearance that Godard does not make
a big deal of; it is simply one of those many autonomous moments in his
films in which he always makes room for incidental occurrences that have
nothing to do with the story.

Like *Le Petit Soldat*, *Made in U.S.A.* ends with the police state uphold-
ing its monopoly on violence. However, a powerful possibility of counter-
violence remains. For Godard declares the film to be a beginning: "la gauche,
année zero" (the left in year zero). This slogan can also be seen as the first
hint of his departure from conventional cinema, which he made in 1968.
The year zero, associated in European postwar film history with Rossellini's
neorealism and the year 1945, that is, with a policy of social change through
cinematic representation of ordinary people, is recast with a view to the

strategies of the activist left. What has changed here is that violence has reemerged as a real political option. In *Made in U.S.A.*, Godard also connects two traditions of American cinema. This connection allows the film to become political: Disney and Bogart refer to two ways of dealing with cinema. The superficial beauty of the Disney films is burst by the heroes whom Bogart played. In *The Big Sleep*, he plays a private detective in whom Godard could see the prefiguration of a leftist who, in a complicated political environment, could also solve matters with guns if necessary. "Years of fighting are ahead," we are told at the end of *Made in U.S.A.*. We never learn the truth about Richard (Dick) P—or, indeed, the facts surrounding the Ben Barka affair.

As if in passing, Godard made a political turn with *Made in U.S.A.* that gradually led from the aesthetic distance of *Le Petit Soldat* to the revolutionary commitment of 1968. In 1960 the Algerian crisis still marked a kind of passage for the hero, from which he emerged as an individual, while Veronica Dreyer fell victim to the police state. Paula Nelson also leaves her film as a victim. Godard came away from the film with the first clear indications of his political radicalization on display.

~

Shot at the same time as *Made in U.S.A.*, *Deux ou trois choses que je sais d'elle* (*Two or Three Things I Know about Her*, 1967) is considered by many to be one of Godard's best. This may have something to do with the fact that here, for the first time, the essay form displaces the form of the feature film, however fractured. Which is not to say that there isn't a protagonist. After all, the title itself refers to a woman. Godard himself later stated that he was interested in "analyzing a region on the basis of one or two persons, that is, a historical, biological, geographical situation, but on the basis of one person—it would have been too difficult with several."[31] This woman's name is Juliette Jeanson, but already in the first shots the character is broken down into its two components: On the one hand, there is the Russian-born actress Marina Vlady and on the other, Juliette Jeanson, married, mother of one son. Both stand on a balcony in one of those Parisian new-build areas that Godard had addressed in successive works, from the original allotment gardens and garage parking lot labyrinths in Joinville-le-Pont (*Bande à part*) to La Défense (*Alphaville*) to new residential buildings (*Une femme mariée*). Now, for the first time, we are in a real *banlieue*, which at that time was not yet a synonym for "problem neighborhood." The "elle" of the title refers to Juliette Jeanson, but it can also refer to Paris, the city (*la cité* or *la ville* or, as an insert in the film indicates, Paris: "la région Parisienne," whose infrastructure was then being comprehensively renewed).

And who is "je," who speaks in the first person? It is Godard himself, who is present throughout the film with his whispering voice and who declares the narrative project to be one of analysis and scientific research (a "film enquête"), whereby individual disciplines merge into one another. "I study the *cité* like a biologist," he says at one point; an insert speaks of an "Introduction à l'ethnologie" (Introduction to ethnology), in the sense of a turning away from "primitives" and toward one's own society, which Jean Rouch also undertook as a filmmaker. For Godard, Juliette is the figure in an experiment; he is the observer who—as in *Vivre sa vie* and *Une femme mariée*—brings together some of the fragments of a woman's life: two or three things, never all of them. Juliette experiences the fragmentary as a burden; she dreams of falling into a thousand pieces.

The experiment is driven by the de Gaulle government, but more by more general institutions: industrial society and capitalism. It leads to a modernization of Paris. Construction work can be seen at many points in the film, and there is as much demolition and destruction as there is construction. The radical reorganization of Paris by Georges-Eugène Haussmann in the nineteenth century is being supplemented by a division of the city into center and periphery. For Godard, this is accompanied by new class discrimination.

The Jeansons are a typical small family, living among thousands of others in the honeycombs of the new buildings. But behind closed doors, there are widely divergent interests at work. The father listens in on enemy communications from the Americans in Vietnam with a friend, while Juliette reveals herself to be a typical housewife. She washes the dishes and talks about Louis-Féraud tights. *Deux ou trois choses que je sais d'elle* covers a day in the life of the Jeansons. The family separates in the morning and comes together again in the evening. In between, Juliette is alone in the city after dropping her son off at a shabby daycare center that doubles as a hotel that charges by the hour. During this time, she lives a different life, but one that coincides with the necessities of everyday family life: that is, she can never make ends meet, and that is why she prostitutes herself.

The scenes are strongly reminiscent of *Vivre sa vie*, the difference being that Godard now gives the matter much more thoughtful treatment. There is no longer an underlying genre formula here (of a fallen girl in a world of crooks) but rather a reflexivity that repeatedly holds up the narrative. "How is it that on August 17, 1966, one has to be thinking about another person in Asia?" Juliette asks herself, in the very scene in which she and a friend visit an American war photographer in the hotel who is on holiday from his missions in Vietnam (a cover of *Life Magazine* with the title "War Goes On" is lying around). Several times Juliette drops out of character and addresses the camera and society directly with a questioning look or a reflection, as if she were trying to answer their questions (i.e., the audience's questions about her own life). *Deux ou trois choses que je sais d'elle* ends with an allegory: a *cité* in green grass, made from detergent boxes (Dash, Persil) and other consumer goods such as a pack of Hollywood chewing gum. It's a bitter gag that reminds us of the morning scene at the Jeansons's home when the boy asks his mother, "What is language?" She answers, "Language is the house in which people live." This allusion to Heidegger's famous definition of language from the *Letter on Humanism* becomes a joke in the final image: people live in boxes and language is reduced to brand names. The American critic Amy Taubin sees in this image a confrontation between Godard and Warhol's Pop Art strategies (declaring a Brillo box to be art), but in Godard's work such citations are always integrated into clearly more complex maneuvers of reference and sublation. The two or three things you can know about a character like Juliette are more than just particles of all-shaping commodity pop culture. They can also still be understood in terms of an existentialist view of life. "What comes next?" "Dying?" "And after that?" "Pas encore mort." Not dead yet.

CHAPTER 3

Revolutionary Cinema

1967 to 1972

One of the most important films about 1968 was made in 1967: *La Chinoise* (*The Chinese Woman*), shot one year before the May events in France. Godard shows great powers of clairvoyance here, inspired by a new love. He had seen Anne Wiazemsky in *Au hasard Balthazar*, in which she had debuted in 1966 at the age of eighteen. "François Mauriac's granddaughter stars in a film by Robert Bresson" was the headline in *France Soir*. The Catholic writer Mauriac was an institution in de Gaulle's France, the conservative antithesis to Jean-Paul Sartre. And in another way, this special status also applied to Robert Bresson, the Catholic filmmaker who filmed Georges Bernanos's *Diary of a Country Priest* in 1951 and presented his version of the French national myth with *Procès de Jeanne d'Arc* in 1962. Bresson's ascetic film language is sometimes associated with his particular religiosity: he was a Jansenist, a follower of a reform movement that derives strongly from the theology of sin set out by the church father Augustine that sees people as completely dependent on divine grace.

Au hasard Balthazar thus represented a kind of cultural summit in which the young actress was the material on which the old masters worked. In her book *Jeune fille*, written many years later, Wiazemsky described Bresson's awkward advances at the time—the age difference was almost forty years— while he was making a film about the mysticism of life. The focus is on a donkey and two children, and Wiazemsky plays the girl Marie, who undergoes a cruel initiation into the world of sexuality.

Visitors arrived during the production. There was a meal with Bresson and Godard in which the two men tried to outdo each other in literary erudition. "Jean-Luc Godard wandered between us for another hour—

with the troubled expression of an orphan hopelessly looking for a family. Every now and then I felt his gaze resting on me for a longer time."[1] In retrospect, Wiazemsky describes an awkward man who approached the well-regarded Bresson with a mixture of ambition and obsequiousness. A year later, he confessed to her the real reason for his visit to the set: "He had fallen in love, he said, with a photo of me that had appeared in *Le Figaro*, and going to see Robert Bresson had only been an excuse to get close to me." Anne Wiazemsky opened up a new world of concepts and slogans for Godard. She lived in Nanterre, a satellite town west of Paris and the headquarters of Guy Debord's Situationist International, and studied philosophy in an extremely politicized atmosphere. One of her fellow students was the young anarchist Daniel Cohn-Bendit, already called "Dany le Rouge" (Red Dany) at that time. One of her teachers was the philosopher Francis Jeanson, a legendary figure from the resistance against conservative policy on Algeria. Godard, who had hitherto been rather ludic about politics, quite spontaneously made *La Chinoise* about these experiences. "For me, it's a documentary, because at the time I was in love with Anne Wiazemsky. . . . I had vague ideas about left and right or whatnot that people had put in my head, or that I had put in my own head. . . . If Anne Wiazemsky had not been a student at Nanterre at the time, and if Francis Jeanson had not been one of her philosophy professors, the film would not exist."[2]

In *La Chinoise*, Wiazemsky, by now Godard's partner, is at the center of a group of young people who lock themselves into the upper-middle-class flat belonging to Véronique's parents. Godard takes the name of the FLN activist from *Le Petit Soldat* for the character played by Wiazemsky, indicating the scope of the enormous change in his political interests over just seven years. The students see themselves as "workers engaged in revolutionary production": Véronique, daughter of a banker; Guillaume (Jean-Pierre Léaud), an actor; Yvonne (Juliet Berto), a country girl; Henri, who works at an "Institut de logique économique" and appears to be the most rational of the group; and Kirilov, who keeps talking about suicide and is named after the character in Dostoevsky's *Demons*. *La Chinoise* starts with the young people making an attempt at analysis. An understanding of social situations is supposed to serve as the basis of practice, and the film takes up this movement of politicization in its form: "un film en train de se faire," a film in the process of being made. In the small-scale factionalized left of those years, the Aden-Arabie cell belonged to the Marxist-Leninists, who were critical of the French Communist Party (PCF) and inspired by the Chinese Cultural Revolution in the mid-1960s. The name Aden-Arabie refers to a youthful pamphlet by Paul Nizan, who had traveled through the southern Arabian peninsula in 1931. The book came out in 1960 with a foreword by Jean-Paul Sartre, and in view of the increasing interest in the "Third World" (French "tiers-mondisme"), it was an important element in the search for political identification.

The second essential point of reference is theater. *La Chinoise* was something of a commission for the renowned Avignon Theatre Festival, born out of Godard's acquaintance with its director Jean Vilar. The five protagonists of *La Chinoise* play revolutionary youths in theatrical form. At the outset of the play, the suspicion is that they want merely to portray something: "Véronique confuses theatre with Marxism; her father worked with Artaud," the script says of her in a polemical remark that incidentally disparages an earlier avant-garde. There is, then, a growing pressure to radicalize at the level of practice. Godard reveals an essential subtext to Jean-Pierre Léaud's Guillaume only late in the film: he identifies him through an insert with Wilhelm (Guillaume) Meister, the main character of Goethe's paradigmatic *Bildungsroman*, an early version of which was conceived as a "Theatrical Mission." The organic storytelling form of *Wilhelm Meister*, however, only fits into the modern age in the form of a citation. *La Chinoise* is an experimental arrangement and at the same time the observation of that experiment, preparations for revolution as a game, in the course of which the documentary character is put to the test by a fictional plot. In the end, Véronique commits a political murder, first hitting another man owing to a trivial mix-up of two numbers, and then killing the Soviet Union's minister of culture on a visit to France. This drastic narrative twist was hardly necessary as a means of demonstrating the nihilistic temptations of student political engagement.

Godard uses the dynamics within the group to work through the basic options. Henri drops out the moment violence becomes a real possibility and retreats to the provinces. Kirilov is serious about his suicide. In addition, there are two guest appearances that significantly shape *La Chinoise*. Senegalese student Omar Diop gives a lecture. Diop was a fellow student of Wiazemsky in Nanterre; he later went back to his home country and died in 1976 in a prison under the government of the liberation hero Léopold Sédar Senghor, which by then had already become oppressive. The philosopher Francis Jeanson, in turn, has a conversation with Véronique about revolutionary violence during an encounter on a local train, similar to the dialogue Nana had with Brice Parain in *Vivre sa vie*. Because of his personal history, Jeanson is an eminent authority on these issues. As a young man he was involved in the Resistance, and during the Algerian War he founded a network to support the Algerian liberation struggle, which made him a "traitor" and supporter of terrorists. Jeanson was one of Sartre's chosen students, and he published a 1947 study about Sartre, addressing the "Problem of Morality." His intellectual and political commitment serves as a voice of reason in the face of the young people's fanaticism. The conversation on the train is remote-controlled by Godard. The professor expresses his views authentically, but Anne Wiazemsky has an invisible button in her ear and hears Godard's voice. He fears she may not always have a good answer ready for Jeanson's challenges. The scene thus becomes a dialogue conducted between Godard himself and an intellectual authority, with Wiazemsky as his ventriloquist's dummy. Here, he speaks in the name of a generation that is engaged in an experiment and whose side he is half taking.

La Chinoise had a broadly negative reception. The revolutionary youth of 1967 felt ridiculed by Godard. His protestations that he saw himself as an ethnologist, as a documentarian of a milieu, were not taken seriously. At a time when clear positions were demanded, Godard made himself impossible through ambiguity.

He reacted defensively: "I know less and less what cinema is," he said at the press conference for the film's presentation in Venice. There is already a hint here of the conclusions he will draw; his doubts about cinema were growing. In the months leading up to and beyond Paris's May 1968, questions of commitment and militancy became so fundamental that he rediscovered himself as a filmmaker—and abolished himself at the same time. The period between 1967 and 1972 is outwardly the most exciting in Godard's life; it is also one that his cinephile followers tend to dismiss or reduce to two feature films: *Week End* (1967) and *Tout va bien* (*Just*

Great, 1972). In between there lies a period in which Godard no longer wanted to use his name and in which he made "invisible films" that were not aimed at the cinema audience but at activists. He disappeared for a while behind the collective name Groupe Dziga Vertov—the name an homage to a pioneering Soviet filmmaker who is said to have held fast to true Leninism longer than Sergei Eisenstein did. Godard's next film marked his departure from his previous status: if his political opponents, essentially strictly dogmatic Marxist-Leninists, were dismissing him as a court jester for the bourgeoisie, then at the very least, his jesting should create some real changes.

On the day *La Chinoise* was screened in autumn 1967 at the Venice Film Festival, Godard had already left. In July, he had married Anne Wiazemsky in Begnins, Switzerland. The mismatched couple—she barely twenty, he in his mid-thirties—had kept the press busy over the summer, and they had arrived in Venice together. But the next project was already waiting in Paris: *Week End*—a film about two bourgeois couples who go to Oinville-sur-Montcient, a small town in the northwest of Paris, one Saturday. Corinne Durand's father is dying, and she wants to see him, together with her husband, Roland, in time to ensure that his will favors her. At the same time, each is making plans to get rid of the other from the very first scene. Corinne's lover is a guest in the flat, while Roland is on the phone with his mistress.

The car journey, which under ordinary circumstances would prove no big deal, in *Week End* becomes an apocalyptic experience of the complete disintegration of civilization. Finally, we encounter a revolutionary primal horde that makes no distinction between pork and human flesh. In the two introductory text panels, Godard presents *Week End* as a film that does not owe its form to any artistic considerations; rather, it is to be understood as something found, ready-made, in a landfill ("trouvé à la ferraille") or as a piece of cosmic debris that had landed on earth by chance. This explanation is contradicted by the fact that *Week End* is also a conventional star production. Corinne is played by Mireille Darc, who was known from commercial productions, especially *Galia*, a psychological thriller by Georges Lautner. She made thirteen films with this veteran of various genres (gangster and police films, comedies). She had become aware of Godard through *Pierrot le fou* and had approached him in the hope of giving her career a little more artistic prestige.

That conversation produced the hoped-for result but also a rejection. Godard flatly stated that he could use Mireille Darc for *Week End* because she was unsympathetic to him—the whole film was supposed to be unsympathetic.

Godard set Mireille Darc's striking sex appeal in a darker context with a long scene at the beginning. In it, she tells her lover, who is filmed against the light, about a sexual encounter with a Paul and a Monique. Godard used a text by Georges Bataille from *Story of the Eye*. This lustful game, sensually stimulated by cat's milk and a breaking egg that trickles down Corinne's legs at the moment of orgasm, stands for something different here than in Bataille, who sought out more comprehensive transgressions in sexual experiments. For Godard, the scene opens a weekend in the spirit of the UNR (the party of Gaullism, i.e., the conservative establishment). The bourgeois orgy is above all a symptom of alienation, an action that acquires its intensity from Corinne's description. The sexual encounter is fulfilled in the retelling of the sentence.

Week End has become famous for one of the most elaborate shots in Godard's oeuvre: a three-hundred-meter tracking shot along a road where traffic has come to a standstill after an accident. Roland and Corinne drive along the gridlocked road, amid incessant honking from all sides. They pass through a carefully choreographed hell of traffic that involves every imaginable vehicle of the time (from a Citroën 2CV, a Shell tanker, and a horse-drawn carriage to an R4), and after nine minutes they have reached the cause: bodies lying on the side of the road, cars wrecked in the ditch or driven into trees. It is an apocalyptic scene that sets the tone for the rest of the odyssey. Corinne and Robert also briefly reach Oinville-sur-Montcient but can't do anything with their ill-gotten inheritance: the world in which they could spend it no longer exists. Instead, a state of affairs prevails that refers back to the beginning of civilization but makes a mockery of the origins of an initially good social system: the idealized communal form of the Iroquois, as Friedrich Engels had described in *The Origin of the Family, Private Property and the State*, is quoted and then made ridiculous. An egg appears again here, but in connection with a rape. The Front de Libération Seine et Oise (FLSO) has established a new, "natural" regime in the "primeval forest" (de facto in a national park outside Paris), which ultimately descends into cannibalism. Roland is emasculated. The "horror of the bourgeoisie" can only be answered by an even greater horror is the message delivered between the lines. The cut phallus (as with the sex at the beginning, the linguistic description here also stands for an act that goes unseen) is also a response to the murder of the mother-in-law, which Godard also shows indirectly: blood splatters on a skinned hare whose eyes have been gouged out.

Week End is an exhausting film, not least because of the aggressive soundtrack. The music by Antoine Duhamel, based on motifs by Mozart, sounds like a defamiliarized version of a melodious orchestral soundtrack. Godard had been thinking about the relationship between image and sound for a long time, but now he increasingly understood this tension in terms of political confrontations: sound is to film what the working class is to class struggle. The sound attacks the image—this constellation, which was to become so essential for the political Godard, is tested in *Week End*. The weekend journey ends in nature and in a state of nature from which no new history (or story) can begin: *Fin du conte* is inserted at the end. And then, even more strongly: *Fin du cinéma*. End of cinema.

～

In October 1967 *Cahiers du cinéma* ran another of their many interviews with Godard. In it, he addresses something that for him stood like a leit-motif over that year: he was now fighting a "battle on two fronts." A film-maker in Paris, if he wants to become politically engaged, has to go through various and multifaceted processes of identification. But in Algeria, in Cuba, in Yugoslavia, he sees fronts to which he would gladly commit himself. At the beginning of the year, he was in fact invited to Algeria, where he used his free time to watch documentaries at the embassy of the People's Republic of China. The more important invitation, however, did not come: Godard's request to travel to North Vietnam and film there was refused. In Hanoi, he said, he was seen as "a person with a somewhat vague ideology." "Yes, I think that is a sufficient reason; they were not wrong."[3]

The disappointment triggered a deep process of reflection. A collective film project gave him the opportunity to come to terms with his rejection from Hanoi. Colleague Chris Marker, one of the most important essayists then working with cameras, invited Godard to contribute something on the subject of Vietnam. *Loin du Viêt-nam* (*Far from Vietnam*, 1967) has seven chapters by such diverse directors as Claude Lelouch (who was in fact despised by the representatives of the Nouvelle Vague, but after *A Man and a Woman* became rather the *cinéaste du jour*), the American photographer William Klein, the communist Joris Ivens, as well as Agnès Varda, Alain Resnais, and Marker from the *rive gauche* group.

Godard wanted to show what bombs can do to a naked woman's body ("the warmest and liveliest thing there is").[4] He didn't consider representing it pictorially; he wanted instead to represent it in the form of a combination of image and sound—the sound is supposed to tear the skin of the image and make the body of the film explode. When he presented this idea to the collective, he was met with rejection: too allegorical, insufficiently concrete, insufficiently political. The film Godard then made is a reworking of this rejection, in which he reintroduces this idea via the back door. He shows himself on a camera filmed from the side and from the front—a reference to *Le Mépris* and to an image he sketched in an interview with the *Cahiers*: "A camera filming itself in a mirror would be the ultimate film." In this case, he is part of the camera, a reflective subject. Godard was thinking about how he could represent Vietnam's cause in Paris, taking up a phrase of Che Guevara's that was on everyone's lips at the time: two, three, many Vietnams must be created to stop imperialism. For the moment, Godard applied this slogan to the narrower context in which he found himself: workers' struggles in France and the fight for a cinema that could escape the imperial context. Godard's contribution to *Loin du Viêt-nam*, however, also shows him in a role that he would also soon reject, that of the thoughtful intellectual. "If it is no longer possible to be an intellectual filmmaker, then I must stop being an intellectual."

~

Paris's May 1968 had had a prelude among cinephiles a few weeks earlier. In February, Henri Langlois, the longtime director of the Cinémathèque française, was abruptly dismissed and a colorless successor appointed. Officially, bureaucratic reasons were given for the change. Langlois had not managed the institution he had created and regarded as his intellectual property with the necessary care and he had not paid sufficient attention to the latest findings in the field of archiving and restoring films. There were certainly plausible motives for this step, but one decisive factor was overlooked:

Langlois was not only the director of the Cinémathèque; he was also its embodiment and inseparable from it. This was also the view of the Parisian cinephiles, who immediately took action. Filmmakers of global renown such as Fritz Lang and Charles Chaplin signed a protest letter. Demonstrations reaffirmed support for Langlois.

Godard was in Cuba at an international cultural congress when news of the Langlois affair broke. Immediately after his return, he took the lead in the protest movement, together with François Truffaut. He had a slogan ready: Now the Cinémathèque française was another Vietnam. This cause offered him an opportunity to inflict a defeat on the Conservative government. "Merde à la culture UNR," represented by Minister of Culture André Malraux, who actually enjoyed great credit as a hero of the Resistance but now became an enemy figure. Paris had a cultural revolution, a guerrilla mobilization that at least somewhat echoed the campaign in Mao's China: "La guérilla continue . . . une révolution culturelle est en train de commencer."[5] The events around the Cinémathèque continued at the Cannes Film Festival, which took place in May and where people tried to ignore the Paris uprising for a while. Godard was once again at the forefront of the agitation. He went to Cannes and, in a tumultuous press conference, forced the festival to be canceled.

Godard did take part in Paris's May 1968 in the narrower sense. But he did not really identify with its goals (which were in any case somewhat unclear). He was a little divided at this stage: on the one hand, he was still attached to a strict Maoism, which made him a sectarian within the multiform French left; and on the other hand, he had already inwardly moved a few steps further on. This was to become evident in his intense productive activity in the second half of this exciting year. A new film had already been shot, but it still had to be edited and finished: *Le Gai Savoir* (*The Joy of Learning*, 1969) was a production commissioned for French state television, an adaptation of Jean-Jacques Rousseau's canonical educational novel *Émile or On Education*. Godard translated the learning processes of a child in a state of nature in the early Enlightenment period into the media present of 1968. *Le Gai Savoir* is an experimental film in a studio setting in which the characters (Jean-Pierre Léaud, as Émile Rousseau, finds himself once again in a role linked to a *Bildungsroman*, following his stint as *Wilhelm Meister*; Juliet Berto as Patricia Lumumba recalls the murdered

Congolese liberation politician) become projection surfaces in front of abstract backgrounds. And above all, they are portrayed through sound. The discrepancy between sound and image that is so characteristic of Godard is turned on its head here in an almost epistemological way. With the rapidly growing possibilities of sound editing, Godard's logocentric side now commands ever-greater opportunities to dominate the image acoustically. He distrusts images because they stand for a realism that the mass media have shaped into an ideology: going somewhere and getting a picture, as reporters do, only leads to images that reinforce the status quo. In *Le Gai Savoir*, Godard is the ghost speaking from the machine, in a sound made of distorted radio waves, while the two actors work away at concepts. For the keyword "faim" (hunger), a French dictionary produced by Gaullist school authorities speaks of a dinner and not the "Third World"—a critical discovery made in the course of this joyful learning by Jean-Luc Godard and his two children, Émile Rousseau and Patricia Lumumba.

∽

Godard took the next step toward a new media practice with his *Ciné-Tracts* (1968). These anonymous leaflet films were a particularly direct reflection of the concerns of the French "68ers" and were shown at meetings, demonstrations, and in factories. The 16 mm prints could be purchased at cost price, which at that time amounted to about fifty francs. Usually around three minutes long, black and white, and with one exception silent, their purpose was twofold: agitation and subversion. Eleven of the forty *ciné-tracts* are attributed to Godard, with further contributions by Chris Marker and Alain Resnais. Many of the later plays on words and inserts in Godard's films, which were heavily peppered with writing, were first tried out here.

∽

In July 1968 in Flins-sur-Seine, where there was a Renault factory, Godard shot material for a film that would eventually be called *Un film comme les autres* (*A film like Any Other*). Today it is seen as the first of his militant (or "invisible") films in the true sense of the word: Godard was no longer functioning as an author but as one among equals in an experimental production process that served as much to find the ideological truth as it did to constantly reexamine itself within a procedure carried out on uncertain terrain. *Un film comme les autres* essentially shows a group of young people sitting in a meadow. Students from Nanterre meet Renault workers. In the background there are residential houses, a French postwar settlement. This neighborhood points to the (*petit*) bourgeoisification of the workforce and thus to a loss of revolutionary potential. The bourgeoisie has created a world in its own image, as the radical group Cinéthique lamented at the time. Here, the tension between image and sound becomes fundamentally skeptical of images. Off-screen voices reveal the content of the debates that took place in Godard's circles.

Thirty years later, Jean-Marie Straub named *Un film comme les autres* "le vrai film 68," the true film of 1968 (i.e., a film that is not about 1968 but embodies the moment itself). However, the committees of 1968 disagreed. On September 4, *Un film comme les autres* was submitted to the Estates General of Cinema, one of the revolutionary bodies formed in Paris that May, and was rejected as "non conforme." With that, the schism was official, and Godard was left so alone within the Left that he had to look for new partners.

~

The year 1968 was a hectic one for Godard, not only because of the flood of events and projects but also because he was also constantly on the move. Invitations and offers reached him from all over the world. While he was busy in Paris with *Ciné-Tracts*, *Le Gai Savoir*, and *Un film comme les autres*, he was preparing another production in London. There was money, and a topic, which soon became obsolete because the abortion laws were changed during the preparations for filming, meant that Godard was unable to— did not have to—deal with this central women's rights issue. One desire, however, still loomed large: Godard wanted to work with the Beatles or the Rolling Stones. This proved possible, because the Stones (at that time still with Brian Jones, the guitarist who died prematurely soon afterward) were at Olympic Studios in London in June 1968 recording their album *Beggars Banquet*. Godard was able to observe the creation of the song *Sympathy for the Devil*, a powerful historical document of popular culture that follows in detail how layer upon layer is laid down, how complex percussion is successively reinforced by instruments, while Mick Jagger worked on his now-legendary lines about the devil's subversive works. *Sympathy for the Devil* also contains a historical image that Godard was able to make something of. An underground perspective that sees world history as being pregnant with a "satanic" progeny is not orthodox in the Marxist sense, but as a deconstruction of the bourgeois ideology of progress, it fit well with Godard's latent apocalyptic inclinations.

In the months that followed, Godard supplemented this material with further building blocks to create a film that was eventually called *One plus One*. But the simple addition alluded to in the title does not work. The Rolling Stones are joined by two prominent representatives of the Black Panthers, Eldridge Cleaver and Amiri Baraka (formerly LeRoi Jones), who hold court on a rubbish dump, as it were, as a continuation of the motifs of *Week End*. They speak in no uncertain terms of the robbery that white pop stars perpetrate against black music, implicitly addressing *Sympathy for the Devil*, because the Rolling Stones would be inconceivable without their borrowings from the blues. Finally, one of the most important aspects of *One plus One* is a kind of travesty of the lyrics to *Sympathy for the Devil*: off-screen, we hear a cutting voice reading from a pornographic novel whose protagonists are the great figures of history. Even the pope has sex in this story.

"'You're my kind of girl Pepita,' said Pope Paul as she lay down in the grass, 'but I'm not in the habit of taking women by force.' 'Caballero,' she replied, 'you are a fool. Do you think you would have got me if I didn't want you?' Paul moved closer and slipped his greasy fingers under the Venezuelan's fancy rain poncho."[6]

The premiere in London became a scandal because the producer had recut the film and given it a new (obvious) title: *Sympathy for the Devil*. While Godard was primarily concerned that the release of the song should not give the game away, Iain Quarrier added the record version of *Sympathy for the Devil*, which was the product of those sessions. Godard was outraged and did his utmost to stop the screening. He accused the producer, and the audience, which was implicated with him, of being "fascists."

~

Godard's travels in 1968 took him mainly to America. He flew to New York as early as the end of February. The Museum of Modern Art was showing a retrospective of his films, and he was expected to attend the opening and then go on tour. Locations on the West Coast, in Texas, and in the Midwest were planned. One reporter compared the reception for the filmmaker to the hysteria caused by the Beatles in 1964. Godard was now a pop star of the art world. Susan Sontag wrote a great text about him in which she compared his renewal of cinema to "Schönberg's rejection of tonal musical language" and also pondered his relationship to language—she saw Godard as being in an endless competition with literature as such.[7]

In Los Angeles, he met two compatriots: Jacques Demy, director of wonderful musicals, and his wife, Agnès Varda, now lived there. Varda had just made a half-hour documentary about the Black Panthers. At a dinner on March 2, 1968, an unusual group of guests came together: the Frenchmen Demy, Varda, and Godard plus the curator Tom Luddy (a man with the best connections to young Hollywood); Rouben Mamoulian, director of classic Hollywood cinema; and Jim Morrison, singer of the Doors. A few days later, *La Chinoise* enjoyed an acclaimed premiere in Berkeley. Two colleagues, documentary filmmakers Richard Leacock and D. A. Pennebaker, had decided to release the film in America. Godard wanted to undertake a joint project with Pennebaker, whose music festival film *Monterey Pop* would soon cause a sensation.

There exists a revealing film documenting this trip to America, which was made by Pennebaker, where Godard meets with a group of students at New York University. *Two American Audiences* was filmed on April 4, 1968, and shows students questioning him in English about *La Chinoise*. Godard takes a particularly clear stand here against Hollywood conventions, which he now equates seamlessly with bourgeois ideology. He makes people laugh with a bon mot: he claims to have spotted a resemblance between the young Marx and Warren Beatty, the leading actor of *Bonnie and Clyde* and one of the outstanding male sex symbols of the era.

In November 1968 Godard and Anne Wiazemsky were in North America together for the first time. They also made a stop in Montreal. The occasion was "Ten Days of Political Film." This was another detour in a year full of unexpected projects. The young French producer Claude Nedjar brought a revolutionary television project in northern Quebec to Godard's attention. In the small town of Abitibi, miners are fighting for better working conditions, and the regional television station has been involved in this struggle. Godard and Wiazemsky traveled to the far north. For a few days, Godard was occupied with the local labor struggle, but he made a rather hasty departure. It is said that Wiazemsky was suffering from the extreme weather conditions, with temperatures of minus twenty-five degrees Fahrenheit. On the long drive back to Montreal, a book project was born, but it never came to fruition. From today's perspective, this may seem particularly regrettable: the title was to have been "On the Connections between Maoism and Climate."[8]

Back in Paris, Godard plunged into the adventure of working collectively. Together with the young Maoist Jean-Henri Roger, he took on two commissions: *British Sounds* (1969) took him back to England, while *Pravda* (1969) collected observations from Czechoslovakia a few months after the suppression of the Prague Spring for German television. Neither film was accepted by its intended client. The most memorable scene from *British Sounds* is the one in which a naked woman walks up and down stairs in a single-family house while a text by feminist Sheila Rowbotham is being read in voice-over. She was originally supposed to take on this role herself, but to her relief an actress with smaller breasts was chosen for the shoot. There had already been naked women in earlier Godard films. Here, however, this special form of disclosure appeared for the first time, which was to run through his entire oeuvre from then on: women were no longer presented as sexual objects in the true sense of the word. Rather, they seem more like moving objects, like walking statues. In his militant phase, nothing remained of the feminine and desirable female body that he had fantasized about with *Loin du Viêt-nam*.

In Prague, Godard found that in Europe, his Chinese socialism had only experienced disappointments. He regarded hopes for a socialism with a human face, such as the reform movement in Prague raised, to be revisionism, a development in which a socialist state deviates from a consistent path. Since this had already occurred in the Soviet Union in the early 1920s, he could only see the invasion by Warsaw Pact troops as an action by the wrong against the wrong. Accordingly, *Pravda* struck a cynical tone: The Groupe Dziga Vertov makes fun of Czechoslovak society.

The most exciting project in the context of the "invisible films" was *Vent d'est* (*Wind from the East*, 1969). This sees Godard in the midst of a group of young people who are trying to make a revolutionary film. The discussions of the time can be heard off-screen: they are about strikes, workers' representation, general assemblies, and bourgeois society and its images. *Vent d'est* represents an attempt to get those narratives through which power reveals itself in society, or with which it distracts itself, into the hands of groups of rebels. Gian-Maria Volontè, an Italian star who had played El Indio in the Italian Western *For a Few Dollars More* a few years earlier, is now a representative of a bourgeois society that finds itself confronted by indigenous people. Godard can also be heard at intervals here. Above all, it can be inferred from his words that *Vent d'est* is to be seen first and foremost as an experiment. Discussions always seem confused: this is part of the program. The film serves the cause by teaching the filmmakers "something about images and sounds." Errors are included. The camera does not belong exclusively to anyone; it is in everyone's hands.

A newspaper page showing Stalin and Mao serves as a basis for discussion for one of the most important reflections in the film: How does one deal with Stalin in Western Europe after 1968, when even the Soviet Union had classified him as a political aberration following the famous "Secret Speech" by the leader of the Communist Party of the Soviet Union, Nikita Khrushchev, in 1956? And does this rebuke also apply to Mao? The response of the Groupe Dziga Vertov suggests that the power relations of the present can also be experienced as "Stalinist," that is, as totalitarian or despotic. This only takes one additional step conceptually, but through the form—through its contrasts between image and sound—*Vent d'est* reveals that there is no easy path from theory (or from words) to practice. At one point you see a woman coming to a crossroads. She meets a man who speaks Portuguese and asks him how to get "to political cinema." This is the great Brazilian filmmaker Glauber Rocha, who himself was greatly inspired by Godard and whom the military dictatorship in his homeland forced into exile in Paris. He gives various directions: one path leads to the cinema of the "unknown" and of "adventures," in another to the cinema of the "Third World."

In a particularly striking sequence, a woman's voice criticizes the changes in Yugoslavia, where the Communist Party was trying to establish state capitalism. In addition, there are pictures of the group in a meadow, with Godard in the center. These picnic motifs are approached using the methods of experimental cinema: they are painted over, the film material is stamped, the similarities to a painting (by Renoir or Manet) are cinematically accentuated. In this way, *Vent d'est* also approaches a rejection of the "bourgeois concepts of representation" in terms of its form. Neither Socialist Realism (Chiffre: Stalin Mosfilm) nor its counterpart in America (Chiffre: Nixon Paramount) is close to what Godard wanted to achieve by abolishing himself as an individual author: film practice as participation in a broader revolutionary process. Elements of his earlier practices of inscription and over-writing can still be seen at points where *Vent d'est* plays with the Western genre. If Spaghetti Westerns were subversive reinterpretations of the old narratives of the founding of culture, here the traces of the Western in *Vent d'est* addressed the founding of a revolutionary society. In the end, however, the "redskins" (clearly identified as painted whites) lie dead in the ditch again. The revolt is always just around the corner.

The film *Lotte in Italia* (*Struggle in Italy*, 1970), which lasted just under an hour, was made in collaboration with the Italian state television broadcaster RAI, thus engaging with part of the ideological state apparatus against which the revolution was to be made. At the center is a young woman named Paola Taviani, whose process of awakening is traced in the film through four steps: Paola has to come to terms with the fact that she is shaped by bourgeois ideas, but she can rise above this through reflection. Sex in the afternoon (while the workers are in the factory) is one such idea. Finally, part of the militant practice is to use the opportunity to speak and broadcast on RAI in such a way that not only reflection results are presented but also their steps. *Lotte in Italia* is that film by the Groupe Dziga Vertov that most clearly reveals the schema of the ideological critique of the time and that is itself somewhat schematic—how to move from false consciousness to a truer one by revisiting what the film started from.

∽

Godard later often said that the Groupe Dziga Vertov essentially consisted of only two people: himself and Jean-Pierre Gorin. For several years, there was indeed an intensive exchange between the partners; as a pair, they complemented each other well. Next to the unsystematic reader and thinker Godard, Gorin was virtually an intellectual strategist. He received his essential formation from Louis Althusser, the leading French Marxist of those years. While a variety of changes in Marx's image were underway in the student movements of the time, above all through the discovery of his early writings, Althusser advocated a consistently ideological Marxism. For him, it was most important to justify positions theoretically, in this specific case from a precise reading of Marx, as he had demonstrated with his books *For Marx* and *Reading Capital*. Via Gorin's Althusser reception, Godard also became an ideologist, albeit an experimental one. For him, discussion was the path to the convergence of reality with analysis—and thus, of image with sound. Cinema, as a medium that combines image and sound, was the best way to achieve this goal. But—caught in a permanently prerevolutionary situation—it always fell by the wayside and never achieved its potential.

Solidarity with liberation movements (even if only through the playful appropriation of names like Patrice Lumumba's in *Le Gai Savoir*) became the most important way of concretizing ideology. In Jordan, the al-Fatah movement under Yasser Arafat had created a potentially revolutionary situation that Gorin and Godard saw as comparable to that in Vietnam. A trip to Jordan followed in 1970. Godard received the invitation from Fatah in Palestine that he had hoped to receive from Vietnam: to participate as an official filmmaker in a liberation struggle. With their film project, however, Gorin and Godard got caught in the middle of dangerous Middle East politics. The Jordanian government put Fatah in its place by means of a commando action that became known as "Black September." Godard was left with a lot of footage from Palestine and felt hard pressed to draw conclusions from it. This moment of disappointed revolutionary hope following participation in a historical event haunted him for the rest of his working life. It took him years to complete the Palestine film, which had the working title *Jusqu'à la victoire* (Until Victory). It was finished with Anne-Marie Miéville as *Ici et ailleurs* (*Here and Elsewhere*, 1970–76). But by that time, the principle of a film practice that sees itself as a constant process of self-revision had been definitively established.

The last (and most controversial) of the Groupe Dziga Vertov films also belongs in this context. *Vladimir et Rosa* (1970), a comedy for German clients, was a parody by Godard and Gorin on the trial of the Chicago Eight (after the removal from the trial of Black Panther Bobby Seale, the Chicago Seven) in the United States. The theater in this film has little to do with "Uncle Bertolt" (Brecht), to whom they refer here. Godard has rarely appeared in so clownish a guise, staging a self-interview with Gorin on the tennis court, with a hair-raising English accent, as if the failure of 1968 meant that all one could do is joke about contemporary events.

One of the defendants at the Chicago trial was anti–Vietnam War activist Tom Hayden. He was now dating a famous woman: Jane Fonda, who was at the height of her fame as an actress. *Barbarella* (1968) was released only a few years earlier, and *Klute* (1971) was to become the epitome of New Hollywood cinema. So there were also political reasons to welcome the idea with which a French American producer approached Godard and Gorin: to make a radical film featuring film stars. *Tout va bien* (*Just Great*, 1972) ended the revolutionary phase of the prolonged May 1968 for Godard, with an epilogue. This parallel is explicitly drawn at the beginning of the film: May 1968 and May 1972 are the framework dates for a review of revolutionary goals. For Godard, they were located above all in a film practice that saw him disappear in a crowd of equal voices. Now, together with Gorin, he had an opportunity to make a revolutionary film amid mainstream cinema.

~

Godard came to the shoot suffering with a serious handicap. In June 1971 he had had a motorbike accident in Paris with the editor Christine Aya, in which he suffered life-threatening injuries. Godard was sitting in the back seat. His convalescence lasted three years, during which he was almost constantly at work. In later statements, however, he let it be known that the trauma of several days of unconsciousness and serious impairment of his physical integrity had changed him profoundly. The year 1971 was also a turning point in his private life. In April, Godard had shown *Vladimir et Rosa* at the Cinémathèque suisse with his old friend Freddy Buache—in a double program with Ėntuziazm (*Simfonija Donbassa*) by Dziga Vertov. He then spent two days in an upper-middle-class house on the edge of the Jura, commonly referred to as a *phalanstère*, a communal building modeled on the work of the early socialist Charles Fourier. The Swiss filmmaker Francis Reusser lived there with Anne-Marie Miéville, a young woman who had made a few records in Paris in 1967. But above all, like Reusser, she was politically engaged in the Palestinian cause especially. Miéville (who had a daughter in Paris from a previous relationship) and Godard fell in love but barely had time to get to know each other better before the accident brought about the great caesura. During Godard's months of slow convalescence, Miéville returned to Paris (also for the sake of her child) and spent much time by his side in the hospital, while all legal decisions were still being made by his wife Anne Wiazemsky. When Godard was finally able to work again, he hired his new companion as a set photographer for *Tout va bien*. So began a relationship that lasted for more than fifty years. Miéville became "ma femme" for Godard, his life partner.

~

In *Tout va bien*, a factory in the French province that had not been "contaminated" by the events of 1968 is belatedly caught up in a workers' struggle. Jane Fonda plays an American reporter; Yves Montand is her husband. *Tout va bien* begins with the signing of checks. There is a budget for each department in the shoot: the production conditions are revealed, and two labor disputes are dealt with simultaneously in a parallel action—the dispute in the factory (which is fought out on a kind of theater set as if Nestroy's *On the Ground and First Floor* had been crossed with Jacques Tati's *Playtime*), and the dispute that takes place during the shoot. Incidentally, as a filmmaker, Godard rarely had to deal with exploitative "patrons," but rather—as in this case—he dealt with rich patrons who wanted to adorn themselves with the appeal of radical chic, which he had by no means lost during his years in the underground.

Jane Fonda and Yves Montand were guinea pigs in a film in which there was a constant reflection on how to get two stars into a story. Montand plays a committed filmmaker who is caught up in publicity after May 1968 and who tries to justify his compromises to himself in a long self-interrogation in front of the camera. Once upon a time, he had written scripts for the Nouvelle Vague, which seems very distant to him now. During the film, Jane Fonda becomes an "American correspondent in France who no longer corresponds with anything."

In an elaborate sequence, the camera travels along a seemingly endless row of supermarket checkouts, observing cashiers and customers as they pack their goods, while turmoil gradually develops between the shelves: young people are interfering in an act of communist agitation. The battles of 1968 are still not settled in 1972. For the couple, the film ends with a positive diagnosis: they have learned to think of themselves "historically."

~

The collaboration with the two stars receives a postscript in 1972: a film lasting just under an hour that declares itself to be an open letter to the American actress—*Letter to Jane: An Investigation about a Still*. In 1972 Jane Fonda traveled to Hanoi, the capital of North Vietnam, the United States' enemy in the war. Her visit was billed as a peace mission and was widely reported in the world media. The Paris illustrated magazine *L'Express* ran a report under the title "Retour de Hanoi" centered on a black-and-white photograph by Joseph Kraft: Jane Fonda in a semi-close-up shot, her head slightly lowered, her mouth closed, with a serious expression; behind her in the middle of the picture a small Vietnamese man, and on the right in the foreground someone of whom only a pith helmet can be seen. This was a classic composition, and Godard and Gorin thought about it at length. Both filmmakers speak English, Godard with his typical accent and slight lisp. They appeal to Jane Fonda to engage with the content and form of this photograph and to enter into a dialogue with them about it. Once again, it is about the role of intellectuals in society but also about the question of what "peace" between North and South Vietnam can mean, and of course it is about revolution.

For Godard, a circle closes here because Jane Fonda made a trip to the Vietcong that had not been authorized for him. Now he was "traveling" to Vietnam after all, by way of a "détour," a diversion. Although the situationists did not have a good word to say about Godard, here he was using one of their key terms ("détournement") in their sense: Godard and Gorin could also have written a letter to Yves Montand, who was involved in socialist politics in Chile under Salvador Allende, but Fonda was a more rewarding target. In *Letter to Jane*, both admit that they are aware of the precarious situation: "We are both men; we criticize your acting in this photo."

This formulates the core idea: the image is read as having been staged. Roland Barthes had provided the tools for such readings with his *Myths of Everyday Life*, and Godard and Gorin also drew on the experiments of Soviet cinema pioneer Lev Kulešov, who had shown that a facial expression can be interpreted differently in various montage contexts. This view of Jane Fonda's image is exciting because Godard and Gorin also read out a historical constellation: In the cinema of the silent era, the expression of the stars was not yet as standardized as it has been since the 1930s. What is the reason for the unification? Here *Letter to Jane* comes to a surprising point: it was the New Deal in the United States, of all things, that led to actors now merely pretending to think. Godard and Gorin derive this "Rooseveltian expression" from Henry Fonda (the star of *Grapes of Wrath*, based on the novel by the "later fascist" John Steinbeck) to his daughter Jane. In the end, the accusation is relatively simple: Jane Fonda was not in Vietnam as a revolutionary subject and was only pretending to think in that picture.

~

In May 1973 Godard wrote a letter to his former friend François Truffaut. He had watched his film *La Nuit américaine*, which is about filming, in which Truffaut himself plays a director called Ferrand. Godard allowed himself to be provoked into a general confrontation. "Probably no one will call you a liar, so I will. That is not a greater insult than fascist, it is a criticism, and films like this and like those of Chabrol, Ferreri, Verneuil, Delanoy [*sic*], Renoir, etc. leave only the absence of criticism, and that is what I deplore." The list of names in which Godard includes his former and most important colleague could not have been more polemical: Jean Renoir was, after all, one of the greatest French filmmakers of the twentieth century (and became very important for Godard in his later period); Chabrol, on the other hand, was, for Godard, not even worth an invective. It was enough to mention Chabrol, one of the former representatives of the Nouvelle Vague, in connection with Marco Ferreri, a veteran like Henri Verneuil, or a representative of the old school like Jean Delannoy (whose name Godard also misspells). The attack on Truffaut also has an underlying motive of sexual rivalry, for Truffaut was involved with Jacqueline Bisset at the time, and Godard "wonders why the director is the only one who, in *La Nuit Américaine*, does not fuck."

The accusation boils down to Truffaut's discreet handling of his sexual privileges as a film kingpin, while Godard preferred shocking clarity about his. But the real competition was about money. While colleagues in France were producing "expensive movies (like you), the money that was reserved for me has been swallowed up by the Ferreri . . . and I'm stuck." So Godard moves directly from a severe rebuke to a possibility of absolution. Truffaut could give him money. "Could you enter into coproduction with us for ten million?" Godard also wants to make a film about the profession, though he wants to include other aspects, such as the sexual behavior of stars (like Marlon Brando in *The Last Tango in Paris*, which caused a furor at the time), but the daily private expenses of the accountant could also be a factor, "and each time we compare the sound with the image, the sound of the sound engineer and the sound of the Deneuve he records."

Truffaut is deeply hurt by the letter and reacts with a much longer overall reckoning that contains something like a character profile of Godard, even if the main point is to make him realize "in my opinion you've been acting like a shit." Truffaut accuses Godard of feigning interest in the behind-the-scenes staff; he often also offended Godard when he said that he was "out of ideas today" on a day of shooting and sent everyone home without a second thought. He insinuates vanity as the real motive behind his revolutionary withdrawal from the film industry and accuses him of being "envious and jealous, even in your better periods. You are an absolutely competitive type." And then Truffaut hints at something very personal. Godard obviously suffered from the failure of this relationship long after his separation from Anna Karina. "For six years I, we all, saw you suffer because of (or for) Anna, and no matter how disgusting you might be, they did not hold it against you because of your grief."[9]

⁓

There was also a break with his companion Jean-Pierre Gorin; *Letter to Jane* was their last collaboration. They fell out because Gorin finally wanted to make his own film and then failed. When he left for America, he left behind a bankrupt production company. The unsystematic thinker Godard had thus lost his systematist—or he had got rid of him. The production company that ruined Gorin was replaced by a start-up: Sonimage, registered on December 1, 1973, was officially set up in the name of Anne-Marie Miéville. Among the many factors that ultimately led to the move to Grenoble, the financial one cannot be underestimated: the Paris authorities refused to grant tax deductibility for video equipment. Godard also left behind a not-inconsiderable mountain of debt when he set off for the provinces with Miéville. He took the studio equipment with him. "I left Paris at the end of 1973, and that was the end of 1968."

CHAPTER 4

Video, Ergo Sum

1973 to 1980

If there is a film that could be something of a hinge point in Godard's oeuvre, a transition between the two epochs in his life and work,[1] then it is *Ici et ailleurs*, created over a period of five years. *Here and Elsewhere* is a meditation on the word "and." The starting point is disappointment. Let us recall: in 1970 Godard was in Palestine with Gorin to make a film about a revolutionary organization—a commissioned work, with a budget from Fatah, the largest group in the struggle for an independent Palestine. What had not been possible in Vietnam for lack of an entry visa or filming permit was now finally taking place: Godard throwing in his lot with a people in the anti-imperialist struggle. But once again Godard had to realize that he had been taken in by a naive notion. In "Black September" 1970, the involvement of the Palestinian Fatah organization in the struggle was brutally curtailed by the Jordanian government. The hopes of the European visitors to witness and participate in a revolution that was just beginning (first against the royal house in Amman and, implicitly, soon also against Zionist Israel, which had taken over the West Bank in the 1967 Six-Day War) were dashed. Fatah had to move to Lebanon, and the PLO, under the leadership of Yasser Arafat, began planning terrorist attacks in Europe that were to attract worldwide attention—especially in 1972 with the taking of hostages and the murder of eleven Israeli athletes at the Olympic Games in Munich. Godard and Gorin returned to France in 1970 with film material from Palestine. There it remained—"in ruins, like Amman," Godard told his colleague Chris Marker when he visited him in the editing room.

It was only much later, after the drastic changes in his life caused by the motorbike accident and the new partnership with Anne-Marie Miéville, that Godard returned to it. What was intended as an example of militant cinema became an exercise in reflexive cinema: retrospective in the literal sense, because at the center of the reflections of the now so-named project *Ici et ailleurs* is the relationship from here (France, petty-bourgeois society, media consumption) to there (Palestine, bondage and homelessness, political struggle). The film is built on conjunctions and entanglements in every respect: "Learning to see here (*ici*) in order to hear elsewhere (*ailleurs*)" is one of the film's many slogans. It links the motif of the title with a second one, namely, the combination of image and sound. One of the central experiences for the work on *Ici et ailleurs* was Godard's belated realization of what they had actually shot in Palestine. The sound recordings of the Palestinians were left in the original, and it was only when Godard and Miéville brought in translators that it became clear that the Palestinians were talking about very different things from what the French revolutionaries would have liked to have attributed to them. They doubted the tactics of their leaders and expected defeat in the uprising against the Israeli occupiers.

In the subsequent review and processing of the film material into essay form, the program mutated into something different: television, in the literal sense of seeing another world from afar. Godard and Miéville, who used their voices in dialogue to guide us through the film, linked the Palestinians' struggle for liberation with the media passivity of a French middle-class family that experiences events in the Middle East as canned and packaged. *Ici et ailleurs* is intended to counter the images of television with an "appropriate image" (*un image propre*). The fact that a reproduction of Picasso's *Guernica* hangs on the family's wall like an empty sign of resistance is a further indication that Godard and Miéville wanted to turn away from common forms of intellectual engagement. For them, Picasso represented an outdated model: a committed painter who conveyed a message with his means (a large-format painting) but did not change his artistic practice. They bristled at this just as they bristled at Sartre, who was still the most important voice in political debates in France around 1970. *Ici et ailleurs* is also, always in dialogue with Miéville, the core of Godard's examination of the role of intellectuals.[2] In a 1972 interview, he commented at length on Sartre, whom he takes as an example:

At the time, I took part with him in some actions for *La Cause du peuple*. And afterward I tried to have a discussion with him, but it was not possible.

I wanted to know how his remarkable statements at the Russell Tribunal . . . and his studies of Flaubert and Mallarmé were connected. He replied that he had two men inside him. One wrote incessantly about Flaubert because he couldn't help it, and one would plunge headlong into the fray and speak to the workers at Renault. I find that Sartre, by setting aside the social conditions of his existence, does not make his work as a revolutionary intellectual, revolutionary. The proletarian also wants to know . . . why Sartre writes about Flaubert the way he does. Why one writes ten hours a day and protests three hours, while the worker is on the assembly line all the time.[3]

Godard thus opposes a division of labor that in Sartre's work functions in a very bourgeois way, according to a schedule. As soon as he has met his daily quota, he can hit the streets.

Palestine and other places in the "Third World" are also of interest because the commitment there is undivided. At one point in *Ici et ailleurs*, the Palestinian poet Mahmud Darwish appears. A boy in the ruins of the city of Karameh declaims one of his poems. Darwish became one of Godard's most important points of reference, as the Palestine-Israel-Orient complex, as an extension and continuation of the Algerian conflict of the early 1960s, runs through his entire oeuvre and remained decisive right up to his most recent feature film, *Le Livre d'image* (*Picture Book*, 2018).

The most controversial "and" in *Ici et ailleurs* is one that is not mentioned explicitly but arises through a montage: pictures from a Jewish village (we must assume that it is on occupied territory) where four Fedayin, Palestinian guerrilla fighters, have been thrown out of a building and set on fire—the French family sees a television report of these events. Godard and Miéville comment on this with the words "there is only one thing to say about that" and follow it with a Hebrew lament, a kind of litany of mourning for the extermination camps: "Auschwitz, Majdanek, Treblinka."

The names alone, sung in pained tones, recall the Shoah. In doing so, they refer to a topic that was still new at the time but that has since emerged in many debates about the limits of criticism of Israel's policies: that Israel, as an occupying power, acts in the same way as the Nazis used to act toward the Jews. History, according to this understanding, becomes a matter of additions or calculations, which is made clear in *Ici et ailleurs* with an almost ironic image. You can see a digital calculating machine that adds up digits, creating a kind of historical signal: from 1917 to 1936 and Hitler, the twentieth century continues until Golda Meir. It is against this backdrop of a polemical algorithm that one must understand the montage linking Auschwitz and Palestine.

Godard adopted a formula that, if one does not wish to understand it directly as antisemitic, can nevertheless be instrumentalized in antisemitic ways: a polemical equation of Israel's occupation policy with the extermination policy of the National Socialists. In *Ici et ailleurs*, for example, he intertwines a picture of Golda Meir, prime minister in Israel from 1969 to 1974, with a picture of Hitler. As early as 1969, there is a short interview passage from the German television channel ZDF, in which Godard, surrounded by members of the Groupe Dziga Vertov, holds a sign toward the camera that reads NAZISRAEL. He insists that the journalists write a check to the group, apparently on behalf of the German state and German television, "which is subsidized by the Zionists." He continues: "We want to take money from the Zionists so that we can buy weapons to attack them." In this passage, Godard wields all the arrogance of a self-confident ideologue but also tries to point away from himself: he does not want to be seen in close-up but only as part of the group. *Ici et ailleurs* is a key work in that in it, Godard recognizes a central historical and theoretical motif in the "Jewish question" (the German term *Judenfrage* itself tends to sound antisemitic), to which he would return again and again. The polemical montage that condenses into the word NAZISRAEL also contains the first beginnings of a universal historical perspective that would shape Godard's later work.

~

With the realization that you can't chase revolutions, that you have to make them "here," Godard was already referring to a tension in his own field of work in 1975. He had turned his back on Paris, the metropolis, and settled with Anne-Marie Miéville in Grenoble. They accepted the invitation of a friend who had a company there that manufactured cameras. Jean-Pierre Beauviala was one of the most important technical innovators in this field. In the mid-sixties, he succeeded in finding a solution for synchronizing picture and sound on 16 mm cameras, thus giving filmmakers more freedom of movement. His next development, the Aaton, was considered a masterpiece of technical innovation: a small, quiet 35 mm camera that could be used without a tripod.

Godard had already begun to take an interest in new technologies as part of the Groupe Dziga Vertov and invested a lot of money in video equipment in the early 1970s. He had set up a studio in Rue de Rochechouart in Paris and applied for funding for an autobiographical film with the working title "Moi, je." The money went back into technology. "Moi, je" plays with the two French terms for "I" but also with the conversational formula that often introduces a sentence: "Moi, je suis une machine" (I am a machine). The script, dated January 1973, is a significant document of this transitional period.[4] Godard promises the film authorities a kind of autobiography, but his draft makes it abundantly clear that his project is highly theoretically inspired and deviates from the usual ideas of self-representation. A long quotation from the anthropological classic *Hand and Word* by André Leroi-Gourhan serves as an introduction and provides the essential categories. According to this understanding, man is a being who operates at different levels: a biological level, which entails automated behavior; a second level of "machine-like behavior, concerning chains of operations that are acquired through experience and education and are simultaneously inscribed in gestural and linguistic behavior"; and the third level of conscious behavior, where language acquires paramount importance.[5] Godard is particularly interested in the second level; here he finds the key phrase that concerns him: automation turns people into machines.

In the drafts of the first part of "Moi, je," Godard takes up a rhetorical gesture that, from today's perspective, can be understood as a rejection of political correctness, although this concept did not exist at the time. Godard plays the taboo breaker:

> So you have to dare to say "I"; dare to say that the fantasies that are on the screen are also mine; dare to say that in '41, eighty million parts of me would have loved the Jew-Susser [*juif-susser*] Hitler; dare to say that in '72 America is forcing Vietnam to die for nothing, and the tragedy is that they also have to say the opposite; dare to say that part of me is a genius moron like Guy Lux and that from it comes the destructive power of television, a power that exploits my weakness, but that it is a weakness in which the power of my desire is organized.[6]

One can also understand the draft of "Moi, je" as a shift: One of the consequences of 1968 for Godard was that he no longer saw himself primarily as a political revolutionary but, increasingly, as a social scientist. He could find inspiration for this in Dziga Vertov, who tried to use cinema as a progressive, revolutionary social technique. Throughout the seventies, Godard spoke from a position that identified him as a reader of demanding texts. He took concepts and theoretical building blocks from books but handled them idiosyncratically and hardly ever as systematically as in "Moi, je."

The self-image as a machine is the utmost exaggeration of his identification with the new, electronic technologies that Godard set himself to studying in this period. Video is "an instrument, a more contemporary, newer technology. It is not yet socially entrenched. . . . And that is why you can perhaps use this instrument a little differently. You can use it rather than be used by it."[7] This also corresponds to his state of mind, because Godard was still convalescing and had become "agoraphobic,"[8] preferring to stay at home.

~

In Grenoble, Godard and Miéville were able to experiment at their leisure. Godard had been thinking about the concept of the chain for some time, about the interlocking "hand in hand" of workers who achieve something together on the assembly line, but also about production steps in the filmmaking process. He was now in a position where he could have a whole chain in one person (or more precisely, in one couple)—the writer as typographer as *cinéaste*. Author and printer in one. *Numéro deux* (*Number Two*, 1975) is the document of this new life and work: a film made in a studio in which Godard can be seen with his apparatus. He is now a "patron," both entrepreneur and worker in a factory that combines images and sounds.

Moreover, *Numéro deux* is once again the document of a misappropriation. Georges de Beauregard had approached Godard with the idea of making a sequel to *À bout de souffle*. He hoped for a return to the source, for an end to political and commercial obscurity. Godard took the money that corresponded to the 1959 budget without inflation compensation and deleted the half of the working title "*À bout de souffle (numéro deux)*" that would have committed him to referring to his 1960 classic.

The fairy-tale opening here becomes a formula for modern media work: "Once upon a time" becomes "Twice upon a time" (*il y'a deux fois*). *Numéro deux* once again tells of the life of a modern family—or as Godard put it in an interview, of the "sexual economy of the residents of the new housing estate in Grenoble."[9] Sandrine and Pierre have two children, Nicolas and Vanessa, and their grandparents are there from time to time. The mother is at home, and she usually wears a white bathrobe that she does not close so that her pubic hair is clearly visible. She smokes and dances to the "Ballata del Pinelli," a popular ballad in memory of the Milanese anarchist Giuseppe Pinelli, murdered in 1969 by "falling out of a window" at a police station. Her permissiveness is a consistent theme of the film. The children want to watch their parents being intimate; before leaving for school, they join their parents in bed and are educated about the sexual organs.

The "primal scene" repeats itself on the video screen: the shot of the couple having sex *a tergo* is superimposed over the image of the daughter. The girl becomes a part of the act. The relationship between the parents is characterized by a casual obscenity. The father worries about his wife's "dirty ass"; the mother loves his "rod." The father finds pornography in his son's room that he brought home from school and reflects on his sexual relationship with his wife. During sex, he sometimes feels as if he is the woman. He wonders why it is allowed to "fuck" his wife but not his children. The context of this scene is a contemporary discussion that will culminate in a petition in 1977: in the left-liberal newspaper *Libération*, numerous (predominantly male) intellectuals pled for the age of consent to be lowered to thirteen.[10]

As always, the sequence of scenes is rather associative; it is not only the images between which links take place, but above all words. A film about an ass and a film about politics become interchangeable. The contrasting pair of factory and landscape runs through the film. One of the most beautiful word creations from Godard's entire oeuvre appears in an insert, a verbalization with high poetic resonance: *Fraternité* (brotherhood) becomes *peuternité*, an eternity of possibility (a "can-do eternity" or "ever-ability"). A possibility for all time.

In *Numéro deux*, the film image inhabits second place after the video image. The scenes from the family's life are never seen in full screen, but in screens at which a film camera is pointed. Often two of these *écrans* are in the picture at the same time. Godard and Miéville create a situation in which they observe the images they have made. The couple in the studio engages with the couple inside the TV.

As in *Ici et ailleurs*, Miéville maintains a certain tone. In *Numéro deux*, Godard shows himself to be a ruler in the kingdom of machines, but he is also in a dark chamber. He speaks explicitly of his tiny, insignificant (*minuscule*) position since emigrating from Paris—he has left the upper-case world behind and become lower case. Later we see him bent over his work, as if asleep or unsure what to do. Miéville remains invisible; she is only present by means of her distinctive voice: "I am number three," she says at one point. To this day, *Numéro deux* is mainly analyzed as a Godard film, although Miéville's contributions are at least as significant as those of her partner. Godard himself has contributed to this one-sided reception. At one point, he described the collaboration in terms of a particularly peculiar image: Anne-Marie Miéville was "both the earth and the oil well" when working on *Numéro deux*; he saw himself as "the refinery."[11]

~

In these first years of Godard and Miéville's relationship and collaboration, films slid into one other: *Ici et ailleurs* was already finished when *Numéro deux* was shot, but it only saw the light of day later. *Comment ça va (How Is It Going?)* was made in 1976 but was only released in 1978, two years after its premiere in Cannes, and thematically, it was strongly related to one event in 1974: the carnation revolt in Portugal. In this old European colonial power, it appeared that revolution was coming home, no longer a phenomenon to be sought in far-flung lands. In *Comment ça va*, Miéville plays Odile, the secretary of a left-wing newspaper publisher with whom she discusses at length the tasks of politically engaged journalism. A "little video" is meant to show how newspaper production and printing function. The film was shot on the premises of the, then, young left-wing alternative daily newspaper *Libération*, but the film is about the central organ of the French Communist Party, *L'Humanité*. Odile questions her boss's decisions. He orders matter-of-factly that a certain cut be made; she protests and asks for an explanation.

The key concept that preoccupies Godard and Miéville during this period emerges here explicitly: "How does information work when it is in the

hands of the communists?" *Comment ça va* marks the final departure from
Marxist-Leninist orthodoxy, which is still present here in the form of the
publisher as a conventional party press. Against the idea of ideologically
correct news prepared for a passive audience, Godard and Miéville create
an intermediate state, as in *Ici et ailleurs*: they build on information in
which they aim to abolish the division of labor between sender and receiver.
Along the way, an important name is mentioned: "Instead of exhausting
yourself in shouting 'Death to Fascism' for fifty years, you would have done
better to study Shannon's theories." A classic volume of media theory, *The
Mathematical Theory of Communication* by Claude Elwood Shannon, had
been published in a French translation in 1975 and became an important
motivation for the turn toward information theory that one can discern in
Godard's work. The move to Grenoble and the collaboration with Miéville
was also accompanied by a comprehensive reorientation of intellectual references. Alongside Althusser, there now emerged Gilles Deleuze and Félix
Guattari (*Anti-Oedipus*, 1972) and Foucault (*Discipline and Punish*, 1975):
contemporary French philosophy that was trying to draw conclusions from
1968. These reference points, however, were still largely concerned with
the big "and."[12] The relationship between Godard and Miéville was realized in their joint work. The conjunction "and," which betokens a form
of togetherness, radiates its influence to all areas: "There are no couple
problems," goes the line in *Comment ça va*. "There is a man problem and
a woman problem and a solution." In the concrete case given in the film,
a turn away from the authoritarian structures of French partisan communism, which had already begun in 1968, is replayed. Miéville the secretary
rebels against the publisher's diktats, and in the end the party rejects the
planned video. The finished film, like *Ici et ailleurs*, documents a film yet
to be made: Perhaps the "elsewhere" (*ailleurs*) is made necessary because
"here" (*ici*) proves impossible. This pairing of concepts forms a constant
refrain for the reorientations of these years.

Revolutionary countries were still in the frame: after Vietnam and Palestine, Chile and Portugal were now of interest, and at the end of *Comment
ça va*, Franco's death in Spain is announced. But Godard understood that
he could no longer approach these world processes with a ready-made
theoretical apparatus. Instead, he had to understand them as something
"other." The fact that he often speaks of Miéville as his "other" ("l'autre"

is not necessarily a tender term) reveals the extent to which he probably also processes experiences of a new relationship in terms of his political analysis, and it testifies to his absolutism that he consistently frames this relationship in categories that relate to work. With Anna Karina and Anne Wiazemsky, he had been in the position of a superior and a mentor: a young actress and a star director who had everything to give except closeness and love. The relationship with Miéville was different. Godard's fame no longer played a role; the pair could meet on a level plane. In *Comment ça va*, Miéville is, significantly, never seen frontally: her face is only ever shown in profile or from behind. She is more present here than in any other of the jointly produced media made in the 1970s, but she is deliberately keeping a low profile.

The preoccupation with the transition from film to video is also about enabling a new way of seeing: Godard and Miéville repeatedly allude to how the image practices of mass media produce corrupted ways of seeing. But it is not enough to just take a closer look. New reflexive categories are also needed. For the two image makers from Grenoble, these start with the basics of grammar: The preposition "between" (*entre*) and the conjunction "and" (*et*) together produce a tension that also captures the pair of producers. "UN FILM ENTRE L'ACTEUR / ACTIF ET LE SPECTATEUR / PASSIF" is displayed at the end of *Comment ça va*. A film "between" two pairs of concepts. Actors and spectators, active and passive—Sonimage's films aim to be on both sides of these distinctions.

～

Despite their departure from Paris, Godard and Miéville could still count on interest in their work. State media policy was also being reoriented after the election of President Valéry Giscard D'Estaing and looked for ways to move beyond centralism. The program of the former Gaullist Giscard included greater consideration for the regions. Grenoble was experimenting with new media channels and an early form of cable television. But Godard found it an object of derision. Once again, content was secondary: Sonimage was about combining the new technical possibilities with new ways of looking at things. With two experimental series for television, Godard and Miéville finally had the opportunity to bring the whole nation up to speed with their media practice. *Six fois deux, sur et sous la communication* (1976) and *France, tour, detour, deux enfants* (1978) are little known; in both cases there are faded versions available on YouTube with relatively good English subtitles, but viewer numbers are low.[13] Frieda Grafe found an apt characterization for the unusual form: she described the two series as a "television primer for producers and for the public. Godard really gets angry when he is accused of didactic motives. He describes his work as the 'production of proto-types.'"[14] His idea was indeed that a new form of television could be developed in the Sonimage laboratory and then be put to use on the assembly line of daily broadcasting.

Six fois deux was broadcast from July to September 1976 on Sunday evening at prime time on France 3 (the French third channel, comparable to the regional third channels on German public television). The series came about spontaneously and had an excuse for looking like a contribution for an open channel thanks to the chaotic circumstances under which it was produced.[15] With a lead-in time of only a few weeks, six broadcast windows had to be filled in France 3's Sunday evening program. Manette Bertin, the head of the newly founded media institution Institut National de l'Audiovisuel (INA), took the opportunity for an inaugural visit to Grenoble; INA was also coproducer of *Six fois deux* together with Sonimage. "Six times two" meant six double episodes, the first of which was more theoretical, while the second introduced something or someone.

In the first half of the first double episode (1a: "Y'a personne" [No one is there]), people sent by the employment office drop by Sonimage, where Godard (who, except for his right hand, which keeps feeling for the ash-tray, is out of shot but is present as a voice) gives an introductory talk. A woman who has worked as a cleaner in Grenoble cinemas is looking for a similar job, but Godard confronts her with a surprising question: "Do you know what information is?" He thinks about what it would be like if she went out on the streets to talk to people for Sonimage. Later, he even thinks that she could be sent to the Soviet Union or China, where women are more involved in the workplace, with a film about the role of women in French working life. The second part (1b: "Louison") is entirely dedicated to the farmer Louison, who—in front of the open landscape of his tenant farm—speaks very reflectively about his profession. Louison has interesting views on the intensification of food production and global food supply—and even makes an anarchist-sounding suggestion toward the end: that it would be possible to transform the ownership of land into "nonowner-ship," namely, not simply to collectivize the land, but to abolish property titles altogether.

More challenging is the second double episode, where in the first half (2a: "Leçons de choses" [Lessons of things]), two half-full coffee cups can be seen, while in voice-over Godard tries his hand at an interpretation of Eisenstein's *Battleship Potemkin* that draws on communications theory. Part 2b again introduces an interesting person, for the sake of simplicity one Jean-Luc, who demonstrates here what one might already suspect: "I can talk for an hour." But he also knows: "People will change the channel away from me, like Louison." One can conclude that the reactions to the double episode a week earlier were not only positive.

The third double episode is (like *Letter to Jane*) about the images of journalism. 3a: "Photos et Cie" ends with Miéville tearing up a copy of *Le Nouvel Observateur* to remove from the magazine all advertising material that interferes with the effect of the image—which immediately drew a letter of protest from a photojournalists' trade association. In 3b an ama-teur filmmaker named Marcel is presented sitting in front of his editing equipment for an hour while Godard interviews him from off-screen. The theoretical questions he asks the man bounce right off him. Marcel doesn't give any thought to his filmmaking: he simply records the seasons in his region as nicely as he can, and then he sets them to music that is close to home: Vivaldi. For this hour, Marcel is seen as an unreachable entity within an installation: the camera is pointed at him, he is pressed with questions, he is even targeted by a slide projector that throws his pictures onto the wall behind him; but Marcel is surprisingly unaffected by all this and seems to be completely absorbed in his naive love of the Super 8 record-ing medium.

As with the interviews with which *Six fois deux* began, the tension between intellectuals and people with whom they want to make contact is evident here. The "installation" in the "Marcel" episode, however, suggests that this tension is the real issue: the involvement of a film enthusiast like Marcel should provide proof of Sonimage's political claims. In *Six fois deux*, Godard is mostly present as a questioner in characteristically ambivalent mode: he tends to grasp everything with his concepts but also repeatedly places himself in situations in which he acts like a translator.

The fourth double program is of particular interest because it reveals a friction between Godard and Miéville. Episode 4b tells of Nanas—women who might be a reference to Zola's character, a prostitute named Nana in 1880, or to Godard's film *Vivre sa vie* (with its protagonist Nana S.). Only one of the women interviewed here is openly a prostitute: she tells of practices that would be classified as perversions in a broader sense. The scene is reminiscent of the conversation with Miss 19 in *Masculin féminin*. The episode ends pointedly with a question that Godard, a lifelong smoker, would certainly not be able to answer himself: "How many worries do you get rid of with each cigarette?" It is striking that the interviews in this episode are framed by two remarks in which Miéville distances himself from Godard: "Your program on girls was a bit weak. You divide them up, you direct their responses." And more fundamentally: "One hour on television after centuries of silence, that's either too little or too much." She also takes issue with the fact that the women are paid for the interviews, which again, as episode 1a revealed, is crucial to Godard's understanding of work. In this context, it is not insignificant that according to an original plan, episode 4b was to be about Anne-Marie. But she didn't want to put herself center stage as one of the characters. The reasons for this change remain uncertain—like so much else in this work relationship.

The climax of *Six fois deux* is episode 5b: "René(e)s," in which Godard meets the mathematician René Thom. The eminent researcher had published a book on *Catastrophe theory* in 1972. You see him sitting in a classical pose in front of a blackboard on which he is drawing a diagram or formula with circles from time to time. Godard asks him questions from offstage and lets it be known that although he does not understand Thom's work in the strict sense, he repeatedly finds levels of shared language with him. Thom also proposes a new way of understanding Claude Elwood Shannon: what is taken to be a theory of information, he understands instead as a theory of "transmission." Godard answers intuitively: could we not be "messages" ourselves? From the beginning, the episode plays with the parallel between the highly complex thinker Thom and the intellect of children. The final two minutes draw an idiosyncratic conclusion from this notion and offer a problematic figuration of a thought. Thom concludes with a remark that Godard takes up as a transition: for a mathematician, the best work would be "to dream of the impossible." The way this episode ends almost seems like a parody of a normal credit sequence: the uplifting mood suggested by the soundtrack is accompanied by shots of a dancing girl. It is Anne, the ten-year-old daughter of Anne-Marie Miéville. She is naked except for her ballet shoes. After the parallel performance of children formulating universal theories, and the mathematician's utopian aspirations, this sexualized image is disturbing.

The last double episode draws a balance sheet. "We did three months of television, we did six shows, that's like a week's work—or a week of school." Thematically, there was "a bit of everything"; the topic of sex proved to be "too vexed," *trop defendu.* The B episodes are all named with first names. For the last hour, they are Jacqueline and Ludovic, two people with mental health problems. With Jacqueline, sex does arise, at least in the form of a defense against it. She does not intend to let things go so far, because she has a special wish: she wants to marry the pope. She would have liked to be Madame Jacqueline de Garandal Montini—Montini was the civil name of Pope Paul VI. She has traveled to Rome several times to have a private audience; she has been drawn back again and again. Jacqueline is not explicitly presented as a patient. But gradually, one notices that she has ideas that must be understood as symptoms of schizophrenia. Ludovic, the male protagonist, is less cheerful than Jacqueline. Godard asks him questions. "If someone cut out your tongue [*langue* = tongue, language], would that worry you?" He wants to get at the pair of terms that serves as the leitmotif for this episode: SILENCE/PAROLE, Silence and Speech. Jacqueline is talkative; Ludovic, on the other hand, speaks rather hesitantly and smokes most of the time. At one point Godard talks about himself: "I was in hospital for three years once. After a while it feels good." The return to everyday life was easier for him than for Ludovic, however, who can't quite imagine how he will ever find his feet again on the outside. "My friends got me a place to live," Godard recalls of his long convalescence. The episode and thus the program end with an insert: LA SILENCE LA PAROLE DES UNES DES AUTRES. Some are silent, others speak, and everything is always crosswise. Sonimage has tried to position itself on both sides of this distinction. Godard himself speaks more than anyone else in these programs but almost exclusively in the form of questions. He gets his point across in different ways: with Louison, he could hardly get a word in edgeways; he bounced off Marcel; but with René Thom he found an

interlocutor with whom he could try out his playful philosophy, in the
manner of a game of table tennis.

~

In episode 6a: "Avant et après" (Before and after) the topic is "What's
wrong with television: we are all alone." This was also felt by the English
author Penelope Gilliatt, who published a portrait of Godard for the August
1976 issue of the *New Yorker* and visited him in Grenoble to write it. She
starts by talking about a little detail that has formed a part of Godard's
image for years: he no longer wears tinted glasses. His view on the world
is now open. His study is described in detail: a Formica desk, an arm-
chair with worn corduroy upholstery, a plaque from China. The communist regime under Chairman Mao is still the most important political point
of reference. But Godard lives in the French present. He discusses with
Gilliatt an English translation for the word *souffle* because it interests him
in connection with his signal theory. "A signal between the transmitter and
receiver goes through a channel, and noise is added in the process." Gilliatt
plays table tennis with Godard and mentions that he plays chess "extremely
well." When she asks him about his daughter's age, she doesn't seem to know
that Anne is not Godard's biological daughter. The partner, incidentally, is
conspicuously absent from this portrait, which has the traits of a celebrity
domestic interview but hardly touches on personal life beyond the detailed
description of the study. Anne-Marie Miéville makes no exception here and
maintains her famous media distance.

Godard, Miéville, and their daughter Anne lived in Grenoble in a typical new-build flat in a dormitory town. They shared the living conditions
of the new middle class that had emerged in France in the decades after
the war. They had almost become a family in the mold of the ones that
Godard had viewed from the outside in his films before 1968: a constellation of two couples, Godard and Miéville, Miéville and her daughter.
$(1+1) + (1+1) = 3$. The number diagrams from *Six fois deux*, the permanent
reflection on how 1 could become 2 or 2 could become 1, thus also had a
concrete basis in real life. Godard became increasingly dissatisfied with these
living conditions, but above all with the isolation of petty-bourgeois family
life. Cameraman William Lubtchansky, who often worked for Sonimage

at the time but always returned to Paris afterward, describes the situation in the mid-seventies as follows:

> Godard, who is living a rather lonely life, said how sad it was that he had to spend 20,000 francs to talk to me. To me or anyone else. He has to make films in order to have people around him. He can't stand the fact that as soon as the film is finished, we go home again. He would like to have some kind of center where people lived together and made films all year round. A kind of commune where you can work every day. From time to time there would be a film, but you would work every day, for example, to find out the best way to film this or that. Godard believes that one should never stop working. . . . Godard would like it if I lived in Grenoble. But you live the way you live. His idea is a utopia.[16]

Utopia had become stale by 1976. Godard and Miéville were looking for a new shared point for their "double solitude." Godard wanted a place where he could be himself, but which was easy to reach—for producers, for example. The couple moved once again, across the border, back to Switzerland. They took up quarters in the small town of Rolle on Lake Geneva. Here they had the Jura at their backs, Miéville's home and the land of Godard's birth. They lived in a remote location and at the same time had good transport connections: it was not far to the airport in Geneva. They had allies in the area like Freddy Buache, who cofounded the Cinémathèque Suisse in Lausanne and directed it until 1996.

As far as the French media was concerned, Godard was hardly inaccessible in Switzerland. Manette Bertin, the head of INA, continued to prove a loyal friend. She brought Sonimage into the picture when discussions were had about a new extended television series. The broadcaster Antenne 2 wanted to have the school textbook *Le Tour de la France par deux enfants*, written by G. Bruno in 1877 and subtitled *Devoir et Patrie* (Duty and Fatherland), made into a film. This patriotic classic was entirely devoted to national reconstruction after the defeat in the war against Germany in 1871. Although no one wanted an adaptation that retained the spirit of the nineteenth-century version, the commission aimed at a popular format: short episodes "as an evening feuilleton between advertising and news,"[17] in which the regions of the country were to be presented as in the original. Godard was interested in the broadcasting slot. He accepted the proximity to the popular women's magazine *Aujourd'hui Madame* as a challenge. The idea of using the opportunities afforded to a public broadcaster appealed to him. *Six fois deux* had 200,000 viewers, which was considered a failure, but this was hardly surprising given the time of year (summer) and the not-especially-accessible nature of most of the episodes. But for Godard it was a success; he saw the broadcast as a mass mailshot: "200,000 letters sent at once."[18]

With *France, tour, détour, deux enfants*, he had once again confounded a client's expectations. While *Six fois deux* could still be understood as an experimental reinterpretation of educational television, *France, tour, détour, deux enfants* missed the central idea of Antenne 2: the client had expected a feature film. Godard and Miéville, however, turned it into a documentary film about two children, Camille and Arnaud, both nine years old, both primary school pupils in Paris. The children also assumed that they should play roles and not be themselves: they wanted to become little stars. Godard turned things on their head and appeared himself, under a different identity. He played the radical left-wing intellectual Robert Linhart, who had published a book in 1976 that fitted in perfectly with Godard's reflections on man as a machine: *Lénine, les paysans, Taylor* traced how the early Soviet Union sought to increase labor productivity by approximating automated movements with the help of American theories. While filming, Linhart wrote *L'Établi*, his second book, in which he recounts experiences in a Citroën car factory. He was one of those students who, after 1968, closed ranks with the working class and went to the assembly lines themselves.

The training of laborers to become docile parts of a large production system underpins the interest for the two children in *France, tour, détour, deux enfants*. They are to be made to evade the "monsters." This polemical word is used in the series to describe the adults who, according to Godard and Miéville, are conditioned from childhood to become wage slaves. Accordingly, the school is an ideological institution, a prison, with children as political prisoners.

Above all this echoes Michel Foucault's *Discipline and Punish*, a history of modern regimes of confinement and classification. The theory of the exercise of power through institutions was an important influence for Godard and Miéville; they combined Foucault's sociohistorical analysis with the technical possibilities of their filmmaking. *France, tour, détour, deux enfants* revolves around the concepts of "*ralentir*" (slowing down) and "*decomposer*" (taking apart).[19] In twelve "*mouvements*" (movements, as in a piece of music), a day in the life of two children is "decomposed," with the aim of creating a spirit of obstinacy in the midst of regimes of uniformity.[20]

In the first movement, Camille is seen getting ready for the night (partly in slow motion), slips into pajamas, and lets Godard question her in the semi-darkness on her bed. Godard has dispensed with a picture "of her arse," an off-screen voice announces. It remains unclear what interest there might have been in such an image, but child sexuality is also a powerful theme in *France, tour, détour, deux enfants*. Godard has a conversation with Camille that could be described as a Socratic dialogue. He begins with a question that fits his materialistic interests: How much is your room? Camille doesn't pay rent, of course, but now she is forced to grapple a bit with her privileged existence as a child. Each of the twelve sentences has a conversation between Godard (as Robert Linhart) and Camille or Arnaud at its center. The topics range from epistemology ("How would you find your way to school if you lost your memory?"; "Do you have an existence?" "Yes." "One or several?") to political agitation (Arnaud is filmed shoplifting). Godard is never in the picture during the conversations. He speaks to the children from outside the frame. Arnaud seems more unselfconscious than Camille, who hardly ever looks at the camera and overall gives the impression that she would rather be done with the whole thing.

The American Godard biographer Richard Brody conducted an interview with Camille Virolleaud in April 2001 and, on the basis of this interview, presented the filming of *France, tour, détour, deux enfants* as a form of abuse. The girl, for example, found a scene in which she had to copy out a sentence ("I am not allowed to be noisy in class") fifty times as punishment shameful: "It looked like I had to do punishment work, but I hadn't done anything wrong. I had to do it for him, it wasn't true, it was his truth, but as far as I was concerned it was a lie."[21] The scene is also significant because the themes of repetition and copying run through the whole series. Camille must act out the monotonous punishment of copying because it makes it clear how much the school cares about creating uniformity. Brody mentions another important aspect that caused Camille great problems:

she was used to questions having a right or a wrong answer at school. But Godard asked questions that allowed for many possible answers. So she was called upon to think for herself. But this was precisely what she had not been prepared for by the school system. "I gave monosyllabic answers to avoid mistakes if possible." Here at least, *France, tour, détour, deux enfants* was able to cite itself as evidence for its own political insinuations.

Each of the sentences ends by switching back to the studio, as it were. The conversations with the children are material that the presenters Betty Berr and Albert Dray then discuss again. The twelfth and last sentence remains open: "Should we say something?" "We are not national television." "You don't want to die an idiot." "That's true."

~

In 1978 Sonimage received an invitation. The government of Mozambique was requesting its help in setting up a state television broadcaster. In this case, the revolution no longer required any preparation: it had already won. The former Portuguese colony had become independent in 1975, a consequence of the Carnation Revolution in Lisbon. Now Mozambique was a popular republic with a Marxist government under Samora Machel, who personally extended the invitation to Sonimage. The offer must have seemed highly attractive to Godard, because in Mozambique he and Miéville encountered a population that had no experience with technically produced images. There was a single film camera. The working title with which Sonimage began could hardly be more telling: "Naissance (de l'image) d'une nation"—The birth (of the image) of a nation. This is a variation on, or better, a correction of the famous film title *The Birth of a Nation* (1915) by D. W. Griffith, which carried a racist idea of white domination in North America. A new nation, or at least the image of one, could now emerge in Mozambique. One year later, Godard took stock with a magazine section in the anniversary issue 300 of *Cahiers du cinéma: Le dernier rêve d'un producteur* (The Last Dream of a Producer) that immediately revealed that this attempt to associate himself with a liberation movement in the "Third World" had also failed.[22]

At least six trips to Mozambique were planned, but ultimately only two took place. Godard and Miéville were not the only intellectuals flown in. First came Ruy Guerra, one of the most important Brazilian filmmakers of the time. He was born in 1931 in (then) Portuguese East Africa in what is now Maputo, later went to Paris to study film, and immigrated to Brazil in 1958. For Guerra, the engagement was a return: he took over the direction of the newly founded Instituto Nacional de Cinema. Under his supervision, a film was made that became a founding document of newly independent Mozambique. *Mueda, Memória e Massacre* (1979) commemorates a 1960 massacre under Portuguese colonial rule that became the starting point for the drive toward independence in Mozambique. The French film ethnographer Jean Rouch, who specialized in West Africa, also accepted the invitation. So Sonimage was met with colleagues and structures: the idea of an institutional fresh start was already outmoded. Godard tried above all to put his experiences with television in Grenoble into practice: he thought of a centralism from below, a state television that should reinvent itself in terms of production technology, ideally without Sony equipment and without broadcasting standards such as Pal or Secam. While Guerra worked pragmatically and produced newsreels alongside *Mueda*, Godard and Miéville remained mired in reflections.

It was not only its theoretical contradictions that were decisive for the termination of the Mozambique project. Godard and Sonimage also had alternative projects: there were offers and considerations for new cinematic productions. A feature film in France was beginning to take shape. Godard was speaking with producers like Marin Karmitz and the young Alain Sarde, and he met actresses like Miou-Miou and Isabelle Huppert. Contacts with America also continued to be important: Tom Luddy had organized the first Godard retrospective in the United States in 1968. He was now working for Zoetrope, Francis Ford Coppola's production company. The latter had finally completed his great Vietnam film *Apocalypse Now* in 1979. Godard had several projects with Zoetrope. The most concrete was "The Story," about the emergence of Las Vegas as a city of entertainment—a gangster film about Bugsy Siegel, but above all a reflection on the birth of American culture from organized crime.

There is an eight-minute video film by Ira Schneider from 1979 that vividly illustrates the atmosphere of this collaboration: a home movie, made on the terrace of a house in Del Mar, California. The Pacific Ocean is only a few steps away; at one point Alice Waters, the chef of the trend-setting restaurant Chez Panisse in Berkeley, can be seen rising from the waves. The society there is glittering: Godard, in swimming trunks and a hat, braced against the sun; Jean-Pierre Gorin, with whom the rift has evidently been mended; Tom Luddy, the host; Wim Wenders, in shirt and trousers and with braces, a little overdressed. The most unexpected guest is sitting on a bench, also respectably dressed, and is reading Bertolt Brecht: Heiner Müller.

Wim Wenders also appears in the script for "The Story."[23] He was working on a film in America about the writer Dashiell Hammett, and Godard immediately incorporates this into his story, which is about the cameraman Roberto, the media professor Diana, and the Mafioso Frankie. Frankie, who is supposed to remain invisible, wants to make a film about Hollywood and wants it to be "the only film Hollywood would never make" because it tells of the connection between crime and spectacle. The Wenders character could never direct this film(-in-a-film) because the entertainment industry has long been in the hands of multinational corporations that have no interest in "showing things, but instead hide them."

"The Story" aimed at building a bridge that was meant to be audacious: Godard wanted to follow the great Mafia films—his script begins with Diana doing a television interview with Mario Puzo, the author of the books on which Francis Ford Coppola's *Godfather* films are based. At the same time, he did not want to give up on his own themes. For example, he made a point of filming the accident (presumably an assassination attempt) in which Frankie dies on Super 8 mm and later recopying it onto video. Roberto has a studio that is half video studio, half sex shop: his father makes a living from pirated porn films. This development in Hollywood is also important to Godard: Roberto's career begins with the classic studio system division of labor, whereby he works as a second-unit cameraman. He then goes to Europe and works on Spaghetti Westerns. After his return to the United States, laziness drives him into the porn industry.

Godard wanted to pack both the myth of old Hollywood and its demythologization into a single film. But he was unable to cast the roles. Diane Keaton canceled. "The Story" remained nothing more than a plan.

CHAPTER 5

The Idiot of Cinema

1980 to 1996

In October 1980 Godard was a guest on an American talk show hosted by Dick Cavett. The program was broadcast on PBS, and it was designed to promote the theatrical release of *Every Man for Himself*. This was the American distribution title of *Sauve qui peut (la vie)*, Godard's first commercially successful film since *Tout va bien* almost a decade earlier. His time of obscurity was coming to an end. Godard rejected the word "comeback," which Cavett used: "I have never been away, and when I have been away, I have been pushed away." A little later, he makes a remarkable statement in fluent but occasionally halting English: "It took me almost twenty years to recover myself."[1] *Sauve qui peut (la vie)* does not refer to the experimental period following his retreat from Paris, or to his period of convalescence after his motorbike accident, but to the beginning of his career. It implies that he had to process his early success in particular. He was coming up on twenty years since *À bout de souffle*, and something new was beginning. Godard accentuated the transition with another phrase: "I am not so anguished anymore." It is not entirely clear whether he meant to say "angry" here, that is, whether he wanted to talk about the calm of a formerly angry young man, or whether he actually meant the nuances of the word "anguish," an emotional state between self-torment, fear, and despair. He was also asked by Cavett about his loneliness and responded: "I am not upset about it anymore." So he is still lonely, but he can stand it better. The conversation with an American presenter can be taken as an example of the image that accompanied Godard at the time. He was portrayed as an innovator ("He broke all the rules," "He changed the grammar of film") but was himself unable to put his innovations together into a proper film.

One can certainly say of *Sauve qui peut (la vie)* that it is a "proper" film and that it has one important characteristic: Godard works with stars. The central character is a filmmaker named Paul Godard, played by Jacques Dutronc. Dutronc had become known as a singer, and in the 1970s he appeared for the first time as an actor, notably with *Nachtblende*. Alongside Romy Schneider, he created a sensation. In *Sauve qui peut (la vie)* he bears the name of Godard's father, and it is not only in this respect that there are clear parallels to the director himself, who was making his "third first film" here. Paul Godard is dating television journalist Denise Rimbaud (Nathalie Baye), who is about to break up with him. Paul lives in a hotel, and one day he brings a prostitute to his room, about whom we learn more, mostly in the third part of the film: Isabelle Rivière, played by Isabelle Huppert, who became famous in the late 1970s with *The Lace Maker* and *Violette Nozière*. Immediately afterward she was hired by Michael Cimino to take part in the—legendarily difficult—filming of his Western *Heaven's Gate* in Wyoming. Godard flew to America especially to prepare her for the role in *Sauve qui peut (la vie)*.

With the figure of a prostitute, Godard returns to a central metaphor in his work: love and work are linked in that love becomes work, while work lacks love. The basis is a screenplay he wrote together with Anne-Marie Miéville.[2] Their partnership in life and work was continuing, and many common themes from the seventies emerge in this film: experiences with what would today be called a patchwork or blended family converge with media politics. Paul Godard's daughter Cécile is from a previous relationship: Jean-Luc Godard is stepfather to a girl of the same age.

In the opening credits, Godard does not identify himself as a director, but as a composer ("un film composé"). Alongside this word, one must bear in mind its antonym *décomposer*, which was so important for video practice: taking something apart for the purpose of closer examination. Here, the most important tool for doing this is slow motion. Again and again in *Sauve qui peut (la vie)* the movement of the images slows down. This makes them more legible. Inserts give the film a structure that refers to four movements, as in a piece of music. The four parts are called *The Imaginary*, *Fear*, *The Business*, *The Music*. The characters also function like motifs in music; they are developed and brought together in various combinations.

Paul meets Isabelle outside a cinema; he works with Denise on television; Denise meets Isabelle because she wants to rent out her flat. Relationships, homes, media, self-realization: everything is connected.

Sexuality is bound to concepts. "*Cul*" remains an obsession here. A bell-boy accosts Paul in the hotel car park, menacing him with his passion: he wants Paul to "fuck him in the arse": "There's nothing nicer than a little arsehole." But Paul has other things on his mind. He picks Cécile up from football practice and talks to the coach about how fathers can't be affectionate with their daughters—while Cécile is getting breasts that Paul really wants to see. "Have you ever felt like fucking her in the arse?" The coach does not answer. This offensive dialogue is later echoed in the anti-oedipal role play that a suitor demands of Isabelle: He wants her to playact incest. A young woman returns to her family. Her breasts, her arse, her pussy (*chat*) arouse the desire of the mother who is only present in an imaginary sense. When Denise Rimbaud watches automated animal feeding taking place in a modern barn in the village, her acquaintance strips off her trousers and stretches her arse out to the cows: she sometimes enjoys being licked by a cow's tongue.

These obscenities are only one theme that winds through the film. *Sauve qui peut (la vie)* is a collage of motifs that occupied Godard and Miéville in the seventies. Denise Rimbaud quotes a text by Robert Linhart about his time as an assembly line worker: "Everything calls softly: I am not a machine."[3] These intense reflections on power and the body now also condition work with the actors. Godard wanted everything from the stars apart from what they thought constituted their talent: he wanted stars who acted like beginners. He wanted them to act "neutrally" and "speak like oracles," Isabelle Huppert said of Godard's directions. "He doesn't want my interpretation, but the affirmation of a thought."[4] Then still in the early stages of her career, Huppert proved better able than anyone else to withstand the impositions of a difficult director and make them productive in her mind. "He showed my fragility and my dependence. I was a young actress in a world of men, power and money." Huppert managed to transform this dependence into sovereignty.

On January 6, 1981, the Césars, the French film awards, were presented in Paris. The ceremony became a demonstration. Godard's longtime friend

Jean-Luc Godard with Isabelle Huppert, 1980 (Keystone Press / Alamy Stock Photo, image no. E12J1C)

and now rival François Truffaut won in all major categories with *Le Dernier Métro*, a classically staged drama about France during the German
occupation, starring Catherine Deneuve. Godard and *Sauve qui peut (la vie)*
only took a consolation prize: Nathalie Baye, who had been discovered by
Truffaut and who had been working with Godard's unconventional methods, received the award for best supporting actress. *Sauve qui peut (la vie)*
nevertheless became a great success, including commercially. For the young
producer Alain Sarde, who had made Godard's renaissance possible, the
venture was a success.[5] Godard now had many opportunities to confirm
his return to the cinema. He no longer had to live off his early fame. He
was in a position to gain new freedoms. Between 1960 and 1967, his films
were experimental in a way that could be linked to developments in popular culture. The Godard of the sixties was a pop artist in the sense of the
term that Andy Warhol had coined. The Godard who reinvented himself

in the 1980s was looking further back than the short epoch since the end of World War II: he was looking into the great history of human culture with its myths and materials.

~

Almost all the cues that define Godard's next film, *Passion* (1982), were also familiar from the seventies. "What is the story?" is the obvious question that people ask when they are told about a film. But answering the question "What is it about?" can be less straightforward than one might think. Godard's works after 1980 are consciously and militantly opposed to permitting a straightforward description of their content. *Passion* is about a film called "Passion" that is to be shot in the "most modern studio in Europe." It is a film for television. Some of the money for it must be raised up front. Jerzy (Jerzy Radziwiłowicz) is a director from Poland. He looks so much like Jacques Dutronc from *Sauve qui peut (la vie)* that one might imagine that this was a sequel. And that impression is indeed intentional. Isabelle Huppert is also back, now playing a factory worker making precision objects. Here, too, she is called Isabelle, like the prostitute who dispensed with working under an assumed name. Isabelle is interested in filming because that offers work too. And she begins to take an interest in Jerzy.

The film within the film, *Passion*, has no story in the conventional sense. It is about paintings that are to be filmed in the form of living pictures: Rembrandt's *Night Watch*, Goya's *Execution of the Defenders of Madrid*, and finally, in a particularly elaborate decoration, *The Entry of the Crusaders in Constantinople* by Eugène Delacroix. For Baudelaire, who wrote extensively about this image, it was above all the elements that were of interest. "What a sky and what a sea." The sky is seen in *Passion* as a background painting in the studio, in front of which a sea of Constantinople houses in 1204 forms a backdrop. Around this *tableau vivant*, Godard stages a cinematic working process: A crane camera (a heavy video device) follows the riders, who move between the buildings rather helplessly and not at all like conquerors. Delacroix shows a half-dressed woman with a child in the foreground. In the painting this is a secondary detail; in *Passion* naked supporting actresses are central. They embody the transition between the forms of labor: factory work, prostitution, cinema work.

In a key scene, a stagehand (Jean-François Stévenin, who made one of the most mysterious French films in 1978, *Passe montagne*) is seen penetrating a young woman from behind. He repeats an order as he does so: "dis ta phrase," say your line—a typical stage direction. The woman, writhing in lustful or even tortured movements, answers dutifully: "Il faut des histoires." Everything depends on stories. The word "histoires" is an echo of *France, tour, etour, deux enfants*; Jerzy's constant complaint about the lighting picks up on discussions Godard had with the boy Arnaud in that film. With *Sauve qui peut (la vie)* and *Passion*, Godard brought his interest in discourse back into cinema. The political situation suited him. In 1980 the socialist François Mitterrand won France's presidential election. His term of office was marked by an ambitious cultural policy. Cinema was an important part of the "cultural exception" that was part of France's self-image in an American-influenced global culture. The directors of the Nouvelle Vague were now at a prime age to become representatives of hopes for a strong French film culture in a Europe that was growing more united. Jerzy, a Pole, of course had no idea of the events of 1989, but he helped prepare them. (The actor Jerzy Radziwiłowicz had already done this in 1977 and 1981 in Andrzej Wajda's *Man of Marble* and *Man of Iron*, the two films that brought him to Godard's attention). *Passion* ends with the film's scattered crew setting off for Poland to get involved in politics.

~

The fact that Godard wanted always to be an exception of his own, within the "cultural exception," was also made clear in his next project: *Prénom Carmen* (*First Name: Carmen*, 1983), an adaptation of Prosper Mérimée's novella, which was made famous by Georges Bizet's opera. Godard's interest is ambivalent, and not only in this case. He explores the gaps in stories and wants to know what Carmen and Don José (here a young policeman named Joseph) do with each other when they are left alone, as it were, by the narrator. "Showing people what a woman does to a man" is how the film puts it. The script is written in collaboration, once again, with Anne-Marie Miéville. The aim is not to achieve coherence so much as to work with fragments; but the outlines of the plot can be clearly discerned.

　　　Godard himself plays a leading role. At the beginning, he is in a sanatorium where he has been admitted in order to be able to work better. He plays the madman and desires his freedom. His niece Carmen comes to see him. She needs money for a film project. "You could help us with your video equipment." In truth, Carmen is a member of a terrorist organization. During a bank robbery she meets Joseph, with whom she flees. Their love affair is passionate, but short, because political work comes first.

An essential aspect of *Prénom Carmen* is the music of Ludwig van Beethoven. A string quartet is repeatedly seen rehearsing intensively, and at the end the musicians perform in a luxury hotel where the final showdown takes place. The musical work is analogous to the director's work: it fills the gaps between the notes and turns an abstract text into a sound structure.

The leading role was given to an almost unknown Dutch actress who was prepared to engage with Godard's methods: Maruschka Detmers. Isabelle Adjani was originally intended for the role. After Andrzej Żuławski's *Possession*, she was an erotic sensation in the French cinema of the time. She came to the shoot, but it quickly became clear that their differences were too great. Adjani had brought her own entourage. She wanted to be made up and filmed like a star. Godard wanted to film as if they were material, frequently in a state of undress. Adjani left. Maruschka Detmers corresponded much better to his idea of a "wild brunette." She had previously played a single film role in a now-forgotten thriller and got involved in Godard's work as it was underway. One memorable scene, memorable also for Detmers as an actress, is a rape in the shower where Joseph masturbates; he doesn't penetrate her, he does not impinge upon her autonomy; and the same goes for Godard, who has her land decoratively on the tiles. The scene is accompanied by Beethoven and incorporates aspects of musical intoxication.

～

In the early 1980s, Godard repeated that surge in productivity that he had brought to cinema in 1960. As then, the films now followed on one another in close succession, each already carrying the germ of the next. Joseph, Carmen's lover, becomes Joseph, the husband of the Virgin Mary. In this next project by Godard and Miéville, one might recall a sentence Godard wrote as a young man in a text on political cinema: "By speaking incessantly of birth and death, political cinema bears witness to the flesh and unequivocally gives a new shape to the sacred word."[6] This time the work did not result in a joint script that Godard then realized or composed into a film. Godard and Miéville were each making their own films, which formed a pair and were usually shown together. Godard's *Je vous salue, Marie* (*Hail Mary*, 1985) and Miéville's half-hour *Le Livre de Marie* (*The Book of Mary*, 1985) have different emphases: Godard goes all-out with the history of Western metaphysics, particularly the body-soul problem. Miéville, on the other hand, stays close to the everyday life of a couple with a daughter who commutes between father and mother after her parents' separation—with Baudelaire as her train reading.

The concept of "flesh" has considerable theological resonance since the Apostle Paul used it to refer to the sinful body, while later in John 1, "the Word became flesh." With Godard, Marie, whose mysterious pregnancy the film relates, can at one point be seen reading a passage about the "flesh itself." Marie is a normal young woman. She plays basketball and helps out at her father's petrol station. Her boyfriend Joseph drives a taxi. Godard retells the childhood stories from Luke's Gospel to the point of introducing literal correspondences: the film begins with the insert EN CE TEMPS LÀ (in those days) and also has correspondences to the miraculous events that precede the birth of Jesus in the Bible. In Godard's work, even before the angel who appears to Marie, a scientist appears who is having an affair with the student Eve or Eva (she persistently corrects pronunciations of her name to Eva). The miracle of the immaculate conception (the technical term from Catholic doctrine does not appear explicitly in Godard's work, but he uses it in interviews about the film) is announced cosmically, with a discourse on chance and the appearance of life in the primeval ocean, musically underscored by the *Toccata and Fugue in D minor* and the *St. Matthew Passion* by Johann Sebastian Bach. Marie herself is also introduced musically. During the basketball game, the beginning of Bach's *Well-Tempered Clavier* can be heard, which Charles Gounod took up for his *Ave Maria*. Along the way, a central concept in Godard's and Miéville's work appears in a new context: life may have come from "somewhere else" (*ailleurs*), from outside the physical world or from another solar system. "We are aliens." For Godard, however, the world is always a cinematic occurrence, that is, a matter of images and sounds. Evolution is a "*scénario*." The term is to be understood here deliberately ambiguously, as a script and as a scientific hypothesis.[7] Images of nature and especially of the sky stand for the cosmic events that befall Marie.

The character of Marie is played by an actress who had been increasingly central to Godard's work since *Passion*. At that time, the production team was looking for "young dancers" for the living paintings. Myriem Roussel was nineteen when she auditioned for *Passion* and went on to star in one of its most important scenes, the reenactment of the Delacroix painting about the Crusaders in Istanbul. She is more than just an extra, even if she has no lines. It is her exposed body that speaks.

In *Prénom Carmen*, Roussel played a member of the Beethoven Quartet. At this point, Godard was already openly courting her. Roussel's descriptions, however, give the impression of an erotic siege.[8] The director and the young actress met together, they traveled together and shared hotel rooms, they went to the cinema. Officially, this was always a work matter. Godard wanted to make a film with Roussel about a father-daughter relationship: "L'Homme de ma vie," the man of my life. A story about incest.

Godard rented a house near Nyon for Roussel so that he would not have to keep traveling to Paris. His siege only became a relationship when Godard abandoned the incest project. Instead, he moved on to a film that took the idea of the Virgin Mary as a structuring premise. As an actress, Roussel, who says Godard called her his "cinema virgin," experienced him in the role of her director-godfather. Godard's long courtship is echoed in the script of *Je vous salue, Marie*. "I am not sleeping with anyone," she says, and not only to her gynecologist. She experiences her pregnancy as a pain, but also as a challenge to think about her existence. For her, being "free" and being "available" (*disponible*) go together. Joseph has to get used to the idea that he will be the father of a child without ever having slept with Marie. He must even fight for the intimate privilege of seeing Marie naked just once.

In the last words of the film, Godard accentuates the film's relation to its biblical model. Every syllable counts: "Moi, je suis de la vierge," says Marie. So, she is not the virgin herself, she is "of" the virgin, descended from her and is in a relationship with her, which makes the following formulation even more complicated: "J'ai marqué l'âme qui m'a aidé." I have "marked" the soul that helped me. "That's all."

In addition to the natural sciences and the vocabulary of theology, *Je vous salue, Marie* is also interwoven with other contemporary preoccupations of

Godard's and Miéville's. In an interesting passage, Godard relates the alea-
tory moment in his work to the artificial intelligence of the computer age,
which he grasped early on: "I would have something for the people at
IBM—I could say to them: Look, I have a book on religion and psychoanalysis by Françoise Dolto, I have two characters, Mary and Joseph, I
have three cantatas by Bach and a book by Heidegger. Write me a program
in which all these things occur together. But they can't do it, so I have to
do it myself, but I don't want to spend twenty years doing it."[9]

As with *Sauve qui peut (la vie)*, there is a video showing the preparatory
work on *Je vous salue, Marie*, which helped with the search for funding.
Three hundred thousand Swiss francs were needed. In these twenty minutes,
you get a direct insight into the workshop: Godard and Miéville sit on the
floor while listening to music by Bach and talking about Françoise Dolto's
book *L'Évangile au risque de la psychanalyse*, which was a major inspiration.
Psychoanalysis played a role at several points in the film's prehistory.

Even the idea of making a film about Freud reappears here. Myriem
Roussel was to play Dora, who is known from the case history of the hys-
teric Ida Bauer. In Godard's work, the founder of psychoanalysis [Freud]
always functions as Dr. Freude [that is, Dr. Joy], creating a motif that makes
its way into the finished film, for there the word *freude* (joy, *joie*) is a fre-
quent subject of Marie's reflections. And it is also the subject of one of
Godard's typical word-sound games, for he brings Maria and her prede-
cessor Eva together in the film through the consonance of the words voice
(*voix*) and way (*voie*). Even the name Jesus can be traced back to the French
in Godard's work: *je suis*.

Myriem Roussel can be seen ironing in the video; she is asked to explain
what difference she perceives between two pieces by Bach. One could think
here once again of the constellation from *France, tour, détour, deux enfants*:
Godard and the child, Godard and the young woman, who together consider Bach's music's relation with Marie's housework—and with the efforts
of a young actress to play this part and work with this material.

This sketch proves once again how strongly the feature films of the early
eighties are rooted in the video practice of the seventies. So it is not surprising that the figure of the archangel is still associated with a "vendeur
du vidéo," a video salesman who does not announce a child to Marie but
instead switches on a television set.

To this collage of motifs is added an autobiographical detail that contains a displacement: "What I remember most from my religious childhood are the gymnastics exercises and football matches we had every Sunday, not far from the church." So instead of Mass, Godard had sports.

～

The production history of *Je vous salue, Marie* was complicated: "I had big debts, so I stopped the film part way through and did another one, *Détective*, to make money. After that, I returned to *Je vous salue, Marie* and finished editing it." For the montage, Godard was able to draw on an unusually large amount of material. He brought up this experimental work, whose result was anything but foreseeable, in an interview regarding his own "father role," which encompasses both the creator God and the "barren" Joseph. "I used 90,000 meters of film—usually enough for four films. I am not a religious person, but I am a believer. I believe in images. I have no children, only pictures."[10]

The interweaving of the two projects meant that Godard met with protests in Cannes in the spring of 1985, which were directed at a film that was not even being screened there: at the premiere of *Détective*, he had to contend with devout Catholics who found his depiction of (at least one) Mary blasphemous. The resistance of religious groups even reached overseas, and the pope himself took an interest in the matter. Godard took advantage of the opportunity and wrote a letter to the head of the Catholic Church in which, among other things, he referred to the "instrument of the papal voice" and specifically to that of John Paul II, who had spoken in Rome on December 12, 1980, about "the fullness of Eros in the spontaneity of human love": "This makes the Holy Father one of the scriptwriters of this film, and he should be able to express his sorrow for this, regardless of all the political difficulties with this serious but incomplete film."[11] The Vatican did not react, and months later, at the American premiere of *Je vous salue, Marie* in New York, five thousand people demonstrated against the film.

～

Godard had often cross-subsidized his own work by simply diverting money to projects for which it was not originally intended. But when it came to

Détective, Alain Sarde had no reason to complain: he got a film with numerous stars and at the same time a piece of chemically pure Godard, which to some critics even recalled the spirit of his sixties works. The focus is on a criminal case in the broadest sense. Jean-Pierre Léaud plays a hotel detective who has set up a surveillance station with his uncle in a room of the luxurious Concorde Saint-Lazare. Using a "ridiculous Japanese video camera," they monitor Françoise (Nathalie Baye), the wife of the pilot and charter flight entrepreneur Emile (Claude Brasseur). They hope to recover a significant sum from the boxing manager Jim Fox Warner (rock star Johnny Hallyday), who is also staying there. However, he also owes money to the mafia.

Godard arranges the complicated plot, which is set both in the present and two years earlier, as a roundel involving four groups. The detectives keep it Shakespearean: they bear names from *The Tempest*; Jim Fox Warner has the name of two major Hollywood studios, but his reading material is by Joseph Conrad (*Lord Jim*). An elegant gentleman, referred to only as "the Prince," whose murder two years ago remains unsolved, reads novels by the Sicilian author Leonardo Sciascia. And Françoise would love to open a bookshop: she picks up numerous books (but only ever for a moment) in *Détective*.

"To each remains his fragment of truth," as the film has it. For Godard, this is the only permissible consequence of the genre he is tearing apart here. Usually detectives solve a case, but here a case is solved by way of a typical Godard movement. The dialogues are about as important as the quotes. The JVC camera is shown once in a close-up, accompanied by a sentence that is a direct reference to *Ici et ailleurs*. Godard is very present in this film, and yet he is also elsewhere in spirit. In any case, he is present in his still-undisguised desire to expose the breasts of young women.[12] In *Détective*, Julie Delpy made her début, and this film provided the second roles for both Emmanuelle Seigner (who would later marry Roman Polanski) and Aurelle Doazan. In a scene in which two breasts serve as elastic resistance for a boxing workout, Godard provides an ironic twist on this fetish. And in a dialogue, he makes the rules of the gendered order clear: "Ah, young girls' breasts," sighs William Prospero, the off-duty detective; in the scene afterward, Françoise "answers" with another sigh, "Ah, men's money."

You can't take the Godard of *Détective* at his word, or indeed at anyone's word. Here, he only ever speaks for himself, and from a certain remove. In the credits, he writes of a film "from . . . to": from John Cassavetes, Edgar G. Ulmer, and Clint Eastwood to Jean-Luc Godard and only then to the audience. In this case, he is the channel through which an idea of cinema that connects with the three directors made its way into the present day of the 1980s. Cassavetes, Ulmer, and Eastwood are not easy to bring together. Godard probably means questions of production in all three cases: the three directors were known for their ability to make "economical" films, namely, cheap ones. And *Détective* is itself also a film above all about missing money. While they can all somehow afford to stay in the expensive hotel, they pay in the ill-founded hope that their fortunes will soon be turned around. The big boxing match on which everything seems to depend does not take place. And the neon sign of the AGFA company, which advertises video cassettes with its neon glow, outshines the literary clique in *Détective*.

~

At the end of the eighties, Godard had to come to terms with a situation that could no longer be ignored: he was approaching sixty and Anne-Marie Miéville was in her mid-forties. If they had ever harbored a shared desire to have children, that wish could now never be fulfilled. "I make pictures instead of children. Does that make me less human?" This rhetorical question is asked in the one-hour documentary *Soft and Hard: Soft Talk on a Hard Subject between Two Friends*, commissioned by the British broadcaster Channel Four in 1985, which is perhaps one of the most intimate moments in Godard and Miéville's work. Here, too, each scene is chosen very deliberately: Miéville irons while Godard, who looks very youthful in these shots, practices, without a ball, with a tennis racket in the living room. You also see him in bed, which brings to mind the phrase "Everything belonged to him, but to whom did he belong?" In the center is a long passage in which Godard and Miéville talk about filmmaking. She sits on the couch in such a way that we can look into her face. We see the back of Godard's head.

Both also reveal childhood memories. For Godard, cinema only began at the Cinémathèque in Paris when he was twenty. When he saw *Ben-Hur* at the age of seven,[13] it didn't do anything for him. Miéville tells—with echoes of Proust—about how, as a child, she projected family photos onto the wall in a darkened room, using a magic lantern of her own invention.[14] They talk about scenes in *Détective*, about the couples and the relationships that are shown in that film. In one of the most touching moments, Miéville reveals that she has such great respect for cinema that she feels inhibited by it in her own work. She is sitting at this moment opposite a man, her husband, who combines the utmost respect for cinema with the utmost willingness to constantly smash it up. "For me, cinema is something fragile," says Miéville. "For you, there is nothing else. I am a slow learner. You think everything you say is interesting." *Soft and Hard* ends with the couple projecting themselves as a shadow play into the final image of *Le Mépris*— a homage to the "lantern cinema" of Miéville's childhood and to Godard's power over the camera and the images.

~

Little has come out about Jean-Luc Godard and Anne-Marie Miéville's relationship in the more than fifty years they shared a life together. This is in part a result of the fact that Miéville has very rarely made any public statements. Her self-effacement is only broken by the films she occasionally makes on her own. In these, she deals with women's issues explicitly. "Toujours le fille de . . ." (a woman is always someone's daughter). That is a comment made by her 1988 film *Mon cher sujet* (*My Dearest Subject*). In it, we get to know women from five generations. Young Angèle has to decide whether to terminate her pregnancy. The story of King Solomon's judgment helps her: she has the child. Her mother, Agnès, struggles with old age, her two husbands, and her in-between position in life. The sixty-year-old, gray-haired entrepreneur Odile fits into the role of the lonely woman with stoic elegance. At one point, she visits the old man from whom they all descend. He sits ill and sullen in his chair, but when the maid comes into the room, he compliments her on her alabaster skin. We are familiar with this sullen, misogynistic idealization of women from Godard's films. Art, like love, cannot rely on men. Miéville captured this poignantly as early as 1983 in her first short film, *How Can I Love* (*A Man When I Know He Doesn't Want Me*). There are five farewell scenes—five failed relationships— from which the men shamefacedly steal away, while the woman usually also has to do the embarrassing work of saying something when there is no longer anything to be said. The scenes have an understated humor, but with Miéville—as with Godard—self-irony offers no escape. Existence only becomes bearable through culture, and culture in turn makes the intolerability of life all the more apparent. Angèle's boyfriend in *Mon cher sujet* is a musician who has no sympathy for her soprano singing. He arranges for her to audition at a recording studio where hit songs are produced. One of these songs appears in its entirety in the film; it is a pathetic, cosmic fantasy of childbirth that—despite the studio production—seems to have a much more direct impact than Angèle's soprano performances. But the impression is deceptive. In front of an initially skeptical singing teacher, Angèle even sings the aria of the Queen of the Night from Mozart's *Magic Flute*—and she is convincing. She expresses herself through her music.

Anne-Marie Miéville examines the mediations in relationships, and in this, too, her elective affinity with Godard is unmistakable. In *Lou n'a pas dit non* (*Lou Didn't Say No*) in 1993, there is a series of different reference systems for the partnership between Lou, a filmmaker, and Pierre, an actor: the correspondence between Rainer Maria Rilke and Lou Andreas-Salomé is cited, two statues in the Louvre play a role, a ballet becomes a scene of impossible togetherness, and music lies like a vast land between the protagonists. *Nous sommes tous encore ici* (*We're All Still Here*, 1997) is even more heterogeneous and consists of three parts that follow one another like movements in a piece of music: a recitation by two women from Plato's *Gorgias*; an excerpt from Hannah Arendt's *Origins of Totalitarianism*, read out by Godard; an everyday scene between an elderly couple, with Godard in the role of the man. However autobiographically inspired this last dialogue may be, the reworking is substantial, and when Miéville makes her own relationship the subject, the motive is not narcissism but rather a late-bourgeois filmmaker's view of herself as a case of a specific culture. There is no togetherness that is not production—of history, of friendship, of descendants.

The theater is the place where this work is still directly seen—perhaps that is why Miéville's last film to date looks a little like a social comedy: *Après la réconciliation* (*After the Reconciliation*, 2000) is set for the most part in a smart Parisian flat. Two women (Miéville herself and Claude Perron) and a man (Godard) pass the time in conversation and coquetry. When a second man joins them, the chemistry seems wrong at first. This supposed globetrotting adventurer turns out to be a philistine, and in the end, the couple is left alone with themselves again. Godard then sits on a bed, exhausted from the game of seductions and also visibly sad about how little he has to give. In that moment, the gap between the character he played and the character he is seems almost to disappear. His tears here are especially exquisite because they come from a bad actor who is a great artist.

From the sixties, there is a television recording of the failed couple Anna Karina and Jean-Luc Godard, which can hardly be surpassed in sadness—but it remains within the framework of television's confessional rituals. Anne-Marie Miéville, on the other hand, has staged an intimate moment, stepping out of her dependence. Godard said of Anna Karina: "I couldn't give her more than the cinema." Miéville has a cinema of her own, so she doesn't have to repress what she is in her solo films: "Toujours la femme de . . ."

~

In *Soft and Hard*, there is also already talk of the next Godard film. The contract for *King Lear* was finally concluded, and Godard could count on monthly remittances from Cannon for a while. But he also had to deliver an adaptation of Shakespeare's drama, with the aim of a 1986 premiere at the Cannes Festival. The year before, when *Détective* was being premiered, Godard had met the two Israeli producers Menahem Golan and Yoram Globus. Along with their American company Cannon, this pair consistently focused on commercial films such as the *Death Wish* series with Charles Bronson or action films with Chuck Norris. Now and then Cannon also got involved in more ambitious productions. Writer and occasional filmmaker Norman Mailer was already on board when Godard joined. They soon arrived at an idea of making a film of Shakespeare's *King Lear*, with a script by Mailer and the old king as a mafia godfather. Godard had already been preoccupied with the father-daughter theme since the seventies. In a script version of *Prénom Carmen*, Godard (as the old man in the sanatorium) called himself Mr. Lear, and a nurse was named Cordelia. Fantasies of a retreat from the world overlap with fantasies of the transmission of a special power.

But in the case of *King Lear*, it took a long time and many twists and turns to get from the original idea to a film. Godard continued to seize almost every opportunity to earn money. In 1986, for example, he traveled to New York to interview Woody Allen on behalf of the Cannes Festival. The New York filmmaker was known for never appearing at festivals. But the festival wanted him to at least be present in the form of a video recorded for the premiere of *Hannah and Her Sisters*. *Meetin' WA* (1986) is staged relatively conventionally by Godard's standards as a classic interview setup: a camera is pointed at Allen on the sofa, while Godard is partially visible in the countershot, surrounded by books and videos, the inevitable cigar in his mouth, and wearing very conspicuous socks. He speaks English but soon falls into French and has himself translated—the aplomb with which he had expressed himself in English on the *Dick Cavett Show* has now deserted him. Godard's questions are also a thesis that has long preoccupied him: television, which destroys creativity with its "radioactivity." Allen tries to answer everything authoritatively, but occasionally cannot hide his helplessness in the face of the complicated questions. Dutifully, he too laments the influence of television and video cassettes on the audience. At the beginning and then again at the end, Godard speaks of Woody Allen as a little bird (*merle*) that he is visiting in his nest. The half-hour document ends with a play on words: "Lucky I ran into you. . . . Lucky Luke. . . . Lucky Jean-Luc."

The interview was shown at Cannes in 1986, when *King Lear* was overdue. But Godard had great difficulty in meeting the deadline, even a year on. The film was finally made at a breakneck pace, within a few weeks in March and April 1987. The convoluted development at least made it possible for Godard's central narrative idea to shift its reference to an event of 1986. Under the shadow of the Chernobyl catastrophe, *King Lear* was now set in a future in which all culture has been wiped out by a nuclear accident. Cinema—like Shakespeare—has had to be reinvented or discovered. A star of contemporary theater took over the search: Peter Sellars had been recommended to Godard by Tom Luddy. He played the role of William Shakespeare Junior the Fifth, a descendant of the author of *King Lear*. In this way, the film adaptation also becomes an investigation into how one can work with a text that is not only lost, but which one lacks the means to understand.

Godard has thus created an ideal constellation for his approach to texts. He does not even have to read all the source material: he can design this

Jean-Luc Godard as Professor Pluggy with playwright Peter Sellars in *King Lear*, 1987
(Entertainment Pictures / Alamy Stock Photo, image no. F6FBNB)

King Lear as an archaeological work, in which passages of Shakespeare appear but there is never any intention of being faithful to the text. Godard is reacting implicitly to a significant intellectual current of the 1980s, but he asserts his own punch line: What one would normally call deconstruction, he makes into a matter of reconstruction. Handling texts in an open manner, which French philosophy had made one of its most important strategies, is in Godard's case something done from a cultural null point.

He also assumes a role himself: Professor Pluggy is a memorable figure, a fool of cinema with a tangle of cables on his head (through which he connects to the "unknown"), a man who sacrifices himself for the sake of the "dawn of our first image." Cinema is rediscovered—at the cost of Professor Pluggy's life. At the end, Woody Allen also reappears, at the editing table, as Mr. Alien. The "image" that *King Lear* rediscovers is at the same time that of a new present, after the human catastrophe, as well as an image of the future, of science fiction and religious eschatology. Once again, the Pauline quotation from 1 Corinthians appears here. Corinthians fascinates Godard: "The image will appear in the time of resurrection."[15]

~

Since 1948, numerous classics of American crime literature have been published in France by Gallimard under the name Série Noire. As a marketing gambit, the name "black series" became so powerful that it led to the naming of an entire Hollywood genre. Film Noir, one of the most important currents in American postwar cinema, was in no small part a phenomenon mediated by its reception in France. By the 1980s the Gallimard series that had begun with Dashiell Hammett and Raymond Chandler had long since moved on to new names—and there was also a spin-off into television crime stories. One of the authors who found his way into the Série Noire was James Hadley Chase. These thrillers had always had some significance for Godard, so the offer to film Chase's novel *The Soft Centre* as part of the TV series *Série noire* was all the more welcome. It may well be surprising that there were still producers who entrusted Godard with their material and expected him to provide at least the rudiments of a conventional production. In any case, the fame of *À bout de souffle*, the high-profile *Détective*, and the commercial successes with *Sauve qui peut (la vie)* and *Je vous salue, Marie* ensured that Godard always had a wide range of options to choose from.

And he accepted them all. This resulted in a productive chaos that bore amazing fruit time and time again. The television film *Grandeur et décadence d'un petit commerce de cinéma* (*Rise and Fall of a Small Film Company*, 1986), which was for a long time almost forgotten about, was just one of its products. Once again, the film became a film about the production of a film. The small company referred to in the title is looking for actors for a commission based on a book by James Hadley Chase. As in the first episode of *Six fois deux*, Godard had people come from the labor office. They go through a casting process, pass by the camera in a long sequence, and must say something, often just one word or a short passage. Godard obviously follows on here from his reflections on assembly line work and concatenation by allowing a text to emerge from a human chain. The casting text is from Chase's work. The duty to the novel thus discharged through this stroke of genius, Godard can devote himself to his other obsessions. Fellow director and cinema maverick Jean-Pierre Mocky plays Jean Almereyda (this was the real name of Jean Vigo—one of the pioneers of the Nouvelle Vague), the boss of the company Albatros Films. His wife, Eurydice, also wants a role in the planned film. She reminds the casting agent Gaspar Bazin (Jean-Pierre Léaud) of an actress from another era: Dita Parlo, known from Vigo's *L'Atalante* and Jean Renoir's prewar classic *La Grande Illusion*. Godard thus marks the difference with which he was struggling most intensely in those years: the cinema he once loved, and which offered him so many formative experiences, no longer exists. The "petit commerce" has become a branch of television—and he took the same path, by accepting the commission for an episode from the *Série Noire*. He distances himself from himself to a certain extent, as is made clear in his short appearance: he shows up in front of the Albatros Films office because he is looking to have a conversation with the producer Rassam. The irony is bitter: Jean-Pierre Rassam, a legendary producer of Lebanese descent and facilitator of several Godard films, had died the year before from drug abuse after an eventful life. Godard disappears after a short dialogue ("We are not pirates"). He does not give Rolle as his address, but Reykjavík.

~

In an interview in January 1985, Godard compared himself to Michelangelo. He was not concerned with his place in art history but rather with his social position: like the great Renaissance painter, Godard lived on commissions. It was not uncommon for him to be involved in several commitments at the same time or to have to squeeze in an assignment to get another thing done—that's how it had been with *Détective*. This was also the case with *Soigne ta droite* (*Keep Your Right Up*, 1987), in which the emotional state of an artist under deadline pressure is radically exaggerated:

> Toward the end of the twentieth century, the idiot's phone rang. He wanted to have one of those quiet evenings that you can still have in the remote European regions between the forests of southern Germany and the lakes of northern Italy. At such a moment, the phone always rings: a polite but unfamiliar voice, with authority. In high places, they are willing to forgive the idiot for his many sins, but he has to hurry: he has to invent a story, film it,

and deliver a copy of the film to the capital that very afternoon. It has to be shown in the cinema that very evening. A car will be waiting for him in the garage in the valley, and a ticket is ready at the local airport. If that works out, and on time, the idiot can expect forgiveness.[16]

The prologue described here by Volker Pantenburg seems like a homage to Kafka made in the context of an accelerated society—and it sets the direction for *Soigne ta droite*. When someone is in a hurry, accidents happen easily. The genre here is slapstick. The film title is clearly an allusion: *Soigne ton gauche* was the name of a short boxing comedy by René Clement in 1936 starring the young comedian Jacques Tati. Godard wanted to make a film in the spirit of Tati. And he plays the leading role himself: the filmmaker Monsieur Godard, who is both a prince (like the idiot in Dostoevsky's novel) and a friendly old man in an old-fashioned three-piece suit who, with film cans in his hand luggage, barely makes it onto the plane to Paris on time. He did indeed complete the requested film in time. It was titled "Une place sur la terre," a place on earth: it is not shown in a cinema, however, but projected into the world—at least that's how it looks, because Godard cuts from a projection room to a view of Paris, with its skyscrapers and the Seine, which serves as a canvas.

Soigne ta droite also consists of several films running concurrently. The story of the idiot has a parallel in the story of a man who is only referred to as an "individual" and who appears in various episodes. The comedian Jacques Villeret's type is rather the opposite of Jacques Tati's: a chubby klutz who always ends up on the losing side. The "individual" is seen as a caddy at a golf game and once in handcuffs on the way to prison (a scene of enormous complexity that refers to communist orthodoxy and individual ethos in the fight against fascism).[17]

Finally, in several sequences, the musicians Catherine Ringer and Fred Chichin from the band Les Rita Mitsouko can be seen recording an album. Godard happened to come across a music video for her hit "Marcia Baila" and was reminded of Cocteau. In the home studio of Les Rita Mitsouko in the twentieth arrondissement, he recognized a working and living relationship similar to the one he shared with Anne-Marie Miéville in Rolle. So, as with the Rolling Stones, he made himself a witness to an act of musical creation, and as with *Sympathy for the Devil / One plus One*, the rest of the film remained unconnected to the musical scene. The two strands share only one theme: death. "Marcia Baila" is a song in memory of a friend of Les Rita Mitsouko who had died of cancer. Dying is the horizon of *Soigne ta droite*, hidden behind the code word *sortir* but also quite obvious in the fact that the idiot/prince collapses upon delivery of his film as well as in clear references to the transports from France to the Nazi death camps in the scenes with Jacques Villeret. And what could Godard have meant by the "sins" for which the idiot hopes to be forgiven? Identification with Les Rita Mitsouko could be a key here. The concentrated yet relaxed way the two musicians interacted illuminates the difficulties that Godard and Miéville encountered in their attempts to share their life and work. Now they had rearranged their living arrangement, with two separate flats next to each other, between which the doors were always open.[18]

This "double loneliness" was at least broken by the fact that Godard had already begun to gather a small team around him at this point. The cinematographer Caroline Champetier did not move to Switzerland for his sake, as Godard had once hoped William Lubtchansky would, but she worked with him regularly. Not even his assistant Hervé Duhamel was available around the clock, as Godard had always pictured in his dreams of a commune. But he was now surrounded by the faithful.

~

In the two years between 1987 and 1989, Godard worked on a plethora of commissions. He also made advertisements—according to his own conditions and using techniques that he had picked up himself. The medium-length video *Le Rapport Darty* (*The Darty Report*, 1989) provides the necessary images from a store operated by the electrical goods chain Darty, along with some of the fashion and flair of the 1980s, combined with reflections on "public happiness" (according to Rousseau) and on the logics of the gift (as outlined by the anthropologist Marcel Mauss). Anne-Marie Miéville directs the video work with her clear, firm voice, while Godard can be heard slurring his words as if he were mentally disabled. Here, too, he presents himself—in voice-over, a gadfly of French consumer culture—as an idiot.

Retrospectively, Godard found a term for this period: a "holiday from fiction." In 1989 he presented the first two episodes of *Histoire(s) du cinéma*, a work that would occupy him for another decade. But now he felt the time had come to make a feature film again. He just needed an idea for it.

It came in the form of a name. Producer Marin Karmitz suggested he make a film with a star. The first choice was Marcello Mastroianni, who after his great roles for Federico Fellini (from *La dolce vita* to *Otto e mezzo* to *Ginger e Fred*) also seemed to fit Godard's ideas around self-reflection perfectly. But the preliminary talks led nowhere, and the contact with Karmitz also fell through. This left only a few alternatives in his price range. Alain Delon was already a little typecast in his image as the eternal *flic* by 1990. He wanted to work with Godard, but he had one condition: he needed a script. Delon knew about Godard's reputation and was careful not to leave himself exposed in front of the camera. A creative strategy would have helped here: Hervé Duhamel created a collage of citations from books in his private library, which in the broadest sense might offer inspiration for an unusual point of departure: a doppelganger fantasy about a man who appears twice, once as a kind of *clochard* and once as a successful businessman.

This is the story of *Nouvelle vague* (1990). Elena, a woman from the very wealthy industrialist family Torlato-Favrini, picks up a man from the roadside and takes him to the family's château. Delon, in shorts and with stubble on his face, stands around largely lost while quotes and pieces of music fill the rooms. He finally dies during a trip on the lake, and a little later a man amazingly shows up at the door again (it is the same Alain Delon, only more cultivated and less melancholic). The story then begins again from the beginning, but with the signs reversed. Now Elena is the passive figure and Delon is in charge.

For Godard, *Nouvelle vague* unfolds out of a childhood memory:

I have lived two dreams in my life. I spent my childhood in an extremely rich family like the one in the film, in a chalet on a lake. I was educated, but also left alone. We had so much money that no one noticed. That was during the war. I didn't get to see anything of the war, which I regret very much today. The consequence of this childhood is that today I don't care if a film makes money. Sarde knows this only too well. The second dream was the Nouvelle Vague as a group. That didn't last long, and you come to terms with it and move on.[19]

The allegorical interpretation of the film, however, is not so straightfor-ward. If Delon's first character was the old cinema and the second one the Nouvelle Vague around 1960, then Godard's second dream of the move-ment of his younger years would be linked to the cold businessman Delon plays after his disappearance. It is probably the case that Godard wanted to recognize himself in the attractive outsider from the first part and that he projected his disappointments with Truffaut and other colleagues onto the second Delon.

~

In the summer of 1989, the producer Nicole Ruellé planned a series on the theme of loneliness (*solitude*) for the television channel Arte. She had an associative anthology in mind and approached important directors: Kubrick, Wenders, Bergman, and Godard. In the end, only one film was made, and it bore only a vague relation to the original idea. For Godard, the keyword *solitude* was all too familiar; it had been a running theme in his work since the late sixties. But this was no longer about his role as an outsider. He had a much bigger idea in mind: he wanted to say something about the soli-tude of a state. At the time he signed the contract, he was still able to con-template a film about the German Democratic Republic, but by the time he actually began work after the usual delay, now acting under time pressure, the GDR no longer existed. Godard had to make a film about Germany as he found it: *Allemagne neuf zéro* (*Germany Year 90 Nine Zero*, 1991)—and loneliness appears from the very first intertitle: *Solitudes, un état et des vari-ations* (a state and variations). It is about Germany's history in Europe, rela-tions with France, America, and Russia. Here, too, Godard transformed a commissioned work into a personal project, but at the same time he was inspired by the world-historical events of 1989 to 1991 to write an essay on the philosophy of history that set out the path toward his later work.

He also went back into his own history: Eddie Constantine took on the role of secret agent Lemmy Caution once again, after *Alphaville*. The actor was well into his seventies and now rarely performed. In the 35 mm film images, he appears downright monumental, especially in the close-ups, with a lizard skin and piercing gaze in the "dragon landscape" of the Bitter-feld open-cast mines. Godard combines various associations with a (never completed) travel film: *Allemagne neuf zéro* is an East-West narrative about a moment in history when the Wall has not yet been torn down in many places but no longer serves to demarcate two systems. Godard addresses the victory of Western democracy and the associated rhetoric with a skeptical eye: he sees a world-historical option disappear and be replaced by an "assault of money on the mind," and eventually by pornography.

Allemagne neuf zéro could be seen as a meditation on history. In the sixty minutes of the edited version, which was eventually completed, motifs accumulate over the course of a journey through Germany. The context is created through reflection. The philosopher Hegel and the writer and scholar Jean Giraudoux are the leading figures here. Count Zelten is the first figure we see: a man with a Mercedes who is looking for the "last spy" in East Berlin. The name Zelten comes from the novel *Siegfried et le Limousin* (1922) by Giraudoux, the story of a Frenchman in Munich who has no memories after World War I and reinvents himself as a German. The actor playing Zelten turned out to be crucial to the whole project: Hanns Zischler, actor and man of letters, had translated Jacques Derrida's *Grammatology* into German in 1974, together with Hans-Jörg Rheinberger, and appeared in films by Wenders, Handke, and Rudolf Thome. He accompanied Godard and his assistant Romain Goupil during filming in autumn 1990 and was in many ways an intellectual mentor to Godard, who found himself in the unusual position of searching for motifs in a country he knew primarily through literature and cinema.

In *Allemagne neuf zéro*, Zelten embodies a figure caught between cultures, as Giraudoux had been in the period before World War II. A book of texts from Hegel's philosophy of history, published in 1968 under the title *La raison dans l'Histoire* (*Reason in History*) by the Estates General of Paris in May of that year, is merged with the original German text in *Allemagne neuf zéro*. The passages quoted here reveal Godard's interest in situating German reunification alongside the historical rupture of National Socialism—the very title alludes directly to Roberto Rossellini's film *Germany at Zero*. At the same time, he wants to reflect on the possibilities of reflection in times of euphoria: "If philosophy is to come to the fore among a people, a rupture must have occurred in the real world." Philosophy only comes into its own when the temporal world no longer satisfies—a clear statement to make so soon after the GDR's accession to the deutsch mark, as German unification was polemically described by its critics.

Most of all, this is a question of translation: Godard's French, the English of Hollywood cinema, and the German that was an important element in Godard's Swiss childhood. His father adored Goethe and Novalis, and now there was an opportunity to return to Weimar Classicism. However, Weimar would be unthinkable without Buchenwald, without the Goethe Oak, which is located on the grounds of the former concentration camp. From Lotte in Weimar, the chain of association leads to a Dora, who kept alive the last German hopes for a superweapon with an underground armaments factory in the Mittelbau-Dora concentration camp.

Hanns Zischler sums up the film's movement:

> It is noticeable that the film goes through a strange double movement: The "inner" (and internal) spaces are the spaces of reading, questioning and studying texts and images (which in turn refer to further imaginary spaces, open them up . . . "en abime"). The translations (of Hegel, for example), the rattling, hammering strokes of the typewriter are just as much a part of this as is the ironic exaggeration of the "study of the classics": a "raccourci ralenti" during the walk through the Goethehaus mirrors the chase through the Louvre in *Bande à part*. The outside, on the other hand, is a disoriented (or orient-less) West, a "terrain vague," which functions either as a red herring or as an abyss (the "dragons" of the giant excavators), as "fake" landscapes (the choir in the artificial ruins) or is obscured by remnants of the wall. The landscape appears as a Breughel image, as an unattainable landscape of longing (the Baltic Sea "before" Pushkin's poem) or as occupied territory (Weimar with Pushkin's monument).[20]

Zischler had already worked with Godard on the short film *Le Dernier Mot* (*The Last Word*, 1988), a commissioned work for the daily newspaper *Le Figaro*. He played a German looking for traces of his father, who had served in the SS in France and was involved in the execution of Valentin Feldman. This young philosopher with Russian roots, a fighter for the Resistance, who was able to publish just one book on aesthetics (1936) and a war diary before being executed by a German firing squad in 1942, became an important figure for the late Godard. Feldman's last words give his murder a logic of sacrifice: "You idiots, I'll die for you!" he replies to the German occupiers' bad joke that the French must always have the last word.

In *Le Dernier Mot*, Godard takes both sides at the same time: that of the German coming to terms with the past, as represented by Zischler's character, and that of the lonely philosophy teacher in the Resistance.

~

In 1992 Godard was given the opportunity to travel to the country he was coming more and more to idealize: Russia. A retrospective of his films was to take place in Moscow in February. When he accepted the invitation, the Soviet Union still existed. After its disintegration, he was once again dealing with the country of Tolstoy and Dostoyevsky, that is, with a nation of culture in which he had great hopes. The Cold War was over. Godard, however, insisted on his own version of the East-West conflict: Russia was the country that had something to offer America other than socialism. For Godard, Russia had become the home of fiction, while the West had long since "run out of things to say." His tendency to speak of nations as if they were individuals was becoming increasingly clear. When he shot an advertisement for the cigarette brand Parisienne in 1992, he had a special use in mind for the fee: he wanted to use it to pay off his "debts to Chekhov, Dostoevsky, Tchaikovsky, Eisenstein, and Solzhenitsyn." Specifically, he had important technology supplied to the famous but poorly equipped Moscow Film Museum with its charismatic director Naum Kleiman, which also helped ensure that his films could be screened in stereo. Only in this way was it possible to experience the full complexity of these polyphonic soundtracks—*Allemagne neuf zéro* was the most recent and particularly significant example of a cinematic discourse on different levels and in different languages. Godard had some passages subtitled and others dubbed (in English or German), but much was left to be deciphered by experts. Viewers had the best access if they could remember individual quotations from books or moments from the history of art and film. Nor was Godard especially concerned with documentary realism or historiography; rather, his concern was with providing a space for his associations and speculations.

When he returned from Moscow, he had a new film in mind—and appropriately enough, a job that he could repurpose to make it possible. The American producer Aaron Spelling is one of the most colorful figures ever to have commissioned a film by Godard. With the soap opera *Beverly Hills, 90210* he launched one of the most successful television series of all time in

1990. He wanted Godard to do a piece on Russia for a series called *Momentous Events*. Werner Herzog was already on the same mission, making a documentary film, *Bells from the Deep—Faith and Superstition in Russia* (1993), about the Russian national myth of the city of Kitezh hidden under water—an Eastern version of the clash between culture and barbarism, with the Tatars taking the place of the imagined enemy, a role long played by "redskins" in America. Godard wanted to make a film about a director who meets figures from Russian literature. He wanted to play the director himself: a character, once again, who acted as an idiot and a prince. The working title pointed the way: "Notre sainte Russie"—Our Holy Russia.

At the premiere in August 1993 at the Locarno Festival, the film was then titled *Les Enfants jouent à la Russie* (*The Kids Play Russian*). Like *Allemagne neuf zéro*, it lasts an hour and, compared with the Deutschland film, goes a step further in the direction of an essay, an argument spelled out in images and sounds. The vestiges of plot serve only as a hook upon which Godard can hang a self-portrait in the visual and acoustic echo chambers of cultural history. In pajamas with a coat and bobble hat, he plays the idiot/prince who meets Anna Karenina and other figures from the Russian "empire de la fiction"—"immense souls from this immense homeland of fiction." In addition to fiction, Russia also invented projection: in 1822, in front of a Russian cell wall, a French prisoner named Poncelet wrote down from memory the formulas on which the entirety of cinema is based.

Godard uses numerous snippets from Russian (and in particular Soviet) films, he cross-fades them and connects different moments from history—for example, he makes as if to reinvent the woman from the Odessa stairs (from Eisenstein's *Battleship Potemkin*) in a porn film. Finally, Godard links Russia's advantage over all other nations to a very far-reaching thought about the history of seeing. In his opinion, the land of icons is also home to a gaze that was turned in a new direction by the first shot/countershot montage in 1910—away from the contemplation of a "true image" and toward a new regime of looking. For Godard, montage in all its conceptual facets is the decisive characteristic of cinema, and he does not just mean the linking of shots into a sequence of moving images. Here he enriches his mythology with an older pictorial tradition that in fact contradicts his views but that he, nevertheless, does not want to abandon.

Godard takes his leave from *Les Enfants jouent à la Russie* in the manner of a comedian: "That's all folks" is the line on which *Looney Tunes*, the animated films from Warner Bros. studios in the United States, traditionally ended. With this quotation, Godard was becoming the Porky Pig of cinema, which in turn is just another identity of the idiot. Holy Russia becomes simply Russia: *notre simple Russie.*

There is something provocative about the way Godard turns the world powers of this stirring period of history into ephemeral constructs, transparent video images and enigmatic voices, while still treating them as if he were dealing with people about whom he can pass moral judgment. In his own way, he is responding to the temptation to apply nineteenth-century categories to events after 1989. Hegel's reflections on the role of reason in history were given a new impetus by the predominantly nonviolent revolutions in the Eastern Bloc and the apparent victory of the "free world." Godard had turned sixty in 1990. He was now on the threshold of a period of mature work that was more than ever concerned with the meaning of history as such. Events in Europe gave constant material for his penchant for speculation: and his next feature film was suffused by the violence of the new age.

~

By the early 1990s, Godard had yet to bag one last big name of the great French stars of his era: Gérard Depardieu. They had already been in contact in 1987 on the occasion of the premiere of Maurice Pialat's *Sous le soleil de Satan* in Cannes. In that film, Depardieu played a priest, with worshipful solemnity. Godard was thrilled with his performance and let Depardieu know. Producer Alain Sarde was also in the frame, and he was also in favor of such a partnership. By 1992 the time had come: that summer, filming took place for *Hélas pour moi* (*Oh, Woe Is Me*, 1993). The idea came out of the story of Amphitryon. Godard knew the ancient myth of the incarnation of the god Zeus, not least thanks to an adaptation by Jean Giraudoux. However, he did not have an adaptation of the myth in mind. *Hélas pour moi* is a presentation of his own philosophy, reflections on the traces of God in the history of humanity and reflections on a world that is perhaps only an image behind which the true world hides, accessible only to those with higher knowledge. This denigration of the earthly and visible world was proposed in early Christianity by Gnosticism, a religious current that became known above all because it was considered heretical doctrine from the orthodox Christian point of view. One of the best-known figures of Gnosis was Simon Magus, a teacher in the first century. Simon is also the name of the character Depardieu plays in *Hélas pour moi*. He seeks out a woman named Rachel. In this encounter, we can see traces of a project that had been on Godard's mind for many years. An adaptation of Racine's tragedy *Bérénice* had already appeared in *Une femme mariée*, where the union of the Roman emperor Titus with the Jewish-Hasmonean queen Berenice stands for an ecumenism that, in *Hélas pour moi*, extends beyond the world of Greek antiquity.

But the film's final form was also dictated by practical considerations. Godard and Depardieu were not on the same wavelength, and a scandal erupted: the star quit the film. Even with creative editing, there was not enough material for the usual one and a half hours. Godard had to reshoot the film, adding a second plot to the story: a man named Abraham Klimt researches the circumstances of Simon's appearance, and his encounter with Rachel.

Hélas pour moi combines Greek antiquity with motifs from the Jewish tradition. Historian of religion Gershom Scholem became a major inspiration, but Godard also picked up on the reception of antiquity in the hymns of Giuseppe Tomasi di Lampedusa. The film "should be about the absence of God. If [he] had succeeded, one would have seen that God is not there. There was this idea (very much coming from Heidegger when he speaks of Hölderlin) that the gods have fled and that in times of need the poets should show the traces of the gods that have disappeared. Then the reverse happened: it became a film about the presence of God."[21]

～

At the end of *Hélas pour moi*, a young man named Ludovic goes to fight in a war that hardly anyone in Europe had predicted. In 1991 the federal state of Yugoslavia began to collapse. Slovenia and Croatia declared themselves independent states, and in Bosnia-Herzegovina, an ethnically mixed population found itself torn apart by Serbian claims to a coherent "national" territory. The war reached its first catastrophic climax in 1993 with the siege of Sarajevo. In the same year, Godard and Miéville sided with the majority of their colleagues in the short video *Je vous salue, Sarajevo* and mourned the fate of the Bosnian Muslims. Alongside the French philosopher Bernard-Henri Lévy, Susan Sontag was particularly committed to making multi-cultural Sarajevo a *cause célèbre*. She staged Samuel Beckett's *Waiting for Godot* in Sarajevo in the middle of the war, thus setting an example of the primacy of culture over weapons.

In 1994 the French intellectual Philippe Sollers published a new edition of Marivaux's classic comedies in the French daily *Le Monde*. In it, he made a point against Susan Sontag, arguing that she should have staged Marivaux, not Beckett, in Sarajevo: she had chosen the wrong genre. At the time, Godard was thinking about a film through which he would tell the story of the American soldier who had unintentionally shot the composer Anton Webern in Mittersill in 1945. His aim was to link this motif (a tragic dramatic moment in the liberation of Europe from fascism) to his interest in Mozart. At the time, he was also interested in the Portuguese author Fernando Pessoa, whose *Book of Disquiet* was rediscovered in France thanks to a new translation. The Portuguese producer Paulo Branco had also set Godard thinking about the Christopher Columbus anniversary in 1992. Five hundred years after the "discovery" of America, Godard wanted to illustrate the relationship between the Old and the New worlds in the form of a very long tracking shot (he thought of three to four kilometers, about eight times as long as the famous shot in *Week End*) that would pass by things that had come to Europe from America. Godard had all this in mind when he read Sollers's text, and all this material found expression in *For Ever Mozart* (1996), a film about war in Europe and about the forms of truth that can correspond to it.[22]

Theater, the novel, morality, philosophy, religion, and finally music all get their chance to tackle the war. The film's form was also shaped by its genesis: the Columbus Project lives on within it, as this film remains linked to the sea; the end concerns Mozart; and Sollers provides the inspiration for the central passage, in which a group of young people travel to Sarajevo to perform a play. At the beginning it is not yet clear which one, but they finally choose *One Does Not Play with Love* by Alfred de Musset, a descendant of Marivaux and one of the French Romantics. Parallel to this expedition into a war zone, the making of a film is also narrated. A director named Vicky Vitalis is shooting "Bolero Fatal." The image for the story is provided by the repetitive musical structure of a bolero. The 1990s appear as a repetition of the 1930s. Godard found this insight in the works of the Spanish writer Juan Goytisolo, who had published *Notes from Sarajevo* in 1993. In the background once again is André Malraux, who immortalized the Republican side in the Spanish Civil War with his film *Sierra de Teruel* (based on his novel *L'Espoir*). This war, which heralded the growing catastrophe of German fascism, was becoming a point of reference—unlike the war in Vietnam.

"Bolero Fatal," the film within the film, fails because it can't find an audience. *Terminator IV* (*Salvation*) does better. And for Mozart, matters become even more complicated. Godard has *For Ever Mozart* end on a concert performance, which is attended by a very mixed audience in a festive venue. Mozart himself is present, played by an actress, and Vicky Vitalis becomes the audience for his music. Mozart plays the solo part of his final piano concerto. Godard underpins this long scene with compositions by cellist David Darling from his album *Dark Wood* (1993). Jürg Stenzl describes this "concert sequence with a resurrected, androgynous Mozart" as "a petrified ritual in a kind of art theater/concert mausoleum."[23]

For Ever Mozart also provided Godard with a late love story. Bérangère Allaux became for him what Ulrike von Levetzow was for the old Goethe: a farewell to erotic closeness with "very young women" to whom he was still being drawn by a "gout épisodique." In an interview, Godard compared himself to Johnny Hallyday in this respect. Allaux, on the other hand, saw in Godard someone who offered himself to her "as a father, a grandfather, and a lover"—and she did not want to have anything to do with him in any of these roles. For Godard, his desire was also linked to an autobiographical motif: the young woman had parents with whom he had a lot to discuss; her mother was a literary scholar and her father had been intensively involved in the FLN during the Algerian conflict. Godard was reminded of his uncles and aunts when he thought of the Allaux family, a "désir de famille, de famille réel" came over him: a desire for family, for real family. Godard saw himself as an orphan, as someone who had left his family. The long-standing theme of his loneliness takes on a new tone in his encounter with Bérangère Allaux and her parents.[24]

Many of Godard's later works have been accompanied by a book published by P. O. L., which illustrates very well how these films were conceived. There are no scripts, but rather simple *phrases*, which are not assigned to a specific character. The whole discourse with its numerous allusions comes to seem like a long, coherent poem from which individual sentences stand out: "Philosophy is almost nothing. You have to have faith."

Is this Godard himself speaking here? In his late work, there is an obvious turn toward matters that fall into realms traditionally overseen by religion. But he is not interested in truths that are hidden behind the visible world. His references to transcendence are part of a Western tradition that found in art the means to address the big questions. Godard emphasizes the connection between art and ethics. In both cases, the prerequisite is a concept of person or subject, which is accompanied by accountability or responsibility. Artists are responsible for their work as people are responsible for their actions. But Godard does something with the form of his films that relativizes his artistic authorship. "I am the living stage on which different actors perform different plays." In *For Ever Mozart*, filmmaker Vicky Vitalis repeats this sentence by Fernando Pessoa. One could apply it to cinema, as Godard understands it: as a medium, it is also a stage on which various "actors" perform (not least the older arts), putting on various plays in which the relationship between person and world is constantly being redefined. In Pessoa, Godard found a key to a self-knowledge that allowed him to speak of himself without becoming the focus, as befits autobiography: an individual places himself and his career at the center. Godard, however, went much further with the autobiography—he had been working for some time on a history of cinema that is deeply personal and at the same time far too big for one person.

CHAPTER 6

The Partisan of Images

1997 to 2020

In February 1977 the German magazine *Filmkritik* published a ten-page spread of facsimile "pages" said to reveal a new project by Godard: a history of cinema and television. It was one of the first public appearances of a project that was to span two decades. Moreover, it supplied a common denominator for Godard's late works. He wanted to use the possibilities of video technology to retell the story of cinema. The sketch for the project anticipated on paper what later become possible with video, namely, combining images and texts into multilayered collages; the soundtrack can only be hinted at on the magazine pages. Godard gave the idea a spin that appealed to the educated middle class: the audience should be able to put the "whole" history of cinema on their shelves at home in the form of ten video cassettes. The notion was in step with contemporary fashion: the increasing spread of video recorders since the 1980s had created a new relationship with film history. In his youth and for a long time afterward, Godard had had experiences that are difficult to convey to today's generation: of films being rare and difficult to access. His first encounters with cinema were even more indirect. He first experienced cinema in 1946 via the film magazine *Revue du cinéma*, whose illustrations left a deep impression on him: "Based on a photo from a film by Murnau that I had never seen, I wanted to make a film myself."[1] *Histoire(s) du cinéma* (1988–98) is largely based on this memory of the period after World War II, when film history began anew. This new start occurred in two different respects. With the borders open once again, America dominated the markets, but films from all over the world were coming into Parisian cinemas and film clubs (among other things via festivals). It became possible to recapitulate. For Godard and his generation, this experience was linked to the history of the Cinémathèque française under Henri Langlois. Film was an event based on copies that had to be saved from oblivion and destruction. Film was an encounter at a screening followed by a discussion.

The fight for the Cinémathèque française in 1968 paid tribute to this heroic period of analogue film culture. Against this background, it is only logical that Godard, together with Jean-Pierre Gorin, conceived the idea of a history of film, in book form, at an early stage: "*Vive le cinéma! À bas le cinéma*" (Long live the cinema! Down with cinema) was intended as a companion volume to the agitational film *Vent d'est* and was supposed to offer something like a treatment in collage of the history of film. In 1972, in *Tout va bien*, they attempted to re-create a famous shot from Eisenstein's *Battleship Potemkin*, a visual quotation that made Godard acutely aware of how much film history takes place in films themselves rather than in books. And as early as 1973, the working title that was to stick for all those years appeared for the first time: "Histoire(s) du cinéma: Fragments inconnus d'une histoire du cinématographe." The first "History of Cinema," published in French, was also written by an author who became increasingly important to Godard during the years he was working on the *Histoire(s)*. In 1935 Robert Brasillach had published *Histoire du Cinéma* together with Maurice Bardèche—a problematic work, nationally conservative in the first edition and openly antisemitic in its 1943 second edition. Godard's regular references to the fascist intellectual, who was executed in 1945 for treason, are among the most ambivalent aspects of his oeuvre.[2]

Like Langlois, but in a different way, Godard wanted to create a tradition. Technical aspects already played an essential role at that time, as can be seen from a later, pointed formulation where he spoke of having "turned into a recording device" during those years. At the same time, he was interested in curatorial matters ("how the management of the Cinémathèque française operates") and the war of formats (between Kodak and 3M or the invention of the SECAM data standard). In the mid-seventies, Godard wrote a detailed concept with Anne-Marie Miéville, but in 1976 another constellation presented itself. Henri Langlois wanted to create an audiovisual film history together with Godard, with help from the producer Jean-Pierre Rassam, who was trying to acquire the film and media group Gaumont at the time. Langlois's unexpected death on January 13, 1977, left a void that gave Godard the opportunity to further develop his project of a history of film.

Particularly important in this connection was an invitation to Montreal, where he lectured and presented film screenings in 1979, in which respect he was also following in Langlois's footsteps. He flew back and forth between France and Canada almost weekly during those months. With Concordia University students, he looked not only at his own films but also at classics from different eras of cinema, sometimes in their entirety, sometimes only as excerpts. The organization and presentation of the celluloid copies—at that time still in individual, approximately twenty-minute reels or "acts"— was taken care of by the Cinémathèque Québécoise.

The result of these weeks was both a deeper understanding of the "montage" between individual works as well as the first fruit of his associations. The book *Introduction à une véritable histoire du cinéma* was published in 1980 and contained transcriptions of the lectures from Montreal. Godard was dissatisfied with the appearance of the work because he had wanted a special aesthetic for the illustrations. He was not interested in glossy illustrations. On the contrary, he wanted the pictures to look as if they had just come out of a black-and-white copier. Indeed, he pushed through a new edition that fit with his aesthetic ideas. This book was also published in German a year later, with these "abstract" illustrations, as *Einführung in eine wahre Geschichte des Kinos*, translated by the cinephile critic Frieda Grafe and Enno Patalas, who was then director of the Munich Film Museum. It became one of the few classic film books in German. However, the books ultimately contradicted the ideal of truth that Godard had in mind for his film history: that is, it could become "true" (*véritable*) precisely if it consisted of images and not illustrated texts.

After the loss of Langlois, the master, Godard found a new ally in Lausanne, Freddy Buache, the long-standing director of the Swiss Cinémathèque. In June 1979 Godard spoke in Lausanne at a conference of FIAF, the International Federation of Film Archives, about the relationship between these collections and film history. In 1980 and 1981 he did a stint similar to Montreal in Rotterdam, where another ally, Monica Tegelaar, was active. Their acquaintance had begun in 1978 when she sought him out in Rolle to win *France, tour, détour, deux enfants* for the Rotterdam Film Festival, where the series had its world cinema premiere in January 1979. Tegelaar organized financial support. With the money from Rotterdam, Godard was finally able to buy an expensive Telecine device that allowed him to copy film material onto video and thus make it easier to edit. In return, he was to take part in a series of events in Rotterdam under the motto "Projection—Discussion." However, the planned series only took place in parts (between autumn 1980 and summer 1981) and not always in Godard's presence. During this time, he was especially busy with his return to feature films, a return documented in one of the most interesting products of this project: an experimental reworking of his recently completed film *Sauve qui peut (la vie)*, which he supplemented in four places with longer passages from films by Sergei Eisenstein, Buster Keaton, Luchino Visconti, and Andrzej Wajda. Under the "upside-down" title *Sauve la vie (qui peut)*, this "version" was shown once in February 1981 as part of the Rotterdam International Film Festival.[3]

During these years, a new title for the later *Histoire(s)* also appeared occasionally: *The Splendor and Misery of Cinema*, based on the title of Balzac's novel from the cycle *The Human Comedy*. Godard thus indicated what he had in mind: nothing less than a representation of the totality of human experience, albeit not in the form of new, invented stories told on film but as a collage of already-existing images and sounds. He recorded as much as he could from the television and thus provided himself with a basic material base, although for the time being it was still unclear how he would deal with the copyright issues.

In 1988 at a press conference in Cannes, he spoke publicly for the first time about the *Histoire(s)* and stated the concrete political context that illuminates a central motif of his history of cinema. In France since 1978, the literary scholar Robert Faurisson had been creating controversy with his claim that the gas chambers in the extermination camps had never been used. The ostensibly scientific arguments of Holocaust deniers such as Faurisson or David Irving in Great Britain found a political basis in the increasingly strong radical right Front National under Jean-Marie Le Pen. For Godard, the role of images in the memory of the death camps was at the center of his film history. The fact that a politician like Le Pen could dismiss the concentration camps as a "detail" was, for him, a function of the way that television took away the basis of seeing and thinking. In 1989 the first two episodes of *Histoire(s)* were broadcast on Canal+, but the eight-part project took almost ten years to complete, interspersed with feature films such as *Hélas pour moi* and, finally, an autobiography.

~

The cinematic "Self-Portrait in December" *JLG/JLG*, released in 1994, belongs on the one hand to the context of *Hélas pour moi* but, on the other, has strong references to the long-standing work on the *Histoire(s) du cinéma*. In this one-hour introspection, Godard reflects on his own individuality and historicity—and on the legends that surround him. He does this using forms that go beyond himself: love and universality are the key words.

Godard begins with a photo from his youth that shows a trace from the past: what dark forces had a hold on this young man? *JLG/JLG* shows a man, Godard, now old, in the dark. He dedicates himself to a work of mourning that precedes death; death has so far failed to appear, although note "on the street in Paris"—an allusion to the motorbike accident that brought him closest to death. Godard reveals himself here as a man who illuminates the darkness a little with his notes. Sometimes his lines on paper are rendered legible only by the light of a match. The motif of fire emerges in an association between lighting a cigar and his parents' generation; they were vectors of a tradition that had made a "Kristallnacht." A book by the natural philosopher Henri Atlan (*Entre le cristal et la fumée*) forms the bracket for this negative and exaggerated treatment of his own family history, which he situates here and elsewhere in the twilight of sympathies for fascism.

Even more idiosyncratic is the next mind game (in this case it is also a drawing game, a sketch with a geometric figure): the name Jeannot, by which Godard is occasionally addressed, rhymes with stereo. He now highlights the "true legend" of stereo: two intertwined triangles (one representing the projection of images, one the corresponding reception) together form a star. Not accidentally, one is reminded of the Jewish symbol, the Star of David. And Godard does indeed apply this figure to historical constellations: Germany "projects" Israel, and Israel reflects this projection (and "has found its cross,"[4] one must add, in the Shoah). This relationship of projection/reflection is repeated with the Palestinians, who "in their own way" also have a cross to bear. Godard thus superimposes on the visible sign of the hexagram the invisible one, evoked by his argument, the symbol of the cross with its Christian connotation; and he turns the triangle into a historical sequence. The concept of projection takes the place of strictly factual causality: From Hitler follows Israel, from Israel, the cross of the Palestinians.

A little sketch with a cleaning lady named Brigitte, whom he persistently calls Adrienne, could be understood as a discreet autobiographical allusion: "The tragedy of sexual relations is the virginity of souls." Julien Green's novel *Adrienne Mesurat*, to which Godard refers here, tells of a young woman who desires a doctor almost thirty years her senior. The possibility that Godard (or JLG) might be a man who reciprocates such a desire refracts shortly afterward in a quote in which he refers to the poet Paul-Jean Toulet and an "immense solitude." The rejuvenation that old artists often achieved at the side of younger women—at least sexually—Godard now sees as impossible precisely because the "souls" of desirable women are so vulnerable. The "imbécile" JLG (a harsher word than his other self-designation, "idiot") finally arrives at the superposition that decisively constitutes *JLG/JLG*: "I must become universal." Shortly before the end of the film, Godard formulates this mission differently, in terms that bring Christianity to mind: "I must sacrifice myself so that through me the word 'love' acquires meaning." One can also see a reinterpreted eroticism in this religiously impregnated philosophy of love: Godard no longer falls in love with young women (although the last word has not yet been said on this matter), which means that he is now available for another love, for an erotic, or mystical, or prophetically charged relationship with history as such.[5]

⌐∿⌐

In 1998 the *Histoire(s) du cinéma* were finally finished in the form in which they exist today: a total of four and a half hours in four double episodes, in other words, eight chapters. They are available both on DVD and as books. A French edition was published by Gallimard, the trilingual version (French, German, and English) officially functions as an add-on to a CD edition of the soundtrack on the ECM label. These different forms of presentation alone are an indication of what we are dealing with in the *Histoire(s)*: a total work of art that deliberately overtaxes the human senses and intellectual capacities. Even if you read the "text" as presented in the

book editions, you would still have to process the significant amount of
text that appears in the form of inserts in images. Often this is just names
or slogans, but sometimes it is wordplay. An example toward the end: SI JE
NE MABUSE. The name of the big-time criminal Mabuse from the German
film classics by Fritz Lang can also be read here as a verb: *si je ne m'abuse* (if
I'm not mistaken). In addition to these linguistic levels, there are also the
images and the music. The images form the source material. Godard draws
on the history of film but hardly ever allows a sequence to run long enough
to be recognized as part of the larger whole to which it originally belonged:
film images are always part of a montage. Here, however, only Godard's
montage counts. Video technology allows him to go much further than
would be possible with an analogue editing table: he not only combines
images from film history to match his own lines of thought, but he also
manipulates them. He "cuts" within the images,[6] and he constantly creates
multilayered new images and often remains present in the background, as
a shadow, as a man at the electric typewriter, as a ghost or a spirit—and
above all as a voice. With his own and many other voices, Godard "speaks"
the material, covering all manner of different registers in his voice-over interventions. The texts are largely unattributed quotations, and here too Godard
draws on a large number of works that have become significant to him over
the years, from Baudelaire (*Correspondences*) to Pierre Reverdy (*L'image*),
from Victor Hugo to Virginia Woolf. Lesser-known names are also important, for example, Denis de Rougemont and Godard's personal central European patron saints Ramuz and Giraudoux. Paintings and photographs enter
into a relationship with the film images. And finally, everything is held
together by the music.[7]

Godard wants the work to be understood in terms of its name: as a
historiographical sketch. He sees himself as standing in a tradition he
shares with the masters of this craft, to whom he also explicitly refers: Jules
Michelet, the historian of the French nation and revolution, who in the
mid-nineteenth century still had contact with contemporary witnesses to
Robespierre and Napoleon; Georges Duby, the medievalist, whose *Dames
du XIIe siècle* Godard read "like a film" because it brought an era to life
in spite of scanty sources;[8] and Fernand Braudel, whose concept of a history of "*longue durée*" (as opposed to one of short steps from one event
to the next) Godard wanted to apply in an almost paradoxical way to the

extreme twentieth century with its overabundance of events. In the field of art history, the central inspiration is André Malraux's "imaginary museum."

At the same time, of course, Godard knows that he is working with a different kind of source material. His material is made up not of archival documents but of secondhand sources, and they are snippets that only offer a glimpse of reality in exceptional cases. For the most part, they stem from fictions—whereas the *Histoire(s)* do everything they can to make this difference, which he had already undermined as a critic, irrelevant. In retrospect, a Godard quote from the American women's magazine *Women's Wear Daily* from 1980 seems like an early complex of concerns from which the *Histoire(s)* grew: "When I started making films, I started with fiction, or what my parents thought was fiction—my actual parents or John Ford. But in the course of the work I felt a need for documentary. Society told me that I had to choose one or the other. But I don't like to decide. I don't like to choose between Cain and Abel, between the Nazis or the Jews—all-too-terrible torturers on the one hand, all-too-terrible martyrs on the other."[9]

Godard also defies the zeitgeist with his historical panorama: postmodernism has done all it can to cut the connection between the unattainable real and images, but he insists on speaking of the reality of the twentieth century using the very methods of this postmodernism—that is, a flood of images seemingly detached from direct references—and on striking it at its essential core. He redeems the renunciation of a "grand narrative," which is one of the central concerns of postmodernism, with a grand narrative that is simultaneously atomized into split-second snapshots and exaggerated in a Hegelian manner.

The reflections on the retrospective capture of the present in *Allemagne neuf zéro* are rethought in the *Histoire(s)*, making extensive (and, as always, unreferenced) use of Hollis Frampton's essay "For a Metahistory of Film":

As one era slowly dissolves into the next, some individuals metabolize the former means for physical survival into new means for psychic survival.

These latter we call art.

Typically, all that survives intact of an era is the art forms it invents for itself. No activity can become an art until its proper epoch has ended and it has dwindled in this way; the art of the nineteenth century helped cinema toward its existence in the twentieth century, which barely existed of itself.[10]

This claim, which Godard formulates a few years before the turn of the millennium, is by no means modest. He not only wants to make cinema the next great medium after painting;[11] he is also looking for a form into which he could incorporate the many total works of modernism (interpreters cite as references everything from Walter Benjamin's *Passages* to *Finnegans Wake* by James Joyce[12]) and at the same time connect the middle of the twentieth century with its end. For inevitably, the *Histoire(s)* also revolve around World War II, the Shoah, and the new beginning in 1945.

Godard, too, sees these events first and foremost as a *cinéaste*. According to him, cinema knew early on what was coming, but "they didn't believe it." Jean Renoir's *La Règle du jeu* (1939) has this prophetic quality for Godard,[13] but that doesn't change the fact that cinema failed in the face of the camps. It didn't film them. In the background of this argument is an inherently contradictory conception of cinema as a mass art ("the only art that has actually been popular"). But this conception experienced a defeat following the American victory in World War II: this victory made it possible "to finance, that is to say, to ruin all of European cinema with the emergence of television."

The year 1945 also marked a change in cinema, because the emergence of popular culture changed the balance of power. Cinema as an art of resistance came under the pressure of commercialism. At the end of chapter 1A, Godard takes up this moment in the form of a provocation: "And if George Stevens had not been the first to use the first 16 mm color film at Auschwitz and Ravensbrück, Elizabeth Taylor's happiness would probably never have found a place in the sun."[14]

The passage lasts forty seconds and is one of the most discussed passages in Godard's work. He interweaves three image complexes: the American filmmaker George Stevens shot scenes in Dachau in 1945 (not in Ravensbrück and Auschwitz, as Godard thought) in which corpses can be seen in an open wagon; in 1951, Stevens, who had returned to Hollywood from his war service and was working as a feature film director, released *A Place in the Sun*, based on Theodore Dreiser's novel *An American Tragedy*—Godard uses a scene from it with Elizabeth Taylor by a lake; and the painting *Noli me tangere* by Giotto, in which Jesus and Mary Magdalene are seen in front of the empty tomb on Easter morning.

In a conversation with the critic Serge Daney, who died in 1992 and was Godard's most important intellectual confidant during these years, Godard explained the context of his montage: "There is a deep sense of happiness in *A Place in the Sun*, which I had encountered in other, even better films. It is a simple, secular feeling of happiness, a moment with Elizabeth Taylor. When I found out that Stevens had filmed the concentration camps and that Kodak had given him their first 16 mm color film rolls for the occasion, it explained to me how he was able to create this large-scale shot of Liz Taylor that radiated a kind of overshadowed happiness."[15]

The superimposition (or overshadowing) of these three motifs contains two possible resurrections: one from the hell of the camps into the heaven of a star system in which Elizabeth Taylor embodies cinema in its transcendent aura beyond human realities; and one from the physical decay of the piles of corpses into the paradoxical incorporeality of the resurrected Jesus, whom Mary Magdalene tries to touch, while he rejects precisely this physical touch. Godard tilts the detail of the painting, however, so that it now looks as if Jesus is grasping *de profundis* and in vain at his disciple's saving hand. Critics such as Jacques Rancière have criticized this passage, accusing Godard of using it to effect a Christianization of the Jewish experience of annihilation and to overwrite the history of the Shoah with a story of salvation. However, it is precisely the intangible body of Jesus's apparition that cannot be held onto, and it is (figuratively) Christianity that plunges into hell.

With this passage and with the entire architecture of *Histoire(s)*, Godard was intervening in a debate that became central to the various ways of coming to terms with the past after the end of World War II: the question of the representability of Auschwitz, the cipher for the Shoah. In 1985 the documentary film *Shoah* by Claude Lanzmann was released, in which remembrance of the National Socialist policy of extermination of the Jews was primarily founded on the testimony of a few survivors. Lanzmann deliberately refrained from using archive material and thus marked a position in the representation of the Shoah: he considered it unrepresentable. When Steven Spielberg released the feature film *Schindler's List* in 1993, Lanzmann reacted harshly: "The Holocaust is unique above all in that it surrounds itself with a circle of flames, a boundary that must not be crossed because

a certain, absolute level of atrocity is incommunicable. Whoever does so
is guilty of the worst transgression. Fiction is a transgression, and it is my
deepest conviction that any representation is forbidden."[16]

Godard made negative comments about *Shoah*. "He didn't show anything, he showed the Germans," he said in a conversation with Marguerite
Duras in 1987, and as if this judgment weren't enough, he followed it up:
"If he had been seen in France, the verdict on Klaus Barbie should not have
turned out the way it did."[17] He was alluding to the trial of the former head
of the Lyon Gestapo, Klaus Barbie, who was extradited from Bolivia in 1984
not to Germany, where Helmut Kohl did not want to create a spectacle,
but to France. In 1987 he was put on trial. He was sentenced to life impris-
onment for crimes against humanity. Barbie was defended by Jacques Vergès,
a star lawyer who had been radically committed to Algeria (and later to the
Palestinians) in his younger years and who defended the anti-Zionist and
Holocaust denier Roger Garaudy in 1998.

After completing *Histoire(s)*, however, Godard sought a conversation
with Lanzmann, with whom he obviously wanted to compete. An offer
from the Arte channel provided an opportunity to do so. Godard was to
contribute to a series of broadcasts titled *Gauche-Droite (Left-Right)*. He
fell upon the idea of meeting Lanzmann in the context of such a program.
The star intellectual Bernard-Henri Lévy was invited as moderator. Based
on an interview with Lévy, Richard Brody reports on four dinners at the
Hotel Crillon, which, if they had actually taken place, must be imagined as
an absurd film scene: "At those four dinners, none of us said a word. Everyone was afraid of making an idiot of themselves."[18] Lévy later corrected this
abbreviated account, which is also adopted by Antoine de Baecque, with a
detailed account.[19] The first meeting between Godard and Lanzmann took
place in private at Lévy's home in a polite atmosphere. At this point, of
course, Lanzmann was already aware of the derogatory statement Godard
had made to Duras, and he was further irritated by an interview in the pop
magazine *Les Inrockuptibles* in which Godard took a particular view on the
question of the representability of the Shoah. He claimed that there must
be footage from the gas chambers somewhere and that it was only a matter
of time ("twenty years") before it was discovered. All it would take was
for someone to give him a commission for the search.[20] With this motif, it
is not clear whether this is a literary confection, comparable to the alleged

pornographic film of Adolf Hitler in the bunker, which Don DeLillo speaks of in the novel *Running Dog*, or whether he really assumed that the existence of such material would correspond to his conception of the testimonial power of images. But it would then not be a film that could erase the historical guilt of cinema, because it would come from the perpetrators ("*ça a été filmé sûrement en long et en large par les Allemands*" [the Germans surely filmed it long and wide], he said in a 1985 interview[21]). If one had one of these films, then "it would be over with Vergès," Godard added, thus distancing himself not only from the "devil's advocate" but also from one of the most important French advocates of the Palestinian cause, which continued to be a key to contemporary history for him as well.

Images of or from Auschwitz were considered the "last taboo" at the end of the nineties, and Godard was one of those who propagated a "religion of the image" against the "censors" Lanzmann and Adorno, who was forever associated with his dictum on the impossibility of poetry after Auschwitz. This is how Gérard Wajcman put it in a text in *Le Monde*, in which he labeled Lanzmann as Moses and Godard as Paul. Godard had already spoken very clearly about Moses in a television program in 1981: "Moses is my nemesis. . . . When Moses brought the Ten Commandments, he first saw pictures—and translated them. So he brought texts, he did not show what he had seen. This is the reason why the Jewish people are cursed (*maudit*)."[22] Wajcman's catchy formulation rendered the matter clear. The Jew Lanzmann and the Protestant Godard stood for two "churches," or more precisely, Godard had founded a church against the Jews, a place of worship for a religion of the image. As nuanced as the debate was in detail, it was also characterized by the oldest stereotypes.

Lévy finally describes how the television project with Godard and Lanzmann fell apart over the course of several meetings. It was to be titled "Pas un dîner de Gala," a reference to Mao ("The revolution is not a banquet"). While Godard makes detailed plans for how his, Lanzmann's, and Lévy's positions could be represented in their program, the conversation between the participants becomes increasingly monosyllabic. Lanzmann's impression of Godard as an antisemite solidifies; Lévy thinks that Godard was "intellectually overwhelmed by Lanzmann." Lanzmann is finally no longer willing to participate in what he considers a "wild psychoanalysis" with an artist for whom he has no affection.

A borderline instance of this last taboo is represented by the four 1944 photographs from Auschwitz, which were taken by members of the Jewish Sonderkommandos and show scenes from the daily routine of the killings. In his reference work on these "images in spite of everything," the image scholar Georges Didi-Huberman discusses Godard's *Histoire(s)* in detail. His reading of the passage with Dachau, Liz Taylor, and Giotto is plausible: "There is no resurrection here in the theological sense, since there is no dialectical completion."[23] Godard sets the images in his montage in endless motion. Didi-Huberman even goes so far as to associate this "endlessness" with the "final solution." And in this movement one must probably also include the antithesis with which Godard contradicts his own intention in the *Histoire(s)*:

cinema, like, Christianity
is not based on a historical truth
it provides us with a narrative[24]

The *Histoire(s) du cinéma* take on a double role not only within Godard's body of work but also within film history overall: they look backward to the nineteenth and twentieth centuries but do so with means that point ahead to the twenty-first century. The digital culture of the present is already taking shape in Godard's work, even if he himself still had to work with video technologies that were comparatively simple. The fact that the project was basically unfinishable can be seen in a series of short films, which Godard later made and which were still entirely influenced by the spirit of collage in the *Histoire(s)*. *De l'origine du XXIe siècle* (*From the Origin of the 21st Century*, 2000) is a sixty-minute abridged version of his historical theses, a run through the twentieth century leading up to the beginning of this "lost century," as he calls it. It begins with a busload of people in Kosovo who are "hors de loi" (outside the law, that is, not protected by any law) and ends with the image of the collapsing dancer from Max Ophüls's *Le Plaisir*. *The Old Place* (2000) and *Liberté et patrie* (*Liberty and Homeland*, 2002), both designed together with Anne-Marie Miéville, are works for exhibition venues: a commission from the Museum of Modern Art in New York and a contribution to the Swiss EXPO national for the Vaud Pavilion, the canton in French-speaking Switzerland that was home and native land to both Godard and Miéville. In the form of a homage to the fictitious painter Aimé Pache, a character in Charles Ramuz's novel, they turn Vaud into a landscape that is both regional and universal. Repeated shots of a TGV high-speed train traveling the Paris-Lausanne route provide the defining image of this world.

~

Godard welcomes the twenty-first century with his "fourth first film" after *À bout de souffle, Numéro deux*, and *Sauve qui peut (la vie)*,[25] *Éloge de l'amour* (*In Praise of Love*, 2001), once again a new beginning. Its story goes back to 1996, when the contract with Canal+ was signed. It took four versions of the script to get to the heart of what Godard had in mind: he wanted to tell of love in its temporality, of the stages of a relationship over the years—getting to know each other, physical passion, separation, rapprochement. A young man named Edgar is looking for actors for a project. The two main characters are to be called Perceval and Églantine, the former after Robert Walser's *The Rose*, the latter after the novel of the same name by Jean Giraudoux.[26] At first Edgar does not get beyond possible actors for the first phase of the relationship; he is looking for a woman for the other stages. It is noticeable that the everyday life of a successful relationship does not appear in this list—from passion it goes directly to separation. This gap corresponds to a recurring remark in the film, namely, that there are no "adults" or there is no "adulthood." Edgar is finally recommended a woman who could be a candidate for his project. He meets her at night at a marshalling yard where she cleans trains—a tedious second job that she is forced to do as a single mother. Edgar and the woman, whose name is not mentioned, realize that they know each other from "two years ago on the coast," when they had first met.

This "two years ago" is the crux of the whole film, as can be seen from the first draft of the script, which revolves around the word "avant" (before, earlier, before).[27] In cinema, one speaks of a flashback when a passage that took place earlier in the internal chronology is inserted into the narrative. *Éloge de l'amour* also contains a long flashback, but it is not an interlude; instead, the entire second part of the film takes place "two years earlier," whereby the indication of "two years" changes because in the first (the "later") part there is also at least one leap in time lasting several years, so that Godard inserts an "even earlier" in between. The chronology loses its secure foundation.

In this second part of the film, which is the chronologically earlier one, Edgar comes to Brittany to meet the well-known leftist historian Jean Lacouture, who was best known for his biographies of de Gaulle, Ho Chi Minh, John F. Kennedy, Gamal Abdel Nasser, and Michel de Montaigne. Edgar wants to find out about the role of Catholics in the French resistance during World War II. He also talks about the project to write a cantata about Simone Weil, a key tragic figure of this resistance. She was a social revolutionary, a mystic, and an agnostic Jew who converted to Catholicism and died of anorexia in England in 1943. Lacouture introduces Edgar to an old couple who run a hotel in the area: the Bayards have just been visited by an agent from Spielberg Associates and his assistant. They want to buy the Bayards' life story (specifically the years 1941, 1942, 1943) and to make a film out of it, with William Styron writing the script. Juliette Binoche, who won an Oscar in 1997 for her role in *The English Patient*, is to star in the film—which the agent expressly emphasizes as an essential condition.

The Bayards have a granddaughter, who annoys the Americans with her politically motivated pedantry: "Which America? There is also a South America. Brazil, Mexico, Canada are also America." She is the woman Edgar wanted to win over for his project in Paris. Her name also comes up in passing: Berthe Bayard. Later it turns out that she was supposed to have the Jewish name Samuel, an allusion to Simone Weil's conversion. It is significant that Edgar never hears her name, and, therefore, he does not in fact know what her name is. All the more important that two years later, when he talks about her after a night at the station, he describes her as "unimpressive"—and then adds, "She is no Berthe Morisot." This allusion to the only woman among the French impressionists can be read in many ways, not least in view of the fact that in the *Histoire(s)* Godard describes cinema as a successor to painting. For the central theme of the film, love, it is essential that Edgar does not "recognize" Berthe (even by name) but almost meets her.

The relationship between Edgar and Berthe fails in a way that Godard probably wanted to see as expressing the essence of love: they miss each other for various reasons, but all of them point to the fundamental impossibility of a love in which two people are absorbed in one another. To put it bluntly, one could say that Edgar and Berthe never live in the same time. The form of the film also indicates that the idea of the stages of love with which Edgar deals is naive. "There is no first time":[28] the two-part film is about "loss and repetition." By the time the audience sees the film in the cinema, the meeting in Brittany is already suspended by the news of Berthe's suicide, which comes at the end of the first part. Nevertheless, before this casually presented but deeply upsetting information, there are still moments in which Edgar and Berthe are so close that they can be considered lovers. But their intimacy is not a private one; it is a historical one. They can be seen in an area of Boulogne-Billancourt where the ruins of early Renault factories point to the end of the workers' movements of the twentieth century (which can also be understood as Résistances). At the same time, this location is linked to Jean Vigo's classic film *L'Atalante* by a *chanson* heard in the scene: it is thus also linked to a time of the innocence of the cinema, namely, the transition from "silent" film to speaking films.

Edgar and Berthe's future, which was impossible from the start, finally ends at the Drancy Avenir regional station, which is forever associated in memory with the deportations to extermination camps that were carried out from there.

Godard himself is present in *Éloge de l'amour* at various stages of his life. He takes the name of the hero from a book he devoured as a teenager and that functions in the film as a link between the two parts.[29] Edgar's journey, which Godard characterizes with an image from this book, is also the adventure of a young man caught between times (it is significant, as is every little detail in this film, and also very cryptic, that at one point the film says of Edgar that he is the only one who will grow up). Godard, however, is present above all as an old man, as someone who not only has already put the four stages of love behind him but has only one love left open to him. The film presents this as an ideal: a transcendent love based on mediations and transgressions, a love of which only an outside narrator knows anything. He also makes these stages visible in an image in which he himself can be seen, sitting on a bench in a square in Paris at night. He sits there, a book in front of him despite the darkness, back-to-back with a young couple.

During the development of *Éloge de l'amour*, Godard also had to come to terms with the disappointment that Bérangère Allaux, with whom he was keen to continue working after *For Ever Mozart*, refused to collaborate with him after the second draft of the script. She had also refused his advances. He was now at an age when he could no longer succeed in winning over young actresses. This mourning for Allaux was already evident in a seven-minute video by Godard in 1998, which was not intended for publication: *Adieu au TNS*. The abbreviation refers to the Théâtre National de Strasbourg, where Allaux was employed. Godard sings a kind of song, in a melancholy *sprechgesang*, accompanied by an instrument that sounds rather like an accordion. The scene is set in a semidark room, Godard wears a suit and hat, and he lights a new cigar with each cut (there are only two). All his self-designations return here, and a few new ones are added: he is the idiot, the refugee "sans domicil," the man in exile. In this short piece, he mourns the failure of his projects with the TNS, where he wanted to work with young actors who were not interested in him, and where he wanted to make a documentary film in the style of Frederick Wiseman, that is, a portrait of an institution. The disappointment of his affection for Allaux is scarcely concealed: "A man following a princess into a theater—what a misfortune."

One would think this painfully private document expressed nothing more than a moment of frank intimacy were it not for one aspect that Richard Brody has highlighted. He pointed out that *Adieu au TNS* is a remake of another video that Godard had produced at the time, in which the actor Philippe Loyrette recited a text by Robert Brasillach, namely his *Will*, written in the days before his execution.[30] For Brody, who is very keen to expose Godard as an antisemite, *Adieu au TNS* is a coded homage to Brasillach. The text, however, does not reveal anything in this regard, for between allusions to Europe (unloved) and AIDS (undefeated), what emerges here above all is a wistful "mission" entrusted to the next generation of young actors not to let the "ship run aground" and to use the means of theater ("sacrifice the body and steal the soul of the character") to unravel a "scientific" mystery. Here we see Godard in his entirety once again.

In *Éloge de l'amour*, Philippe Loyrette, a follower of Brasillach, plays an important supporting role. And Godard quotes from Brasillach's *Will*. He puts the words into the mouth of an old woman who is a candidate for Edgar's project. Some American critics have interpreted this as an identification with Brasillach's fascist ideology and *Éloge de l'amour* as being therefore an antisemitic film. This is an inadmissible abridgment. *Éloge de l'amour* is a film about the theme of resistance against the backdrop of the question of French national identity. In *La France Libre*, Berthe writes on a boat, in a central, allegorical scene. The great opponent of 1968, de Gaulle, now becomes a conceivable partner for Godard: "Celui qui a dit non" (the man who said no) is written on a neon sign advertising a contemporary biography of de Gaulle. Berthe reads a book by the humanist Étienne de La Boétie (*Discours de la servitude volontaire*); an insert refers to the Orchestre Rouge, the Rote Kapelle, a communist cell in the German resistance against the Nazis. In *Éloge de l'amour*, Godard forges a broad coalition not only against fascism but (from Boétie's point of view) against an absolutism that he redefines using the figure of Hollywood.

Éloge de l'amour also has two faces in terms of film technique. The first part is shot on 35 mm film and in elegiac black and white; the second part is shot with MiniDV cameras, that is, in a cheap-looking format whose artificiality Godard increases even further by making the colors look as garish as possible. He thus achieves a quality that he in turn associates with painting—a digital fauvism. Contemporary critics especially liked the first part; they saw *Éloge de l'amour* as a return to the Paris of the sixties, to Godard's "halcyon days." Audiences were not won over by the predominantly positive reviews. The film was a commercial flop. The experience with students from Strasbourg, who were no longer interested in Godard, had likely been no accident. The contact between the generations had been severed. Two children collecting signatures for a Breton dubbing of the then-popular blockbuster *The Matrix* in one of the final scenes of the film are a sign—though again an ambivalent one—for just this process, especially when one considers the subversion of French centralism that is going on here.

~

Even at the premiere of *Éloge de l'amour*, Godard spoke of a new project through which he wanted to tell of his friendship with Manfred Eicher: *Notre musique* (*Our Music*, 2004). This title could be understood quite concretely, because for some years now the releases on the ECM label, which Eicher had made into a leading home for jazz and modern classical music coming out of Munich, had become a fixture of Godard's films.

Eicher shared his music with Godard and received a very special brand ambassador in return. The project changed gradually, however, in the way that Godard increasingly turned his films into scrapbooks recording his invitations, travels, and preoccupations. In 2002 he was in Sarajevo at a literary congress and had the opportunity to meet the Palestinian poet Mahmud Darwish and the Spanish writer Juan Goytisolo. Godard also gave a lecture that later makes a central appearance in *Notre musique*. Music from ECM continued to play an important role; the list of contributors (from Hans Otte to David Darling) is long. But the term "our music" had now taken on a broader meaning: it is "the principle of cinema to turn toward the light and direct it toward darkness." The "musicality" of this movement is the theme of *Notre musique*.

The film consists of three parts or "realms" (*royaumes*): hell, purgatory, and heaven. Purgatory clearly lasts longer than heaven and hell (the latter a collage of shrine images that looks like a sinister dungeon from the margins of the *Histoire[s]*). The plot of the film, shot in Sarajevo, centers on two young women: Judith Lerner and Olga Brodsky. Judith is a young journalist from Tel Aviv who is looking for a "place of reconciliation" in Bosnia. She meets the French ambassador, who she knows saved a Jewish boy during World War II, her future father ("Lyon. 1943. Gestapo," she calls out to him as cues, implicitly turning the man into an opponent of Klaus Barbie). This ambassador named Naville is a "just man" (*un juste*), even if he is very modest about it. Judith conducts an interview with Mahmud Darwish, in which the poet talks about how Israel has inflicted defeat on the Palestinians but also made them famous, because all the world looks at Israel and thus also at its opponents. To this statement, Darwish adds an association: Troy never told its story. It is only known from Homer, that is, from the Greek perspective. So the Palestinians would be the Trojans of today.

The same could be said about the Indians who haunt Sarajevo. Godard once again plays with transitions: For him, Bosnia-Herzegovina, which was brought to a provisional peace in 1995 with the Dayton Accords, becomes a vantage point from which he can look at a long line of historical victors and vanquished. He owed the jump from the Palestinians to the "Redskins" to Elias Sanbar, an ally from the time he visited Fatah in 1970. Sanbar's book *Le Bien des absents* was published in 2001. In it, he formulated a classic theme for the anti-American left: the birth of America (with the extermination of the indigenous people) found a parallel in the birth of the state of Israel, which turned the Palestinians into "redskins," with support from Washington.[31]

In his lecture in Sarajevo, Godard speaks of the cinematic means of the shot/countershot combination: with a cut, the camera changes position and now looks at the person who was the point of origin of the gaze in the previous shot. Dialogues are very often "resolved" in this way in the cinema. In 1948 there was a historic shot/countershot constellation on the coast of Israel: people left ships and went ashore through the water, while Palestinians were driven into the sea (a reversal of Egyptian President Nasser's threat against the state of Israel).

It is by no means clear, however, whether Godard takes a position with this juxtaposition of two images that also further develop his idea of historical "projection" from *JLG/JLG*. Richard Brody reads *Notre musique* as an antisemitic "diatribe." But in Judith Lerner's interview with Mahmud Darwish, Godard shows himself to be far from partisan. The poet makes it clear that the reconciliation Lerner seeks comes at a very high price for him and his people—to represent themselves historically, as Israel does without difficulty, is a distant goal for the Palestinians, even though Darwish was invited to Sarajevo. His counter art and the dedication of *Notre musique* to Elias Sanbar indicate that Godard is looking back on the constructions of his revolutionary phase. Little has changed since 1970, except that China has fallen away as a political option. The fact that, more than ever before, the whole world lives under the sign of "horror" is especially significant for the second female character: Godard had to invent Olga Brodsky because Sarah Adler, the actress playing Judith Lerner, did not want to play this part of the story. Olga is a terrorist. She wants to end the "horrors" through a shocking act. Godard first filmed her on the streets of Sarajevo, and she also attended his lecture, but they never really came into contact. Before he leaves, she hands him a DVD. He hears about her attack later by phone, by which time he is already back in Switzerland filming himself as a flower grower.[32] In a cinema in Jerusalem, Olga Brodsky threatens the audience with a bomb. She gives people five minutes to leave the room and at the same time invites them to join her planned symbolic action—to die for peace. No one stays, and Olga is shot dead by a police team. The bomb she was supposedly carrying turns out to be a bag of books.

With this act of antiterrorism,[33] Godard also places a Jew in a clear relationship to events of the present day. The attacks of September 11, 2001,
and perhaps more clearly, the Chechen nationalist hostage crisis in Moscow's
Dubrovka Theatre in October 2002, with its brutal ending, make Olga's
symbolic act all the more powerful. The concept of paradoxical intervention, which arguably fits here, can also be applied to Godard's own strategy. In *Notre musique*, there is definitely such a thing as progress. The peace
secured by Stabilisation Force in Bosnia and Herzegovina (SFOR) soldiers
in Sarajevo is one example. The bridge in Mostar is being rebuilt, and some-
day the city will have books again (an important scene in the film takes
place in the imposing ruins of the destroyed library building). But there is
also a way out of the story by means of a leap. In the third, concluding part
of the film, Olga Brodsky finds herself in a heaven that is perhaps also just
an enclave in nature. One could think of the revolutionary "tribe" at the end
of *Week End*. The apple which began the disaster in paradise has already
been bitten.

∼

While *Notre musique* was taking shape, Godard was also working on an
exhibition for the Centre Georges Pompidou in Paris, inspired by the curator Dominique Païni, with whom he had been in close contact for some
time. The working title was tinged with a bitter irony: in the mid-1990s,
there had been talk of Godard being admitted to the Collège de France,
the highest distinction in the intellectual life of the Republic during his
lifetime. However, this did not come to pass, and one (albeit not clearly
legible) reaction can be seen in the fact that Godard organized the exhibition "Collage(s) de France. Archéologie du cinema."[34] After all, the invitation to present something in the Beaubourg, as the museum is colloquially
called, was also a form of ennoblement. Godard thus moved up into the
visual arts; he was able to give cinema a new home in a place where modernity took on corporeal form.

The project was marked by many delays and revisions and was not realized until 2006, now under a new title: *Voyage(s) en utopie. Jean-Luc Godard,
1946–2006. À la recherche d'un théorème perdu* (Journey(s) into utopia, in
search of a lost theorem). With the concept of the theorem, Godard once
again makes clear his attempt to grasp cinema as a science, now in an art

space, that is, at the other end of the developmental possibilities of modernity. The sciences are bound to the facts; art is the highest form of autonomy. For Godard, cinema stands between these two commitments or utopias. The exhibition was also archaeological in that it incorporated the earlier concept and showed its revision. Nine rooms with titles like "The Myth (Allegory)" or "The Assholes (Parable)" suggest that the unnamed theorem is to be found in Godard's key concept of montage. Through the installation, Godard makes it clear that cinema has become placeless. From the *Histoire(s)*, he adopts the skeptical position of an unattainable history, pre-formulated in Charles Péguy's history book *Clio*.

~

One of the participants at the literary conference in *Notre musique* was the intellectual and cultural functionary Jean-Paul Curnier, with whom Godard remained in loose contact afterward. The title of *Film Socialisme* (2010) is taken from a letter by Curnier in which he responds in detail to Godard's sending of images and notes on a film project called "Socialisme." Owing to a misunderstanding, Curnier read the papers as if they were about film and socialism in direct connection. This inspired Curnier to reflect on cinema and socialism, "these phases of the past century," taken together. "That socialism and cinema, after having served such bad hands and such unsophisticated souls, have found each other exhausted, is well known."[35]

Godard's revitalized interest in a supposedly obsolete and historically discredited idea takes the form of a reflection on Europe as a civilization on the Mediterranean in *Film Socialisme*. The French historian Fernand Braudel, already an important guiding figure for the *Histoire(s) du cinéma*, had made a name for himself and found a focus for his life's work in 1947 with a major work, *The Mediterranean and the Mediterranean World in the Era of Philip II*. A list of cities and countries on the Mediterranean, which are significant in *Film Socialisme*, immediately reveals the multitude of motifs that can be associated with that sea: Barcelona (Spanish Civil War, antifascism, internationalism), Algiers (decolonization), Odessa (revolutions in Russia), Egypt (birth of culture, Napoleon, European imperialism), Hellas/Greece (beginning of culture, a focal point of financial crises in 2010 but also since 2008 more generally), and Palestine (the place where, for Godard, the "Muslims" from the concentration camps, emaciated to the bone, are

to be found in the world of today). These places are first of all tourist des-
tinations in *Film Socialisme*. The first part is set on a cruise ship that sails
the Mediterranean as a world unto itself (a "floating Las Vegas," according
to Manohla Dargis, the *New York Times* critic). Godard shoots aboard the
Costa Concordia as if he were a guerrilla filmmaker: All around, the daily
routine unfolds; passengers eat at the buffet or attend Mass with an Italian priest. But no one is interested in a lecture by the philosopher Alain
Badiou, who talks about geometry as the origin of civilization. Later, in an
interview, Godard connected—or even confused—the subject of geometry
with that of Aristotelian logic. He said that Europe owed inferential logic,
that is, the word "therefore," to ancient Greece and should basically pay
royalties for it. This would solve the financing problems of the Greek state
budget in one fell swoop. Badiou would probably not have been on board
had Godard not engaged him for *Film Socialisme*, but in the world of this
film it is a part of the standard cruise offer that there should be a philosopher on hand for passengers to consult with. Amid the hustle and bustle
on the ship, among Southeast Asian staff and passengers who are predominantly from affluent Western countries, Godard does his own thing.

Here he recycles another film about the Mediterranean, to which he had
already alluded in *Le Mépris* in 1963: *Méditerranée* by Jean-Daniel Pollet,
with a narrative text by the writer and philosopher Philippe Sollers. In 1969
there was an intense debate about this film between the two magazines *Tel
Quel* and *Cinéthique*. The *Cahiers du cinéma* had already published a special issue on the subject in 1967, which also included a review of Godard:
Impressions anciennes. "What do we know of Greece today?" he wrote at the
time. "What do we know of this outstanding moment when some people,
how shall we put it, no longer wanted to play Darius or Genghis Khan, but
to live in solidarity, solidarity with the light that not only radiated from
the gods but which they reflected, solidarity with the sun and with the
sea?" Remarkably, at the end of this text, Godard compares Pollet's film to
Orpheus, the figure whose looking back was to become a major inspiration
for him in *Histoire(s)*.[36]

The transition to the second part (or the second movement of the sym-
phony) of *Film Socialisme* is an insert: Quo Vadis Europe? Now the scene
is in the south of France, with a Martin family who run a garage and petrol
station. This is about questions of political representation: can the children

run for political office? One may think of the family from *Numéro deux* and those from *Je vous salue, Marie*. Family intimacy, however, is no longer characterized by a rejection of the petty bourgeois way of life, as it was in the 1970s, because in Godard's hands the Martins become a laboratory for communal living. Toward the end of the second part there is also a kind of resolution: the Martins are assigned a place in the historical landscape. They are descendants of a "Martin family" who maintained a Resistance group in the Combat network in southern France. The motto of Combat was *libérer et fédérer* (liberate and unite)—and it can be directly related to the European present after the financial crisis of 2008. That this is an important part of the background is made clear from the first sentence: "Money is a public good." History moves according to the rhythms or conjunctures of precious metals, as Braudel wrote. For *Film Socialisme*, one particular historical event is significant: when the left was defeated in the Spanish Civil War, the National Bank's gold was taken out of the country, but a large part of it was lost on the way to the Soviet Union. A similar story circulates about the gold (the reserve on which monetary stability was based until well into the twentieth century) held by the Bank of Palestine, only in this case it is said to have been the British who appropriated it. In *Film Socialisme*, a man going by the name of Otto Goldberg, formerly a spy for the Nazis, is now tasked with bringing the gold back to Cartagena.

"Freedom is expensive, but it is not bought with gold," is a line in the third part of *Film Socialisme*, in which Godard presents a further variation on the *Histoire(s) du cinéma*. It is titled *Nos Humanités* (Our Humanities). In one ugly polemical moment in this sequence of images, a crocodile is briefly seen devouring a goose. The word "Palestine" comes up. In these passages, Godard also develops something like a vision for peace in the region. It is hidden away deep in the folds of a customarily difficult montage. At one point, acrobats can be seen performing a trapeze act against the backdrop of a blue sky—the scene is borrowed from the autobiographical film *Les Plages d'Agnès* (2008) by Agnès Varda. Two female voices are heard, one reciting the Talmud, the other the Koran. This is also taken from a film, *Le Chant des mariées* (*The Wedding Song*, 2008), a story of Jewish-Muslim friendship under Nazi occupation in Tunisia. While the acrobats continue to fly through the air as if unencumbered by gravity, the two female voices are replaced by the voice of Marlene Dietrich. She sings "Where

Have All the Flowers Gone," a song by Pete Seeger that became an anthem of the peace movement in the sixties. Dietrich recorded the song first in French, then in English and German. On her tour in Israel in 1966, she sang the German version—at a time when the use of the language of the perpetrators was still a taboo in the Jewish state. She was able to take this risk because she had taken a firm stand against Germany during World War II—she was therefore, in the inner logic of *Film Socialisme*, part of a broad Resistance network.

In a later interview, Godard dealt rather lightly with this complex montage, in which he brusquely denounced the state of Israel as a crocodile and revealed a vision for community in Palestine. He suggested: "Israelis and Palestinians should open a circus together and perform as trapeze acrobats. Then everything would be different in the Middle East, everything would be harmonious."[37]

~

A new Godard film was presented in Cannes in May 2014. Godard himself was not present on the red carpet, and the ovation went to the two actresses Zoé Bruneau and Héloïse Godet and their colleagues Kamel Abdelli and Richard Chevallier. *Adieu au langage* is a film in 3D, though not the thin kind of 3D that Hollywood has been using since 2010 to repackage its blockbusters but rather the handicraft version of a three-dimensional film experience, produced with two cameras mounted side by side. In other words, this is a film in visual stereo, in which one is also reminded of how the human brain compiles a spatial experience from the sensory impressions of two eyes. Godard makes clear from the very first sentence that he is interested in a theory of epistemology proper to this medium: "It remains to be known how nonthinking contaminates thinking."[38] Are there nevertheless traces, within consciousness or outside of it, that lead to nonthinking?

The title of the film is also in stereo. "Adieu" is generally considered a word of farewell, but Godard explicitly pointed out that in his region, Vaud, it is also used as a greeting. A logical chain of associations leads from "Adieu" to Emmanuel Levinas, one of the most important of Godard's philosophical inspirations. The play on words "Adieu/Ah Dieux," which only functions on the page as a text image, is one of the axioms of *Adieu au langage*— saying goodbye to life is also a greeting to the gods. By *langage*, Godard means conceptual language. In this case, too, the farewell is at the same time the greeting of another language: cinema is transformed into a technology without a world, in other words, into a language without reference.

In a film in which almost everything is duplicated, the connecting moment is provided by the only character who stands for themselves: Roxy Miéville, the couple's dog from Lake Geneva. Godard has once again shot a film on his doorstep. The real momentum in the film is provided by the walks with Roxy. The dog explores a landscape by the lake and the vegetation, which becomes an artificial paradise thanks to the special cameras Godard uses: a luminous, colorful, porous nature based on a digital calculation of the world. Roxy drifts in a raging river, sniffs through the undergrowth, in other words does everything a dog does whose master must be imagined as a no-longer-too-agile, soon-to-be-eighty-four-year-old man smoking a cigar. A dialogue at the end of the film indicates that Godard was thinking of a paradisical landscape: "He looks melancholy," someone says of Roxy, and Anne-Marie Miéville replies: "Not at all. He is dreaming of the Marquesas Islands, like in the novel by Jack London."[39]

The key word "think" is also explicitly attributed to Roxy. In many scenes, the dog is the "person" we are to imagine being behind the camera, which explicitly makes thinking a stereo concept: seeing is thinking, a common theme with Godard. But if a dog is able to think and see, then much depends on how a human (its owner) is able to respond to that thinking.

At the same time, *Adieu au langage* can be seen as another of Godard's many farewells to cinema and the totalitarian twentieth century and as welcoming a new, posthumanist civilization in which a digital GoPro camera can function as an animal consciousness. The film is disturbingly intimate in that this animal, which has no civilized inhibitions, is the focus. The many scenes in which the two women Josette and Ivitch are naked are given a different feel through Roxy's perspective. Godard was explicitly concerned with showing that nudity is a culturally determined form that would not exist if it were not for ideas of shame, appropriate clothing, and licentiousness. He thus picks up a thought from Jacques Derrida's book *The Animal That Therefore I Am*, which was also the inspiration for *Adieu au langage*: "There is no nakedness in nature."[40]

~

Many had assumed that *Film Socialisme* would be Godard's last film, and with *Adieu au langage*, the title itself suggested that this would mark a fare-well performance. But in 2018, the Cannes Film Festival presented another Godard picture—and also awarded him a Special Golden Palm. The use of the singular in the title *Le Livre d'image* (*Picture Book*) requires an explana-tion. Why not *The Book of Images*? Why only one picture? And which one?

There is every indication that Godard speaks of *image* here the way he spoke of *langage* in the previous film. The image he means here is not sim-ply another of humanity's artistic languages but, instead, a power, a funda-mental human faculty. If one were to understand the film as a chapter of the *Histoire(s) du cinéma*, *Livre d'image* would represent a direct leap from the nineteenth to the twenty-first century; from Flaubert's novel *Salammbô* to the propaganda and execution videos of the Islamic State.

It begins with a figure from the history of salvation: Leonardo da Vinci's depiction of John the Baptist. The important element here is the finger on the right hand pointing upward. From there, from heaven, comes the answer to the Baptist's speech about the end of times: Jesus of Nazareth. The last prophet. For now. Godard begins *Le Livre d'image* with two quo-tations: a passage from Georges Bernanos's diary *Les Enfants humiliés* and an excerpt from Leonardo's painting. Godard only shows the hand from this image. What interests him about the biblical figure is the gesture—and the body part, the hand, that Godard, the craftsman of cinema, has been using as a genuinely human implement at least since the days of the *Nouvelle vague*. "There are the five fingers, the five senses, the five parts of the earth, yes, the five fingers of the fairy. Together they make the hand. And man's true condition is to think with his hands." This is followed by the image of hands handling pictures at a cutting table. And then there is the voice of the singer Scott Walker, whom Godard sees as a modern Orpheus. The way back out of the underworld is indicated by an Ariadne's thread: an unwinding roll of film material. The image of the hand is also for him, as in certain traditions of philosophical anthropology, a sign of the capac-ity of a deficient being to transcend itself, to transcend itself toward some-thing greater. To John, this greater thing was heaven. For Godard, who is not a confessing Christian, heaven is not something that stands above his-tory. Rather, it consists of the countless testimonies that remain of this history. For Godard, heaven is the archive, and in times of global networks, the archive is an inexhaustible reservoir of snippets. With these "clicks and cuts" (as the corresponding procedure in electronic music is referred to), Godard creates the signature of an era.

"As one era slowly dissolves into the next, some individuals metabolize the former means for physical survival into new means for psychic survival. These latter we call art. Typically, all that survives intact of an era is the art forms it invents for itself." There are good grounds for seeing an element of self-description by the later Godard in the use of this phrase taken from the American filmmaker and critic Hollis Frampton, which has been taken up and slightly adapted several times since *Histoire(s)*. However, here he adds another layer: he would like the old means of physical survival, which could be transformed into arts in due course—painting, literature, cinema, music—to be transformed again, or transformed back, into a new means of survival. Despite the use of the singular in the title, *The Image Book* is a (further) excerpt from an unfinishable film, with which Godard attempts to take account of the unfathomability of history and, at the same time, the infinity of digitalizable testimonies.

The two formative experiences of the twentieth century—the extermination camps and decolonization—are still present, but now under the sign of a new and yet also more ancient star, which points back to Godard's "ancestral" century: to the time when people still spoke unabashedly of the Orient and the Occident, and when historicism first developed as an understanding of history that attempted to infer conceivable ends of world-historical movements from a mass of ubiquitous testimonies.

The nineteenth and the twenty-first centuries find themselves brought together in *The Image Book* in a long reflection on a "happy Arabia"—a classic, Western motif that broaches an "orientalizing" question: "Can the Arabs speak?"[41] Or to be more precise: Can the Arabs (and Godard explicitly alludes to European domestic politics with "Islam is of political interest") speak for themselves? Will they be permitted to speak? The "Arabs," for him, are the other side of a Middle Eastern country whose name he does not mention (Israel is the blind spot in *Le Livre d'image*). But they are also the other side of a political projection that only wants to see "Islam" in 2018 and not Muslims or Arabs. He explicitly sets his image book against the religions of the book. This work is at once motivated by global political concerns and also highly intimate. For he also evokes Anne-Marie Miéville, his wife, whose voice was present in his work for fifty years. He quotes her in passages taken from her book *Images en parole*, in which she points in the opposite direction to Godard and his *Image Book*: she creates images in (or from) words.[42]

Godard finds an ambivalent answer to the question of whether and how Arabs can speak by giving the floor throughout the long final section of *Le Livre d'image* to a man who himself stands on both sides of every conceivable divide between a happy and unhappy Arabia and the Occident: the Egyptian Francophone writer Albert Cossery. In his novel *Une ambition dans le désert*, Godard takes a revolutionary parable that marks the beginning of the *Image Book*: half a century after 1968, when Godard first said goodbye to cinema in order to overturn existing conditions, he now finds in his own form of cinema the medium that allows him to finally think of revolution in a truly all-encompassing way.

This marks out the *Image Book* as a film of the end times, and the circle with John the Baptist is closed. Godard himself recorded a soundtrack for the German distribution version, because a prophet's most important organ is his voice. This is a fragile style, marked by old age, but at the end of the film it once again rises to biblical power. The heaven to which John referred is empty, because it can only ever be a placeholder for the history that humanity writes with its own bloody, tender hands. Godard is the prophet of this history: no longer a Hegel, no longer a Ranke, but a trembling collector of details, still one with the spirit of Brecht, from whom he has inherited a tendency to prefer the fragment to the totality. He trembles with anticipation: "We who once, when we were young, had such fervent hopes, . . . and even if things did not turn out as we had hoped, this would not change the hopes at all." But one's expectations also include (one's own) death. *Le Livre d'image* ends with the scene from *Le Plaisir* by Max Ophüls, which has also accompanied him since *Histoire(s)*: a dancing man in a mask who collapses in the midst of exuberant movements. Happiness is not fun but carries horrors within it.

Conclusion

The Joy of Learning

In April 2020, after the start of the coronavirus crisis in Europe, Godard gave an interview to a lecturer at the Lausanne Film School, which was played as a live video on one of the most important digital outlets of the day: JLG was on Instagram. After a press conference via FaceTime at the Cannes Film Festival 2018, he had now joined the platform that facilitates the self-presentations of self-optimized people like no other—in an era in which, economically, one's very appearance is often the commodity. In the course of one and a half hours, Godard is visible as a frail man who hardly has the power in his voice to pronounce a weighty word. His ever-present cigar is thicker than ever. He reviews motifs from his thinking and work. He talks about the project of a new film dedicated to the photography pioneer Joseph Nicéphore Niépce. He also hints at an idiosyncratic conspiracy theory: the Iraq war of 2003 was really about the Americans wanting to conquer the place where humanity learned to write (not a war for oil, but one for the "Chaldean script").[1]

The impact of the coronavirus pandemic encouraged him in his endeavors to practice cinema as one would a science. This idea goes back a long way in his work: its original inspiration was the encounter with Jean-Pierre Gorin, who introduced Godard, an unsystematic thinker, to scientific materialism. He calls cinema the "antibiotic of words." He wants to resolve the war on icons, in which he takes the side of the iconophiles once again, by rebuilding language on the basis of a (hieroglyphic) alphabet, for which the painters would be responsible.

For Godard, cinema is the panacea. Cinema is a form of thinking. In a nutshell, this is the claim he has made not only for his own work but also for the medium that has changed so radically since Godard's debut around 1960. It is also a demand that he makes *of* this medium. He expects more from cinema than a spectacle to distract the masses, more than the exploitation of people's historical experiences, because in the slipstream of this exploitation, history drops away into oblivion (as with Steven Spielberg). What he expects of cinema, as a medium existing at the end of all arts, is precisely that it should assume full responsibility for all arts: from Leonardo the path-breaking hand; from Brecht the urgent intrusions of the fragmentary; from Péguy the view of history.[2]

His long life provided Godard with the opportunity to repeatedly relate political and technical revolutions to each other. In 1945, as a child of the Libération, he was able to free himself from the ambivalent legacy of a family that sympathized with authoritarian rather than democratic systems. In 1968 he himself went through the dogmatic and totalitarian temptations of the radical left. As with almost all members of this generation, this passage proved to be the work of a lifetime, which to this day is still not completed. Godard began to write the history of the twentieth century as the history of his art, just as it was losing its substance: the pictures he always regarded as evidence became material for him to play with. With the *Histoire(s) du cinéma* and the mature work that emerged from it, Godard radically increased the scope of such play. Here, too, he follows a paradox: to a culture that can do anything with images, he demands that it should take images as seriously as it does science, while at the same time casts the sciences as a sorcerer's apprentice who doesn't want to let go of his old apparatuses.[3] When he went to Palestine in 1970, he thought he knew exactly how the revolution should go: the Palestine Liberation Organization would create freedom for the people of Palestine. The question of how this could be reconciled with the right of the state of Israel to exist, he preferred to answer through (aggressive) implications. His self-enlightenment—which is always also a counter-enlightenment—put him on the trail of a revolutionary theory that no longer needed to be put into practice through force of arms. He found the key to his understanding of history in the young German novelists who, under the influence of the French Revolution, developed a way of thinking about infinity, and a universal poetry. The best way to do justice to Godard's work is to regard it as a form of universal poetry that substitutes images for language. The images are under the spell of what has been, but they also have the potential to break this spell. That is the revolutionary power of this art.

Afterword

In August 2014, the Iranian filmmaker Mitra Farahani had an idea. She wanted to restage a meeting between two people that she believed to have taken place in the 1960s: Jean-Luc Godard and Ebrahim Golestan, the former the now world-famous French filmmaker, and the latter his colleague from Iran, who had begun with industrial films and in 1964 had created a highlight of Iranian cinema with his work *Brick and Mirror*. The two could have met in Venice at the film festival, but this never happened, and they did not meet in person in 2014 either. Instead, correspondence began by email, through written pieces and attachments, and even small films. Farahani assembled the material into a film that premiered at the Berlinale in February 2022: *À vendredi, Robinson* is a multilayered work that may be seen as a farewell gift from Jean-Luc Godard. In 2014 the filmmaker offered a much more personal view of himself than had previously been seen, even in his "private" films—from *Soft and Hard* to *JLG/JLG*. He was already reflecting intensively on death at that time—especially on a "mort volontaire," a voluntary or willful death, which he took great care to distinguish from suicide. As we know, Godard sought help in September 2022 to end his life in a self-determined way: "Mr Godard has availed himself of the legal assistance available in Switzerland to make a voluntary departure," as an official statement had it. A supplementary remark appeared in the daily newspaper *Libération* saying that Godard was not terminally ill but "simply exhausted [*epuisé*]." He did not want to leave the time of his death to the biological processes of an old body, but instead to determine it himself. "It was his decision, and it was important to him that it became known." A representative of the organization Exit, to which Godard had turned, added—probably also for legal reasons—that there very much had been a *motif médical*: Godard died a victim of polypathologies related to his advanced age—he was ninety-one—which had rendered him an invalid.

In the first reactions to the news of his death, comments also emerged suggesting that he had a lifelong proximity to thoughts about suicide and pointing to the prominence of this motif in his work. In particular, the entry relating to this term in Jean-Luc Douin's *Dictionnaire des passions* has been quoted in several places: the key phrase is "Godard is fascinated by suicide." An example of this ostensible fascination: The 1982 book *Suicide, mode d'emploi* appears five years later in *Soigne ta droite*. At that time, legal battles over this work were still ongoing and it was eventually banned as part of wider legislation against incitement to suicide. Jean Narboni also reports in the posthumous special edition of *Cahiers du cinéma* on a conversation about suicide that Godard had with him back in 2004: "Dying is not everything: you also need to know how" (*Mourir en effet n'est pas tout, commentait Godard, encore faut-il savoir comment*). Even then, Godard had shown a preference for assisted suicide.

In *À vendredi, Robinson*, Godard places his reflections on "mort volontaire" in a broader context. He quotes (in English translation from the French) the Austrian writer and language theorist Fritz Mauthner, whose work he knew through the volume *Le langage* as translated by Jacques Le Rider: "The act of redemption would be accomplished if one could drive criticism till self-death, quietly desperate, of our thinking/talking, if we ought to not conduct that criticism with words which have only the appearance of life—all the best, your boy Friday, September 2014, JLG." The quote is challenging in its complexity. Strictly speaking, self-death ("Freitod" in Mauthner's original; all these terms have different emphases in different languages, between act of will, demonstration of freedom, and acceptance of the inevitable) here does not refer to physical life at all but only to thinking and speaking (*penser/parler*), which gives critique a "semblance of life." In *À vendredi, Robinson*, Godard thus reflects on dying, but his thoughts on death have a context that refers back to his entire work: to find a form for his "critique" that not only has "the semblance of life" but actually points beyond (biological) life.

In Mauthner, the figure of the shipwrecked European Robinson is a man cut loose from institutions and society, a form of radical autonomy from which Godard distances himself by identifying with the "boy" Friday, with whom Robinson eventually creates a new society. The generosity and the technologically sociable way with which Godard engaged in correspondence with Golestan at the time, the small films in which he addressed the camera in ways that were unexpectedly heartfelt by his standards, make it conceivable that in his preparations for death he had arrived at a philosophical position that he finally realized in 2022.

He did not want to complete another film with his energy almost drained—in the case of his last film, *Scénario*, on which he worked intensively in the months leading up to September 2022, one can hope that it may be released in some form. He was still able to complete a twenty-minute short, *Film annonce du film Droles de Guerres (1er tournage)*. He died—one could take up the Mauthner quote—in the hope of a "redemption" that could go beyond the death of thought and speech. One can see behind this quotation both a fantasy of grandeur (Godard himself as the redeemer of all discourse of conceptual critique) and a motif of supra-personal historicity: self-death as the death of a self that, behind the "semblance of life," could at least accept the unknowability of his future legacy, as a continuation of his own lifelong engagement with that which lies beyond words.

October 2022

Notes

Introduction

1. *Vaste* (huge) is one of Godard's favorite terms.

2. The title of Peter Aspden's story in the *Financial Times* is also telling: "From Mao to Prada," *Financial Times Weekend*, December 21/22, 2019, 13.

3. Hartmut Bitomsky, "Der letzte der *Cahiers du Cinéma*," *Filmkritik* 7–8 (1984): 204.

4. Pantenburg, *Film als Theorie*, 14.

5. Bazin, *Was ist Film?*, 47.

Chapter 1. Modern Times

1. Tom Milne, "Ah! Je l'ai trop aimé pour ne le point hair," *Sight and Sound*, 38, no. 2 (Spring 1969): 63.

2. Godard, *Godard, Kritiker*, 9.

3. Liandrat-Guigues and Leutrat, *Godard simple comme bonjour*, 235.

4. Baecque, *Godard*, 33.

5. Baecque, *Godard*, 32. The film *Les Dernières Vacances* (1948) by Roger Leenhardt is characterized by the atmosphere Godard alludes to here, itself a retrospective pregnant with elements of film history.

6. Baecque, *Godard*, 47.

7. Baecque, *Godard*, 35.

8. Godard, *Godard, Kritiker*, 57 (quotation on Vadim) and 62.

9. *Les Trente Glorieuses* is the French term for the period of economic boom between 1945 and 1975, which Daney coins as a term relating to cinema history.

10. Bazin, "Der Mythos vom totalen Film," 47.

11. The relevant standard work is Baecque, *La cinéphilie*. On Bazin, see the chapter "Un saint en casquette de velours," 33–62.

12. Bazin, "Découverte du cinéma," 326.

13. Georges Sadoul, quoted in Baecque, *Godard*, 82.

14. Godard, *Godard, Kritiker*, 12–13.
15. Godard, *Godard, Kritiker*, 14.
16. Sartre, "Die kinematographische Kunst," 149, 148, 152.
17. Astruc, *Le Montreur d'ombres*, 155.
18. Godard, *Jean-Luc Godard*, 1:76.
19. Godard, *Godard, Kritiker*, 17–22.
20. Godard, *Godard, Kritiker*, 20–21.
21. Truffaut, *Die Lust am Sehen*, 305–18, quotation on 310.
22. Godard, *Godard, Kritiker*, 21–28.
23. Godard, *Godard, Kritiker*, 30.
24. Godard, *Godard, Kritiker*, 37.
25. Godard, *Godard, Kritiker*, 38–40.
26. Godard, *Godard, Kritiker*, 117, 73, 72.
27. Truffaut, *Die Lust am Sehen*, 335.
28. Godard, *Godard, Kritiker*, 81.

Chapter 2. Pop Art

1. Farber, *Negative Space*, 20.
2. Godard, *Godard, Kritiker*, 144.
3. Christopher Pavsek sees in Godard a "reverse chronology from post-modernism to modernism." *Utopia of Film*, 47.
4. Godard, letter to Pierre Braunberger describing his progress on *Breathless*, August 23, 1959, quoted in Hayward and Vincendeau, *French Film*, 206.
5. Godard quoted in *Arts*, March 1960.
6. "Ce que je voulais, c'était partir d'une histoire conventionelle et refaire, mais différemment, tout le cinéma qui été avait déjà fait." Godard interview in *Cahiers du cinéma*, no. 138 (December 1962), quoted in Godard, *Jean-Luc Godard*, 1:218.
7. *Mythologies* (*Myths of Everyday Life*) by Roland Barthes, where among other things a Citroën model is analyzed, was originally published in 1957.
8. MacCabe, *Godard*, 123.
9. Godard quoted in "Hiroshima, notre amour," *Cahiers du cinéma*, no. 97 (July 1959): 5.
10. On the subject, see Richard Raskin, "Five Explanations for the Jump Cuts in Godard's *Breathless*," *p.o.v.: A Danish Journal of Film Studies*, no. 6 (December 1998): 141–53.
11. For a French cinephile, cinema was an obvious way to disappear. The flight into the Napoléon is perhaps also a direct quote: in Carol Reed's *The Third Man*, Holly Martins and Anna Schmidt save themselves from an angry Viennese crowd by fleeing into a cinema.

12. "La photographie c'est la verité. Le cinéma c'est vingt-quatre fois la verité par seconde." The sentence that Godard supposedly wrote spontaneously on a tablecloth was used in the first advertisements announcing *Le Petit Soldat* in the trade press. See Baecque, *Godard*, 157.

13. Godard, *Einführung in eine wahre Geschichte des Kinos*, 44.

14. See Mary, *La Nouvelle Vague*. The term *Nouvelle Vague* originally came from journalism. In 1957 Françoise Giroud described a new generation in France, the eighteen- to thirty-year-olds who represented, among other things, a consumer phenomenon with new views on fashion and lifestyle.

15. "Ein Regisseur ist auch ein Missionar: Jean-Luc Godard läßt Roberto Rossellini sprechen," in Godard, *Godard, Kritiker*, 138–42, quotation on 142 (originally in *Arts* 716 [April 1, 1959]).

16. Enno Patalas, "Godards Film vom Krieg," *Filmkritik* 5 (1965): 259.

17. Available in Brenez et al., *Jean-Luc Godard Documents*, 29–49.

18. Baecque, *Godard*, 216.

19. Moravia, *Die Verachtung*, 77.

20. See Joseph Vogl, "Schöne gelbe Farbe," 256: "The red yes and the blue no—as the two marks of counterposed changes of fortune in the narrative—not only shift continuously across the various characters and objects until the blue void at the end, they are also supplemented by the third basic color, the yellow—of Penelope, of the bathrobe, of Francesca's jumper—that keeps an empty field open."

21. Godard took his inspiration for this from the medium-length film *Méditerranée* (1963) by Jean-Daniel Pollet, who later became significant again in *Film Socialisme*.

22. The scene can also be seen as a response to a critique of the Nouvelle Vague, which Jean Cau, Sartre's longtime secretary at *Les Temps Modernes*, reproached for showing "France reduced to the dimensions of a bed on which a couple entangle themselves hand and foot, oh recreation, oh happiness, what death! We understand that young cinéastes have little or nothing to say." Quoted in Baecque, *Godard*, 195.

23. See Marcia Landy, "Just an Image: Godard, Cinema, and Philosophy," *Critical Quarterly* 43, no. 3 (2001): 9–31.

24. Rembert Hüser calls *Une femme mariée* "one of the most intelligent cinematic representations of the Shoah" in his essay "Augen machen," which also discusses exactly why it had to be a pilot who could make the, then, still "unattainable evidence" of Auschwitz attainable. See Bannasch and Hammer, *Verbot der Bilder*, 260.

25. Brody, *Everything Is Cinema*, 221.

26. There are few examples of a comparable move among contemporary colleagues: Jacques Demy and Agnès Varda returned from Los Angeles after a few years; Barbet Schroeder had a Hollywood career.

27. Godard, *Godard, Kritiker*, 66–67.
28. See Baecque, *La cinéphilie*, 199–209. Moullet coined for Fuller the inimitable term "philopod," that is, a director who "loves feet"—feet being the part of the body from which human movement emanates.
29. Godard quoted in Grafe, *Nouvelle Vague*, 7.
30. Godard, *Einführung in eine wahre Geschichte des Kinos*, 212.
31. Godard, *Einführung in eine wahre Geschichte des Kinos*, 200.

Chapter 3. Revolutionary Cinema

1. Wiazemsky, *Jeune fille*, 186.
2. Godard, *Einführung in eine wahre Geschichte des Kinos*, 222.
3. Jean-Luc Godard, "Loin du Vietnam: Vietnam in uns," *Filmkritik* 10 (1967): 586.
4. Godard, "Loin du Vietnam," 586.
5. Godard quoted in Baecque, *Godard*, 399.
6. The entire text appeared in January 1970 under "Eins und Eins" in the magazine *Film + Fernsehen* (quote on p. 14). From today's perspective, what is most striking about this transcript is the consistent titling of African American civil rights activists as "Negroes." When *One plus One* was shown on German television in 1970, the "pornographic" passages had been made unintelligible through the use of bleeps.
7. Sontag, "Godard," in *Gesten radikalen Willens*, 182–223.
8. MacCabe, *Godard*, 214 (interview with Claude Nedjar).
9. Both letters in Truffaut, *Briefe, 1945–1984*, 458–59.

Chapter 4. Video, Ergo Sum

1. For periodization, see Witt, *Jean-Luc Godard*. A more recent classification has been proposed by the Cinémathèque française on the occasion of its major retrospective in early 2020: Nouvelle Vague (1954–65), Fables Sociologiques (1965–66), Travaux Révolutionnaires (1967–72), Expérimentations Vidéo (1975–78), Dialogue entre les arts (1979–92), and Méditations Historiques (1993–2019). *Ici et ailleurs* belongs to the revolutionary films. Stefan Kristensen has delineated a number of Godard's philosophical periods, but in the same breath rejected this schema as too simplistic: Phenomenologist (1960–67), Marxist (1967–72), Deleuzian (1973–78), psychoanalytic theologian (after 1979), and Benjaminian (since the 1990s).
2. See especially Emmelhainz, *Jean-Luc Godard's Political Filmmaking*.
3. Godard, *Jean-Luc Godard*, 1:374. *La Cause du peuple* was a radical left-wing newspaper that was banned in 1970.
4. Brenez et al., *Jean-Luc Godard Documents*, 195–245.

5. Leroi-Gourhan, *Hand und Wort*, 288.

6. Volker Pantenburg translates the untranslatable pun "juif-susser Hitler" as "that 80 million parts of me would have given Hitler a blowjob" (the verb *sucer* has this meaning in French). "Moi/Je/JLG," 272.

7. Wilfried Reichart, "Ein Interview mit Jean-Luc Godard," *Filmkritik* 2 (1977): 56.

8. Brody, *Everything Is Cinema*, 374.

9. Brody, *Everything Is Cinema*, 380.

10. Daniel Cohn-Bendit wrote in his 1975 autobiography *The Grand Bazaar*: "It happened to me several times that some children opened my flies and started stroking me. I reacted differently depending on the circumstances, but their wish posed problems for me." These and similar passages led to a pedophilia debate in Germany in 2013. The writer Gabriel Matzneff, one of the signatories of the 1977 petition, became the subject of a controversy about abuse and libertinage in 2020 as a result of the publication of the book *Le Consentement* by Vanessa Springora, who had met him at the age of thirteen.

11. Brody, *Everything Is Cinema*, 380.

12. For details on theoretical influences, see Witt, "On and Under Communication," 318–50; and generally, Kristensen, *Jean-Luc Godard philosophe*.

13. Enthusiasts have published a German-language transcription of *France, tour, détour, deux enfants*: *Frankreich Weg Umweg zwei Kinder*, Zweitausendeins (Frankfurt am Main, 1982). It is one of the rarest Godard collector's items in existence today.

14. Grafe, "Die Klippschule der Nation," 100.

15. On public channels, the public could make their own television network. In the German-speaking countries, there were various attempts to set up a citizens' networks. In Austria, this began in 1975, exactly at the time when Sonimage was experimenting with such forms.

16. Manfred Blank, Harun Farocki, and Susanne Röckel, "Conversation with William Lubtchansky," *Filmkritik* 9 (1982): 429.

17. Grafe, "Die Klippschule der Nation," 99.

18. Grafe, "Die Klippschule der Nation," 100.

19. One could write a separate study on the term *decomposer*. It appears in *Le Gai Savoir*.

20. Michael Witt has convincingly explained how *France, tour, détour, deux enfants* combines an interest in cinema techniques (the chronophotography of the film pioneer Étienne-Jules Marey) with an analysis of society. See Witt, "Going through the Motions."

21. Brody, *Everything Is Cinema*, 401.

22. A concise summary with references to all relevant sources can be found in Daniel Fairfax, "Birth of (the Image) of a Nation: Jean-Luc Godard in Mozambique," *Acta Univ. Sapientiae, Film and Media Studies* 3 (2010): 55–56.

23. The excerpts in Godard, *Jean-Luc Godard*, 1:418–41, give a comprehensive exposition of the project. The script consists of a text-image collage.

Chapter 5. The Idiot of Cinema

1. The complete conversation, originally in two parts, is available on the DVD edition of the Criterion Collection of *Every Man for Himself*.

2. The script concepts (partly with the collaboration of Jean-Claude Carrière) and further material can be found in Godard, *Liebe Arbeit Kino*.

3. Linhart, *Eingespannt*.

4. Brody, *Everything Is Cinema*, 426.

5. The American *Rolling Stone* wrote in November 1980 of a "born again filmmaker."

6. Godard, *Godard Kritiker*, 14.

7. In particular, the passages that speak of chance (*hasard*) can also be traced back to a book by Jacques Monod from 1970, *Le hasard et la nécessité: Essai sur la philosophie naturelle de la biologie moderne*. Godard thus quotes the most prominent member of his mother's family.

8. Roussel told biographer Antoine de Baecque in detail about her experiences with Godard. See Baecque, *Godard*, 623–26.

9. Brody, *Everything Is Cinema*, 460.

10. Quoted from Godard's *Hail Mary: Women and the Sacred in Film*, 1.

11. Godard, *Hail Mary: Women and the Sacred in Film*, 6.

12. On the question of nudity in Godard, see Bergala, "Le nu chez Godard."

13. This refers to the 1925 film adaptation by Fred Niblo, one of the greatest successes of the silent film era. Where and under what circumstances Godard may have seen this early spectacle film in 1937 remains buried in the obscurity of a fleeting childhood memory.

14. A magic lantern can be found in the first pages of Marcel Proust's novel *In Search of Lost Time*.

15. The quotation haunts Godard's thinking in different formulations and is based fundamentally on a misunderstanding if one looks at the translation of the passage in 1 Cor. 15:49: "As we have been fashioned in the image of the earthly, so we shall be fashioned in the image of the heavenly." Godard takes a religio-anthropological hope about the transformation of bodily existence into resurrection and turns it into a hope grounded in the theory of images—or possibly in a mystical quality of images.

16. Volker Pantenburg, "Der Idiot: *Soigne ta droite* und Jean-Luc Godards burleske Phase" (unpublished speech notes).

17. For an excellent discussion of this difficult-to-understand scene, see Morgan, *Late Godard and the Possibilities of Cinema*, 84–89.

18. The detail comes from Godard's assistant Hervé Duhamel, whom Brody interviewed for his book *Everything Is Cinema*, 486–87.

19. Brody, *Everything Is Cinema*, 526.

20. Stenzl, *Jean-Luc Godard*, 411–12.

21. Godard, *Jean-Luc Godard*, 2:321.

22. See the account of the history of its origins in Stenzl, *Jean-Luc Godard*, 367–68. Important sources are cited there that are no longer accessible today.

23. Stenzl, *Jean-Luc Godard*, 366.

24. Godard, *Jean-Luc Godard*, 2:22–23.

Chapter 6. The Partisan of Images

1. Witt, *Jean-Luc Godard*, 159.

2. For *Histoire du Cinéma* by Brasillach and Bardèche, see Kaplan, "Fascist Film Esthetics: Brasillach and Bardèche's *Histoire du Cinéma*," *Modern Language Notes* 95, no. 4 (May 1980): 864–88.

3. See Michael Witt, "In Search of Godard's 'Sauve la vie (qui peut),'" *Necsus*, June 10, 2015, https://necsus-ejms.org/in-search-of-godards-sauve-la-vie-qui-peut/.

4. "Car la stéréo existe aussi en histoire . . . et la loi de la stéréo continue Israel a *projeté le peuple palestinien et le peuple palestinien à son tour a porté sa croix.*" See Godard, *JLG/JLG*, 28.

5. Friedrich Schlegel once said that historians are backward-looking prophets turned toward the future.

6. The best discussion of Godard's concept of image and montage can be found in Kristensen, *Jean-Luc Godard philosophe*. Thanks to Selin Gerlek for recommending this book.

7. The "transcription" or "score" of the *Histoire(s) du cinéma* by Céline Scemama has four tracks: Image, voice, sound/music, text. Available via the author's website at the Université Paris 1 Panthéon-Sorbonne, http://cri-image.univ-paris 1.fr/celine/celinegodard.html. Céline Scemama also wrote one of the standard works on the *Histoire(s)*: *Histoire(s) du cinéma de Jean-Luc Godard: La force faible d'un art*.

8. Duby also came up with the idea of an audiovisual series in connection with the Bibliothèque de la Pléiade, the renowned French classics series. Witt, *Jean-Luc Godard*, 43n145.

9. Brody, *Everything Is Cinema*, 559.

10. Godard, *Histoire(s) du cinéma*, 4:80. Cf. Hollis Frampton, "For a Metahistory of Film: Commonplace Notes and Hypotheses," *Artforum* 10, no. 1 (September 1971): 33.

11. In a striking passage, Godard takes a text by the art historian Élie Faure, whom he admired, and replaces the name of the painter Rembrandt with the term "cinema."

12. A particularly interesting piece to read against these works would be Hollis Frampton's comprehensive *Magellan* film cycle. See Witt, *Jean-Luc Godard*, 122.

13. For Godard, the animal hunt in the 1939 film has an ominous character. His interpretation clearly corresponds with a remark by Peter Handke from the seventies in his book *Das Ende des Flanierens*: "Jean Renoir made the film before the Second World War, *La règle du jeu*, which perhaps offered the purest reflection of the feelings and desires of that era, which were still heavily disguised at the time."

14. Godard, *Histoire(s) du cinéma*, 1:29.

15. Godard, *Son + Image 1974–1991*, 165, ıuoted from the translation by Blümlinger, *Kino aus zweiter Hand*, 193–94.

16. Claude Lanzmann, "Ihr sollt nicht weinen," 175.

17. Godard, *Jean-Luc Godard*, 2:46.

18. Brody, *Everything Is Cinema*, 588.

19. "Dossier: Godard est'il anti-semite?," *La Règle du Jeu* 45 (January 2011): 199–252; or in English, Bernard-Henri Lévy, "Is Jean-Luc Godard Antisemitic?," *Huffington Post* (online), November 13, 15, and 18, 2010.

20. "One always discovers the archives a long time afterwards. . . . I have no proof of this at all, but I think that if I were to set out on a search with a good journalist, I would find pictures from the camps over the course of twenty years. You would see the deportees entering the camp and you would see the condition in which they left it." Quoted from the translation by Peter Geimer in Didi-Huberman, *Bilder trotz allem*, 201. The passage "the condition in which they left it" is insensitive, to say the least.

21. *L'Autre Journal* 12 (January 1985), quoted in Gérard Wajcman, "'Saint-Paul' Godard contre 'Moïse' Lanzmann," *Le Monde*, December 3, 1998.

22. Godard on the television program *L'Invité du jeudi*, September 17, 1981, quoted in Brody, *Everything Is Cinema*, 559.

23. Didi-Huberman, *Bilder trotz allem*, 213.

24. Godard, *Histoire(s) du cinéma*, 1:63.

25. Baecque speaks of a "pivotal moment." Brody sees it differently; for him it is the "third first film." Brody, *Everything Is Cinema*, 589.

26. In *Masculin féminin*, the name Églantine had appeared for the first time as a quote from Giraudoux, one of many indications of how strongly Godard's work is determined by his long-term memory.

27. See the four drafts in Godard, *Jean-Luc Godard*, 2:447–69.

28. Douglas Morrey, "History of Resistance/Resistance of History," *Studies in French Cinema* 2 (2003): 129.

29. Godard refers to the book for young readers *Le Voyage d'Edgar* (1938), by Édouard Peisson. He also has childhood memories of Brittany.

30. On the Brasillach trial and execution, see Kaplan, *The Collaborator*.

31. Sanbar, *Le Bien des absents*, 92–93.

32. On Godard as gardener, see Bergala, "Autoportrait de Godard en jardinier."

33. The self-sacrifice also alludes to Godard's interpretation of Valentin Feldman's death.

34. The concept of archaeology in this context was suggested notably by Michel Foucault, who taught at the Collège de France from 1970.

35. Godard, *Film Socialisme*, 109–10.

36. *Cahiers du cinéma*, no. 187 (February 1967): 38.

37. Conversation with Daniel Cohn-Bendit, *Télérama*, May 13, 2010, quoted in Conley and Kline, *A Companion to Jean-Luc Godard*, 541.

38. "Reste à savoir si une non-pensée contamine une pensée." Godard quotes from a text by Hadrien France-Lanord, "Heidegger: Une pensée irréductible à ses erreurs," *Le Monde*, January 28, 2014. The source reference comes from Ted Fendt, www.mubi.com, who has not only decoded the quotations in *Adieu au langage* with enormous meticulousness but also compared them down to the exact wording.

39. Godard had already spoken of his love of Jack London's dog story *Michael, Brother of Jerry* (the French title is *Michaël, chien de cirque*) when he met Anne Wiazemsky. Wiazemsky, *Jeune fille*, 186.

40. Derrida, *Das Tier, das ich also bin*, 22.

41. The question echoes postcolonial theory. *Can the Subaltern Speak?* (1988) is the title of a famous text by the Indian literary scholar Gayatri Chakravorty Spivak.

42. The passage, which remained untranslated for the German subtitles, deals with the tension between eye (image) and ear (word): "La terre abandonnée, surchargée de lettres de l'alphabet, étouffée sous les connaissances et plus guère d'oreilles qui soient à l'écoute."

Conclusion

1. Godard speaks of the "birth of writing" (*la naissance de l'écriture*) and in the same breath of "Chaldean writing" (*l'écriture chaldéen*). He probably means the

early advanced civilization of the Sumerians, which had its center in the city of Ur. According to the legends, the biblical Abraham came from Ur "in Chaldea."

2. The book *Clio* has not been translated into German. *Dialogue de l'histoire et de l'âme païenne* (1909) by Charles Péguy is a key text in Godard's oeuvre and, together with Walter Benjamin's "Angel of History" and the figure of Orpheus, forms the basis for his artistic understanding of history. Joseph Hanimann writes of a "floating permanent present" beyond historical causality that, for Péguy, comes to constitute history, and of a search for consequences, which is also quite a good fit for Godard. Hanimann, *Der Unzeitgenosse*, 188.

3. Fabrice Aragno, Godard's longtime collaborator during his late phase, described the production process on *Le Livre d'image*: Godard edits and designs the film on what from today's perspective looks like old, almost antique video equipment (presumably from the stocks he built up in the early 1970s) and then sends the material to Aragno, who prepares it for release in today's digital programs, with Godard closely supervising the effects.

Bibliography

Astruc, Alexandre. *Le Montreur d'ombres*. Paris: Bartillat, 1996.

Baecque, Antoine de. *Godard*. Paris: Pluriel, 2010.

Baecque, Antoine de. *La cinéphilie: Invention d'un regard, histoire d'une culture 1944–1968*. Paris: Fayard, 2003.

Bannasch, Bettina, and Almuth Hammer, eds. *Verbot der Bilder—Gebot der Erinnerung. Mediale Repräsentationen der Schoah*. Frankfurt am Main: Campus, 2004.

Bazin, André. "Découverte du cinéma: Défense de l'avant-garde." In *Le Cinéma français de la Libération à la Nouvelle Vague*, edited by Jean Narboni, 325–29. Paris: Cahiers du cinéma, 1984.

Bazin, André. *Was ist Film?* Berlin: Alexander Verlag, 2004.

Bellour, Raymond. "L'autre cinéaste: Godard écrivain." In *L'entre-images 2: Mots, Images*, 113–38. Paris: Éditions P. O. L., 2012.

Bergala, Alain. "Autoportrait de Godard en jardinier." In *Jean-Luc Godard: Documents*, edited by Nicole Brenez, David Faroult, Michael Temple, James Williams, and Michael Witt, 414–41. Paris: Éditions du Centre Pompidou, 2006.

Bergala, Alain. "Le nu chez Godard." In *Nul mieux que Godard*, 125–41. Paris: Cahiers du cinéma, 1999.

Blümlinger, Christa. *Kino aus zweiter Hand*. Berlin: Vorwerk 8, 2009.

Brenez, Nicole, David Faroult, Michael Temple, James Williams, and Michael Witt, eds. *Jean-Luc Godard: Documents*. Paris: Éditions du Centre Pompidou, 2006. [Catalog on the occasion of the exhibition *Voyage(s) en utopie. Jean-Luc Godard, 1946–2006*.]

Brody, Richard. *Everything Is Cinema: The Working Life of Jean-Luc Godard*. New York: Metropolitan Books, 2008.

Conley, Tom, and T. Jefferson Kline, eds. *A Companion to Jean-Luc Godard*. Chichester: Wiley-Blackwell, 2014.

Derrida, Jacques. *Das Tier, das ich also bin.* Vienna: Passagen Verlag, 2010.

Didi-Huberman, Georges. *Bilder trotz allem.* Munich: Fink, 2007.

Emmelhainz, Irmgard. *Jean-Luc Godard's Political Filmmaking.* Cham: Palgrave Macmillan, 2019.

Farber, Manny. *Negative Space.* New York: Praeger, 1971.

Godard, Jean-Luc. *Einführung in eine wahre Geschichte des Kinos.* Translated by Frieda Grafe and Enno Patalas. Munich: Hanser, 1981.

Godard, Jean-Luc. *Film Socialisme.* Berlin: Diaphanes, 2011.

Godard, Jean-Luc. *Godard, Kritiker: Ausgewählte Kritiken und Aufsätze über Film (1950–1970).* Edited by Frieda Grafe. Munich: Hanser, 1971.

Godard, Jean-Luc. *Hail Mary: Women and the Sacred in Film.* Edited by Maryel Locke and Charles Warren. Carbondale: Southern Illinois University Press, 1993.

Godard, Jean-Luc. *Histoire(s) du cinéma.* 4 vol. Munich: ECM Records, 1999.

Godard, Jean-Luc. *JLG/JLG: Autoportrait de décembre.* Paris: Éditions P. O. L, 1996.

Godard, Jean-Luc. *Liebe Arbeit Kino: Rette sich wer kann (Das Leben).* Berlin: Merve Verlag, 1981.

Godard, Jean-Luc. *Jean-Luc Godard.* Vol. 1, *1950–1984.* Edited by Alain Bergala. Paris: Cahiers du cinéma, 1984.

Godard, Jean-Luc. *Jean-Luc Godard.* Vol. 2, *1984–1998.* Edited by Alain Bergala. Paris: Cahiers du cinéma, 1998.

Godard, Jean-Luc. *Son + Image, 1974–1991.* Edited by Raymond Bellour with Mary Lea Bandy. New York: Museum of Modern Art, 1992.

Grafe, Frieda. "Die Klippschule der Nation: Godards Videoarbeiten fürs Fernsehen." In *Ausgewählte Schriften 3: Nur das Kino—40 Jahre mit der Nouvelle Vague,* edited by Enno Patalas, 97–106. Berlin: Brinkmann & Bose, 2003.

Grafe, Frieda, ed. *Nouvelle Vague.* Vienna: hundertjahrekino/Viennale, 1996.

Handke, Peter. *Das Ende des Flanierens.* Vienna: Davidpresse, 1976.

Hanimann, Joseph. *Der Unzeitgenosse: Charles Péguy—Rebell gegen die Herrschaft des Neuen.* Munich: Hanser Edition Akzente, 2017.

Hayward, Susan, and Ginette Vincendeau, eds. *French Film: Texts and Contexts.* 2nd ed. London: Routledge, 2000.

Kaplan, Alice. *The Collaborator: The Trial and Execution of Robert Brasillach.* Chicago: University of Chicago Press, 2001.

Kristensen, Stefan. *Jean-Luc Godard philosophe.* Lausanne: L'Age d'Homme, 2014.

Lanzmann, Claude. "Ihr sollt nicht weinen: Einspruch gegen Schindlers Liste." In "Der gute Deutsche," Dokumente zur Diskussion um Steven Spielbergs

"Schindlers Liste," *Deutschland*, edited by Christoph Weiss, 173–78. St. Ingbert: Röhrig Universitätsverlag, 1995.

Leroi-Gourhan, André. *Hand und Wort: Die Evolution von Technik*. Frankfurt am Main: Sprache und Kunst, Suhrkamp, 1980.

Liandrat-Guigues, Suzanne, and Jean-Louis Leutrat. *Godard simple comme bonjour*. Paris: L'Harmattan, 2004.

Linhart, Robert. *Eingespannt: Erzählung aus dem Innern des Motors*. Berlin: Verlag Klaus Wagenbach, 1978.

MacCabe, Colin. *Godard: A Portrait of the Artist at 70*. London: Bloomsbury, 2003.

Mary, Philippe. *La Nouvelle Vague et le cinéma d'auteur*. Paris: Seuil, 2006.

Moravia, Alberto. *Die Verachtung*. Berlin: Wagenbach, 2007

Morgan, Daniel. *Late Godard and the Possibilities of Cinema*. Oakland: University of California Press, 2012.

Pantenburg, Volker. *Film als Theorie: Bildforschung bei Harun Farocki und Jean-Luc Godard*. Bielefeld: Transcript, 2006.

Pantenburg, Volker. "Moi/Je/JLG." In *Automedialität: Subjektkonstitution in Schrift, Bild und neuen Medien*, edited by Jörg Dünne and Christian Moser, 261–82. Munich: Fink, 2008.

Pavsek, Christopher. *The Utopia of Film: Cinema and Its Futures in Godard, Kluge, and Tahimik*. New York: Columbia University Press, 2013.

Sanbar, Elias. *Le Bien des absents*. Arles: Actes Sud, 2001.

Sartre, Jean-Paul. "Die kinematographische Kunst." In *Mythos und Realität des Theaters*, 147–53. Reinbek bei Hamburg: Rowohlt, 1979.

Scemama, Céline. *Histoire(s) du cinéma de Jean-Luc Godard: La force faible d'un art*. Paris: L'Harmattan, 2006.

Sontag, Susan. *Gesten radikalen Willens*. Frankfurt am Main: Fischer Taschenbuch, 2011.

Stenzl, Jürg. *Jean-Luc Godard—musicien: Die Musik in den Filmen von Jean Luc Godard*. Munich: edition text + kritik, 2010.

Truffaut, François. *Briefe, 1945–1984*. Munich: Heyne, 1994.

Truffaut, François. *Die Lust am Sehen*. Edited and translated by Robert Fischer. Frankfurt am Main: n.p., 1999.

Vogl, Joseph. "Schöne gelbe Farbe: Godard mit Deleuze." In *Gilles Deleuze— Fluchtlinien der Philosophie*, edited by Friedrich Balke and Joseph Vogl, 252–65. Munich: Fink, 1996.

Wiazemsky, Anne. *Jeune fille*. Munich: C. H. Beck, 2009.

Witt, Michael. "Going through the Motions: Unconscious Optics and Corporeal Resistance in Miéville and Godard's *France/tour/détour/deux/enfants*." In *Gender and French Cinema*, edited by Alex Hughes and James S. Williams, 171–94. Oxford: Berg, 2001.

Witt, Michael. *Jean-Luc Godard, Cinema Historian*. Bloomington: Indiana University Press, 2013.

Witt, Michael. "On and Under Communication." In *A Companion to Jean-Luc Godard*, edited by Tom Conley and T. Jefferson Kline, 318–50. Chichester: Wiley-Blackwell, 2014.

Filmography

The following filmography was compiled by Regina Schlagnitweit in the course of her three-part Godard retrospective (2015 to 2017) at the Austrian Film Museum. The feature films are taken not from the traditional literature but, in most cases, from the actual film and video materials. Works made since 2017 and works by Godard that have resurfaced since have been added. The trailers for his films, which he often designed himself, were not recorded. Directed and scripted, unless otherwise stated: Jean-Luc Godard.

Cinematic Films

À bout de souffle (*Breathless*) (1960)
Script: Jean-Luc Godard, based on a story by François Truffaut; Cinematography: Raoul Coutard; Music: Martial Solal; Cast: Jean-Paul Belmondo, Jean Seberg, Daniel Boulanger, Jean-Pierre Melville, Jean Douchet. 35 mm, b/w, 89 minutes.

Le Petit Soldat (*The Little Soldier*) (1960, released 1963)
Camera: Raoul Coutard; Music: Maurice Leroux; Cast: Michel Subor, Anna Karina, Henri-Jacques Huet, Paul Beauvais, László Szabó, Jean-Luc Godard. 35 mm, b/w, 86 minutes.

Une femme est une femme (*A Woman Is a Woman*) (1961)
Camera: Raoul Coutard; Music: Michel Legrand; Cast: Jean-Claude Brialy, Anna Karina, Jean-Paul Belmondo, Marie Dubois, Jeanne Moreau. 35 mm, color, 83 minutes.

Vivre sa vie (*My Life to Live*) (1962)
Script: Jean-Luc Godard, Marcel Sacotte, after Sacotte's study *Où en est la prostitution*; Camera: Raoul Coutard; Music: Michel Legrand; Cast: Anna Karina, Sady Rebbot, André S. Labarthe, Henri Attal, Peter Kassovitz. 35 mm, b/w, 83 minutes.

Les Carabiniers (*The Carabineers*) (1963)
Script: Jean-Luc Godard, Jean Gruault, Roberto Rossellini, based on the stage play by Beniamino Joppolo; Cinematography: Raoul Coutard; Music: Philippe Arthuys; Cast: Marino Masè, Patrice Moullet, Geneviève Galéa, Catherine Ribeiro, Barbet Schroeder, Jean Gruault, Jean-Louis Comolli. 35 mm, b/w, 80 minutes.

Le Mépris (*Contempt*) (1963)
Script: Jean-Luc Godard after *Il disprezzo*, by Alberto Moravia; Cinematography: Raoul Coutard; Music: Georges Delerue; Cast: Brigitte Bardot, Michel Piccoli, Jack Palance, Fritz Lang, Jean-Luc Godard. 35 mm, color, 102 minutes.

Bande à part (*Band of Outsiders*) (1964)
Script: Jean-Luc Godard, based on *Fool's Gold* by Dolores Hitchens; Cinematography: Raoul Coutard; Music: Michel Legrand; Cast: Anna Karina, Claude Brasseur, Sami Frey, Danièle Girard, Louisa Colpeyn. 35 mm, color and b/w, 94 minutes.

Une femme mariée (*A Married Woman*) (1964)
Camera: Raoul Coutard; Music: Ludwig van Beethoven, Claude Nougaro; Cast: Macha Méril, Bernard Noël, Philippe Leroy, Roger Leenhardt, Christophe Bourseiller. 35 mm, b/w, 93 minutes.

Alphaville (1965)
Camera: Raoul Coutard; Music: Paul Misraki; Cast: Eddie Constantine, Anna Karina, Akim Tamiroff, Jean-Louis Comolli, Jean-Pierre Léaud. 35 mm, b/w, 99 minutes.

Pierrot le fou (1965)
Script: Jean-Luc Godard, based on *Obsession* by Lionel White; Cinematography: Raoul Coutard; Music: Antoine Duhamel; Cast: Jean-Paul Belmondo, Anna Karina, Henri Attal, Samuel Fuller, Jean-Pierre Léaud. 35 mm, color and b/w, 109 minutes.

Masculin féminin (*The Children of Marx and Coca-Cola*) (1966)
Script: Jean-Luc Godard, based on *La Femme de Paul* and *Le Signe* by Guy de Maupassant; Cinematography: Willy Kurant; Music: Jean-Jacques Debout; Cast: Jean-Pierre Léaud, Chantal Goya, Marlène Jobert, Michel Debord, Brigitte Bardot, François Hardy. 35 mm, b/w, 106 minutes.

Made in U. S. A. (1966)
Script: Jean-Luc Godard, based on *The Jugger* by Richard Stark; Cinematography: Raoul Coutard; Music: Robert Schumann, Ludwig van Beethoven, Mick Jagger and Keith Richards; Cast: Jean-Pierre Léaud, Anna Karina, Marianne Faithfull, László Szabó, Yves Afonso. 35 mm, color, 84 minutes.

Deux ou trois choses que je sais d'elle (*Two or Three Things I Know about Her*) (1967)
Screenplay: Jean-Luc Godard, based on the series of articles "La Prostitution dans les grands ensembles" by Catherine Vimenet; Camera: Raoul Coutard; Music: Ludwig van Beethoven; Cast: Marina Vlady, Joseph Gehrard, Anny Duperey, Jean Narboni, Juliet Berto, Claude Miller, Jean-Luc Godard. 35 mm, color, 87 minutes.

La Chinoise (*The Chinese Woman*) (1967)
Camera: Raoul Coutard; Music: Karl-Heinz Stockhausen, Franz Schubert, Antonio Vivaldi; Cast: Anne Wiazemsky, Jean-Pierre Léaud, Michel Séméniako, Lex de Bruijn, Juliet Berto. 35 mm, color, 96 minutes.

Loin du Viêt-nam (*Far from Vietnam*) (1967)
A collaborative film by Chris Marker (overall director), Alain Resnais, Jean-Luc Godard, William Klein, Joris Ivens, Agnès Varda, Claude Lelouch; Cinematography: Jean Boffety, Denis Clerval, Ghislain Cloquet, Willy Kurant, Alain Levent, Bruno Muel, Théo Robichet, Bernard Zitzermann. 35 mm, color and b/w, 116 minutes.

Week End (1967)
Camera: Raoul Coutard; Music: Antoine Duhamel, W. A. Mozart, Guy Béart; Cast: Mireille Darc, Jean Yanne, Jean-Pierre Kalfon, Valérie Lagrange, Jean-Pierre Léaud, Jean Eustache. 35 mm, color, 103 minutes.

Sympathy for the Devil / One plus One (1968)
Camera: Anthony Richmond; Music: Mick Jagger, Keith Richards; Cast: The Rolling Stones (Mick Jagger, Keith Richards, Brian Jones, Charlie Watts, Bill Wyman), Anne Wiazemsky, Ian Quarrier, Frankie Dymon. 35 mm, color, 101 minutes.

Un film comme les autres (*A Film like Any Other*) (1968)
Together with Groupe Dziga Vertov; Camera: Jean-Luc Godard, William Lubtchansky (unnamed); with three students from the University of Nanterre and two workers from Renault Flins. 16 mm, color and b/w, 102 minutes.

One P. M. (1968, released in 1971)
Together with D. A. Pennebaker and Richard Leacock; with Jean-Luc Godard, Anne Wiazemsky, Rip Torn, Eldridge Cleaver, Tom Hayden, the Jefferson Airplane. 16 mm, color, 80 minutes.

Le Gai Savoir (*Joy of Learning*) (1969)
Script: Jean-Luc Godard, after *Émile ou de l'éducation* by Jean-Jacques Rousseau; Camera: Georges Leclerc; Cast: Juliet Berto, Jean-Pierre Léaud; Narrating voice: Jean-Luc Godard. 35 mm, color, 92 minutes.

Pravda (1969)
Together with Jean-Henri Roger (Groupe Dziga Vertov); Camera: Paul Burron; with Věra Chytilová, Jean-Luc Godard. 16 mm, color, 60 minutes.

British Sounds (1969)
Together with Jean-Henri Roger (Groupe Dziga Vertov); Camera: Charles Stewart; with workers from the British Motor Company, students from Oxford and Essex, militant workers from the Dagenham area. 16 mm, color, 51 minutes.

Vent d'est (Wind from the East) (1969)
Together with Jean-Pierre Gorin (Groupe Dziga Vertov); Screenplay: Jean-Luc Godard, with Jean-Pierre Gorin, Daniel Cohn-Bendit, Gianni Barcelloni, Sergio Bazzini; Cinematography: Mario Vulpiani; Cast: Gian Maria Volontè, Götz George, Vanessa Redgrave, Anne Wiazemsky, Glauber Rocha. 16 mm, color, 93 minutes.

Lotte in Italia / Luttes en Italie (*Struggle in Italy*) (1970)
Together with Jean-Pierre Gorin (Groupe Dziga Vertov); Camera: Armand Marco; Cast: Cristiana Tullio-Altan, Anne Wiazemsky, Jerome Hinstin, Paolo Pozzesi. 16 mm, color, 59 minutes.

Vladimir et Rosa (1970)
Together with Jean-Pierre Gorin (Groupe Dziga Vertov); Camera: Armand Marco; Cast: Juliet Berto, Anne Wiazemsky, Yves Afonso, Jean-Pierre Gorin, Jean-Luc Godard. 16 mm, color, 96 minutes.

Tout va bien (*Just Great*) (1972)
Together with Jean-Pierre Gorin; Camera: Armand Marco; Cast: Yves Montand, Jane Fonda, Vittorio Caprioli, Pierre Oudry, Anne Wiazemsky. 35 mm, color, 95 minutes.

Letter to Jane: An Investigation about a Still (1972)
Together with Jean-Pierre Gorin; with a photo of Jane Fonda; Voices: with Jean-Pierre Gorin, Jean-Luc Godard. 16 mm, color, 52 minutes.

Ici et ailleurs (*Here and Elsewhere*) (1970 footage, released in 1976)
Together with Anne-Marie Miéville; Participation 1970: Jean-Pierre Gorin; Camera: William Lubtchansky; Music: Jean Schwarz. 16 mm, color, 54 minutes.

Numéro deux (*Number Two*) (1975)
Together with Anne-Marie Miéville; Camera: William Lubtchansky (35 mm), Gérard Martin (video); Music: Léo Ferré; with Sandrine Battistella, Pierre Oudry, Alexandre Rignault, Rachel Stefanopoli, Jean-Luc Godard. 35 mm, color, 88 minutes.

Comment ça va (How Is It Going?) (1976)
Together with Anne-Marie Miéville; Camera: William Lubtchansky; Music: Jean Schwarz; with Anne-Marie Miéville, Michel Marot. 16 mm, color, 78 minutes.

Sauve qui peut (la vie) (Every Man for Himself) (1980)
Script: Anne-Marie Miéville, Jean-Claude Carrière; Cinematography: William Lubtchansky, Renato Berta, Jean-Bernard Menoud; Music: Gabriel Yared; Cast: Isabelle Huppert, Jacques Dutronc, Nathalie Baye, Cécile Tanner, Roland Amstutz. 35 mm, color, 89 minutes.

Passion (1982)
Camera: Raoul Coutard; Music: W. A. Mozart, Antonin Dvořák, Maurice Ravel, Ludwig van Beethoven, Gabriel Fauré; Cast: Isabelle Huppert, Hanna Schygulla, Michel Piccoli, Jerzy Radziwiłowicz, Jean-François Stévenin, Myriem Roussel. 35 mm, color, 88 minutes.

Prénom Carmen (First Name: Carmen) (1983)
Script: Anne-Marie Miéville; Camera: Raoul Coutard, Jean Garcenot; Music: Ludwig van Beethoven, Tom Waits; Cast: Maruschka Detmers, Jacques Bonnaffé, Myriem Roussel, Hippolyte Girardot, Jean-Pierre Mocky, Jean-Luc Godard. 35 mm, color, 84 minutes.

Je vous salue, Marie (Hail Mary) (1985)
Camera: Jacques Firmann, Jean-Bernard Menoud; Music: W. A. Mozart, Antonin Dvořák; Cast: Myriem Roussel, Thierry Rode, Juliette Binoche, Philippe Lacoste, Manon Andersen. 35 mm, color, 79 minutes.

Détective (1985)
Script: Alain Sarde, Philippe Setbon, Anne-Marie Miéville, Jean-Luc Godard; Cinematography: Bruno Nuytten, Louis Bihi, Pierre Novion; Cast: Nathalie Baye, Johnny Hallyday, Jean-Pierre Léaud, Laurent Terzieff, Claude Brasseur, Alain Cuny, Emmanuelle Seigner, Julie Delpy. 35 mm, color, 98 minutes.

Soigne ta droite (Keep Your Right Up) (1987)
Camera: Caroline Champetier; Music: Les Rita Mitsouko; Cast: Jean-Luc Godard, Jane Birkin, Jacques Villeret, Michel Galabru, François Périer, Les Rita Mitsouko (Catherine Ringer, Fred Chichin). 35 mm, color, 81 minutes.

King Lear (1987)
Script: Jean-Luc Godard, based on the play by William Shakespeare; Cinematography: Sophie Maintigneux; Music: Ludwig van Beethoven, J. S. Bach; Cast: Jean-Luc Godard, Peter Sellars, Burgess Meredith, Molly Ringwald, Norman Mailer, Woody Allen, Julie Delpy, Leos Carax, Freddy Buache. 35 mm, color, 90 minutes.

Nouvelle vague (1990)
Camera: William Lubtchansky; Music: Paul Hindemith, Heinz Holliger, Meredith Monk, Werner Pirchner, Arnold Schönberg; Cast: Alain Delon, Domiziana Giordano, Laurence Côte, Christophe Odent, Roland Amstutz. 35 mm, color, 89 minutes.

Allemagne neuf zéro (*Germany Year 90 Nine Zero*) (1991)
Camera: Christophe Pollock, Andreas Erben, Stepan Benda; Music: W. A. Mozart, J. S. Bach, Igor Stravinsky, Paul Hindemith, Ludwig van Beethoven; Cast: Eddie Constantine, Hanns Zischler, Claudia Michelsen, André S. Labarthe. 35 mm, color, 62 minutes.

Hélas pour moi (*Oh, Woe Is Me*) (1993)
Camera: Caroline Champetier; Music: J. S. Bach, Dmitri Shostakovich, Ludwig van Beethoven, Pyotr Ilyich Tchaikovsky; Cast: Gérard Depardieu, Laurence Masliah, Bernard Verley, Roland Blanche, Louis-Do de Lencquesaing. 35 mm, color, 84 minutes.

JLG/JLG—Autoportrait de décembre (*JLG/JLG—Self-Portrait in December*) (1994)
Camera: Yves Pouliquen, Christian Jacquenod; with Jean-Luc Godard, Geneviève Pasquier, André S. Labarthe, Bernard Eisenschitz. 35 mm, color, 56 minutes.

For Ever Mozart (1996)
Camera: Christophe Pollock, Katell Dijan, Jean-Pierre Fedrizzi; Music: Ben Harper, György Kurtag, Ludwig van Beethoven, W. A. Mozart; Cast: Madeleine Assas, Bérangère Allaux, Ghalhia Lacroix, Vicky Messica. 35 mm, color, 84 minutes.

Éloge de l'amour (*In Praise of Love*) (2001)
Camera: Julien Hirsch, Christophe Pollock; Music: Maurice Jaubert, Arvo Pärt; Cast: Bruno Putzulu, Cécile Camp, Jean Davy, Françoise Verny, Noël Simsolo. 35 mm, color and b/w, 98 minutes.

Notre musique (*Our Music*) (2004)
Camera: Julien Hirsch; Cast: Sarah Adler, Nade Dieu, Rony Kramer, Simon Eine, Jean-Luc Godard. 35 mm, color, 80 minutes.

Film Socialisme (2010)
Camera: Fabrice Aragno, Paul Grivas; Cast: Jean Marc Stehlé, Catherine Tanvier, Patti Smith, Lenny Kaye, Alain Badiou. DCP/35 mm, color, 101 minutes.

Adieu au langage (2014)
Camera: Fabrice Aragno; Cast: Héloise Godet, Kamel Abdeli, Richard Chevallier; Narrating voice: Jean-Luc Godard. DCP [3D], color, 70 minutes.

Le Livre d'image (*The Image Book*) (2018)
Camera: Fabrice Aragno; Narrating voices: Jean-Luc Godard, Anne-Marie Miéville.
DCP, color, 84 minutes.

Long Television and Video Works (from 30 Minutes Runtime)

Six fois deux, sur et sous la communication (1976)
TV series. Together with Anne-Marie Miéville, 13 episodes. 1a: "Y'a personne," 1b: "Louison"; 2a: "Leçons de choses," 2b: "Jean-Luc"; 3a: "Photos et Cie," 3b: "Marcel"; 4a: "Pas d'histoires," 4b: "Nanas"; 5a: "Nous trois," 5b: "René(e)s"; 6a: "Avant et après," 6b: "Jacqueline et Ludovic." Edited episode: "Claude-Jean Philippe." Video, color, 623 minutes.

France, tour, détour, deux enfants (1978)
TV series. Together with Anne-Marie Miéville, 12 episodes. 1: "Obscur/Chimie"; 2: "Lumière/Physique"; 3: "Connu/Géométrie/Géographie"; 4: "Inconnu/Technique"; 5: "Impression/Dictée"; 6: "Expression/Français"; 7: "Violence/Grammaire"; 8: "Désordre/Calcul"; 9: "Pouvoir/Musique"; 10: "Roman/*Économie*"; 11: "Réalité/Logique"; 12: "Rêve/Morale." Video, color, 300 minutes.

Voyage à travers un film (*Sauve qui peut [la vie]*) (1981)
Extended and annotated TV version. With Isabelle Huppert, Christian Defaye, Jean-Luc Godard. Video, color, 98 minutes.

Scénario du film Passion (1982)
With Jean-Luc Godard. Video, color, 54 minutes.

Soft and Hard: Soft Talk on a Hard Subject between Two Friends (1985)
Together with Anne-Marie Miéville; with Jean-Luc Godard, Anne-Marie Miéville. Video, color, 49 minutes.

Grandeur et décadence d'un petit commerce de cinéma (*Rise and Fall of a Small Film Company*) (1986)
Script: Jean-Luc Godard, based on a novel by James Hadley Chase; Cinematography: Caroline Champetier, Serge Le François, Pierre Binggeli; Music: Béla Bartók, Leonard Cohen, Bob Dylan, Janis Joplin, Joni Mitchell; Cast: Jean-Pierre Léaud, Jean-Pierre Mocky, Marie Valéra, Nathalie Richard, Jean-Luc Godard. Video, color, 92 minutes.

Entretien entre Serge Daney et Jean-Luc Godard (1988)
Video, color, 129 minutes.

Histoire(s) du cinéma (1988–98)
TV series. Narrating Voice: Jean-Luc Godard; 8 episodes. 1A: "Toutes les histoires," 1B: "Une histoire seule"; 2A: "Seul le cinéma," 2B: "Fatale beauté"; 3A: "La

Monnaie de l'absolu," 3B: "Une Vague Nouvelle"; 4A: Le Contrôle de l'univers," 4B: "Les Signes parmi nous." Video, color, 263 minutes.

Le Rapport Darty (*The Darty Report*) (1989)
Together with Anne-Marie Miéville, on behalf of the electronics chain Darty. Video, color, 41 minutes.

Les Enfants jouent à la Russie (*The Kids Play Russian*) (1993)
Camera: Caroline Champetier; with Jean-Luc Godard, László Szabó, André S. Labarthe, Bernard Eisenschitz. Video, color, 60 minutes.

Deux fois cinquante ans de cinéma français (*2 × 50 Years of French Cinema*) (1995)
Together with Anne-Marie Miéville; with Jean-Luc Godard, Michel Piccoli, Cécile Reigher, Dominique Jacquet, Xavier Jougleux. Video, color, 50 minutes.

The Old Place (2000)
Together with Anne-Marie Miéville, commissioned by the Museum of Modern Art, New York. Video, color, 46 minutes.

Moments choisis des Histoire(s) du cinéma (*Selected Moments from the History of Cinema*) (2004)
Narrating voice: Jean-Luc Godard. Video/35 mm, color, 83 minutes.

Reportage amateur (maquette expo) (2006)
Together with Anne-Marie Miéville. Video, color, 46 minutes.

Vrai faux passeport (2006)
With Jean-Luc Godard. Video, color and b/w, 55 minutes.

Short Films, Episodes, Short Video Works (up to 30 Minutes)

Opération "Béton" (1954)
35 mm, b/w, 17 minutes.

Une femme coquette (*A Flirtatious Woman*) (1955)
Script: Jean-Luc Godard, after *Le Signe* by Guy de Maupassant; Cast: Maria Lysandre, Roland Tolma, Jean-Luc Godard. 16 mm, b/w, 10 minutes.

Tous les garçons s'appellent Patrick (Charlotte et Véronique) (*All the Boys Are Called Patrick*) (1957)
Script: Éric Rohmer; Cast: Jean-Claude Brialy, Anne Colette, Nicole Berger. 35 mm, b/w, 20 minutes.

Une histoire d'eau (*A Story of Water*) (1958)
Together with François Truffaut; Cast: Jean-Claude Brialy, Caroline Dim. 35 mm, b/w, 12 minutes.

Charlotte et son Jules (*Charlotte and Her Boyfriend*) (1958)
Cast: Jean-Paul Belmondo, Anne Colette, Gérard Blain. 35 mm, b/w, 13 minutes.

"La Paresse" (Sloth) (1962)
Episode from *Les Sept Péchés Capitaux* (*The Seven Deadly Sins*). Cast: Eddie Constantine, Nicole Mirel. 35 mm, b/w, 13 minutes.

"Il nuovo mondo" (The New World) (1963)
Episode from *RoGoPaG*. Cast: Alexandra Stewart, Jean-Marc Bory, Michel Delahaye, Jean-André Fieschi, André S. Labarthe. 35 mm, b/w, 20 minutes.

"Le Grand Escroc" (1964)
Episode from *Les Plus Belles Escroqueries du monde* (*The World's Most Beautiful Swindlers*). Cast: Jean Seberg, László Szabó, Charles Denner, Jean-Luc Godard. 35 mm, color, 24 minutes.

"Montparnasse-Levallois" (1965)
Episode from *Paris vu par*. Cast: Joanna Shimkus, Serge Davri, Philippe Hiquilly. 35 mm, color, 18 minutes.

"Anticipation, ou l'amour en l'an 2000" (1967)
Episode from *Le Plus Vieux Métier du monde*. Cast: Jacques Charrier, Anna Karina, Jean-Pierre Léaud. 35 mm, color, 20 minutes.

Mouchette (Bande-annonce) (1967)
Trailer for *Mouchette* by Robert Bresson. 35 mm, b/w, 2 minutes.

"L'Aller et retour des enfants prodigies" (1967, released in 1969)
Episode from *Amore e rabbia* (*Love and Anger*). Cast: Catherine Jourdan, Christine Guého, Nino Castelnuovo. 35 mm, color, 29 minutes.

Ciné-Tracts (1968)
Forty unscripted pamphlet films by various filmmakers. Issues no. 7, 8, 9, 10, 12, 13, 14, 15, 16, 23, and 40 are considered to be the work of Jean-Luc Godard. 16 mm, b/w, each approx. 3 minutes.

Schick after Shave (1971)
Advertising film (aftershave). Together with Jean-Pierre Gorin; with Juliet Berto. 16 mm, color, 1 minute.

Faut pas rêver / Quand la gauche aura le pouvoir (1977)
Music: Patrick Juvet; with Anne-Marie Miéville, Camille Miéville. Video, color, 4 minutes.

Scénario de Sauve qui peut (la vie) (1979)
Video, color, 21 minutes.

Une bonne à tout faire (1981)
With Andrei Konchalovsky, Vittorio Storaro. 35 mm, color, 10 minutes.

Lettre à Freddy Buache (*A Letter to Freddy Buache*) (1982)
With Jean-Luc Godard. 35 mm, color, 11 minutes.

Passion, le travail et l'amour: Introduction à un scénario (1982)
With Isabelle Huppert, Jerzy Radziwiłowicz, Hanna Schygulla, Jean-Claude Carrière. Video, color, 30 minutes.

Changer d'image: Lettre à la bien-aimée (1982)
With Jean-Luc Godard. Video, color, 10 minutes.

Petites notes à propos du film Je vous salue, Marie (1983)
With Myriem Roussel, Anne-Marie Miéville, Jean-Luc Godard. Video, color, 21
minutes.

BBNY (1985)
Advertising film (perfume). Video, color, 1 minute.

Meetin' WA (1986)
With Woody Allen, Jean-Luc Godard. Video, color, 26 minutes.

"Armide" (1987)
Epsiode from *Aria*. Camera: Caroline Champetier; Music: Jean-Baptiste Lully; Cast:
Marion Peterson, Valérie Allain. 35 mm, color, 11 minutes.

Closed (1987–88)
Series of commercials (fashion). Video, color, 7 minutes.

On s'est tous défilé (1988)
Commissioned by the fashion label Marithé + François Girbaud. Video, color, 13
minutes.

Puissance de la parole (*The Power of Words*) (1988)
Camera: Pierre Binggeli, Caroline Champetier; Cast: Jean Bouise, Laurence Côte,
Lydia Andréi, Jean-Michel Iribarren. Video, color, 26 minutes.

Le Dernier Mot (1988)
Video, color, 12 minutes.

Metamorphojean (1990)
Series of advertising films (fashion). Video, color, 2 minutes.

Pue Lulla (1990)
Commercial (trainers). Video, color, 1 minute.

"L'Enfance de l'art" (1990)
Episode from *Comment vont les enfants/How Are the Kids?* Together with Anne-Marie Miéville. Video/35 mm, color, 8 minutes.

"Pour Thomas Wainggai" (For Thomas Wainggai) (1991)
Episode from *Contre l'oubli* (*Against Forgetting*). Together with Anne-Marie Miéville. Video/35 mm, color, 3 minutes.

Parisienne People (1992)
Advertising film (cigarettes). Together with Anne-Marie Miéville. Video, color, 34 seconds.

Je vous salue, Sarajevo (1993)
Video, color, 2 minutes.

Le Monde comme il ne va pas (1996)
Contribution to a television talk show. Video, color, 4 minutes.

Plus Oh! (1996)
Music video. With France Gall. Video, color, 4 minutes.

Adieu au TNS (1998)
With Jean-Luc Godard. Video, color, 7 minutes.

De l'origine du XXIe siècle (*From the Origin of the 21st Century*) (2000)
Camera: Julien Hirsch. Video, color, 16 minutes.

"Dans le noir du temps" (2002)
Episode from *Ten Minutes Older: The Cello*. Together with Anne-Marie Miéville; Camera: Julien Hirsch. Video/35 mm, color, 11 minutes.

Liberté et patrie (*Liberty and Homeland*) (2002)
Together with Anne-Marie Miéville; Cast: Jean-Pierre Gos, Geneviève Pasquier. Video, color, 21 minutes.

Prières pour réfuzniks (2004)
Video, color, 10 minutes.

Ecce Homo (2006)
Video, color and b/w, 2 minutes.

Journal des réalisateurs (2008)
Video, color, 3 minutes.

Une catastrophe (2008)
Festival trailer (Viennale). Video/35 mm, color, 1 minute.

Il y avait quoi (pour Éric Rohmer) (2010)
Digital, color, 3 minutes.

"Les Trois Désastres" (2013)
Episode from *3×3D*. DCP [3D], color, 17 minutes.

"Le Pont de soupirs" (2014)
Episode from *Les Ponts de Sarajevo*. Digital, color, 8 minutes.

Khan Khanne, sélection naturelle (2014)
Digital, color, 9 minutes.

Bande-annonce pour le festival de Jihlava (2018)
Festival trailer. Digital, color, 1 minute.

Sang titre (2019)
Version of *Dans le noir du temps* for audiences in Gaza and Ramallah. Video, color, 10 minutes.

Additional Films

The following list includes the films mentioned in the book that are not by Jean-Luc Godard. It gives the original title (as it appears in the text), the official distribution title, the year of the premiere, and the director. In a few cases, English distribution titles are mentioned in the text—these can also be found in the list, with references back to the original titles.

Apocalypse Now (1979, Francis Ford Coppola)
Après la réconciliation (2000, Anne-Marie Miéville)
L'Atalante/Atalante (1934, Jean Vigo)
Au hasard Balthazar (1966, Robert Bresson)
Barbarella (1968, Roger Vadim)
The Battle of Stalingrad. See *Stalingradskaya bitva*
Battleship Potemkin. See *Bronenosec Potemkin*
Le Beau Serge (1958, Claude Chabrol)
Bells from the Deep—Faith and Superstition in Russia (1993, Werner Herzog)
Ben-Hur (1925, Fred Niblo)
The Big Sleep (1946, Howard Hawks)
Birth of a Nation (1915, D. W. Griffith)
Bitter Victory (1957, Nicholas Ray)
Bonjour Tristesse (1958, Otto Preminger)
Bonnie and Clyde (1967, Arthur Penn)
Bronenosec Potemkin / Battleship Potemkin (1925, Sergei Eisenstein)
Le Chant des mariées / The Wedding Song (2008, Karin Albou)
Citizen Kane (1941, Orson Welles)
Cléo de 5 à 7 (1962, Agnès Varda)
Les Cousins (1959, Claude Chabrol)
Człowiek z żelaza / The Man of Iron (1981, Andrzej Wajda)

Człowiek z marmuru / *The Man of Marble* (1977, Andrzej Wajda)

La Dentellière / *The Lace Maker* (1977, Claude Goretta)

Les Dernières Vacances / *The Last Vacation* (1948, Roger Leenhardt)

Le Dernier Métro / *The Last Metro* (1980, François Truffaut)

Le Dinosaure et le bébé (1964/67, André S. Labarthe)

La dolce vita (1960, Federico Fellini)

The English Patient (1996, Anthony Minghella)

Ėntuziazm (Simfonija Donbassa) (1930, Dziga Vertov)

Et Dieu créa la femme / *And God Created Woman* (1956, Roger Vadim)

The Fall of Berlin. See *Padenie Berlina*

For a Few Dollars More. See *Per qualche dollaro in più*

Forty Guns (1957, Samuel Fuller)

For Whom the Bell Tolls (1943, Sam Wood)

Die freudlose Gasse (1925, Georg Wilhelm Pabst)

Galia (1966, Georges Lautner)

Germania, anno zero / *Germany Year Zero* (1948, Roberto Rossellini)

Ginger e Fred / *Ginger & Fred* (1986, Federico Fellini)

The Godfather (1972, Francis Ford Coppola)

The Godfather: Part II (1974, Francis Ford Coppola)

The Godfather: Part III (1990, Francis Ford Coppola)

La Grande Illusion (1937, Jean Renoir)

The Grapes of Wrath (1940, John Ford)

Hannah and Her Sisters (1986, Woody Allen)

The Harder They Fall (1956, Mark Robson)

Heaven's Gate (1980, Michael Cimino)

Hiroshima, mon amour (1959, Alain Resnais)

Un homme et une femme / *A Man and a Woman* (1966, Claude Lelouch)

How Can I Love (A Man When I Know He Doesn't Want Me) (1983, Anne-Marie Miéville)

L'Important, c'est d'aimer / *The Most Important Thing: Love* (1975, Andrzej Żuławski)

Journal d'un curé de campagne / *Diary of a Country Priest* (1951, Robert Bresson)

Jules et Jim / *Jules and Jim* (1962, François Truffaut)

Klute (1971, Alan J. Pakula)

The Lace Maker. See *La Dentellière*

The Last Tango in Paris. See *Ultimo tango a Parigi*

Le Livre de Marie / *The Book of Mary* (1985, Anne-Marie Miéville)

Lola (1961, Jacques Demy)

Lou n'a pas dit non / *Lou Didn't Say No* (1994, Anne-Marie Miéville)

M (1931, Fritz Lang)

The Maltese Falcon (1941, John Huston)

A Man and a Woman. See *Un homme et une femme*

The Man of Iron. See *Człowiek z żelaza*

The Man of Marble. See *Człowiek z marmuru*

Man of the West (1958, Anthony Mann)

The Man Who Knew Too Much (1956, Alfred Hitchcock)

The Matrix (1999, The Wachowski Brothers)

Méditerranée (1963, Jean-Daniel Pollet)

Metropolis (1927, Fritz Lang)

Moi, un noir / *I, a Negro* (1957, Jean Rouch)

Mon cher sujet / *My dearest subject* (1988, Anne-Marie Miéville)

Monterey Pop (1968, D. A. Pennebaker)

Mueda, Memória e Massacre / *Mueda, Memory and Massacre* (1979, Ruy Guerra)

Nachtblende. See *L'Important, c'est d'aimer*

Die Nibelungen (1924, Fritz Lang)

No Sad Songs for Me (1950, Rudolph Maté)

Nous sommes tous encore ici / *We're All Still Here* (1997, Anne-Marie Miéville)

La Nuit américaine / *Day for Night* (1973, François Truffaut)

Nuit et brouillard / *Night and Fog* (1956, Alain Resnais)

On the Waterfront (1954, Elia Kazan)

Otto e mezzo / *8½* (1963, Federico Fellini)

Padenie Berlina / *The Fall of Berlin* (1949, Mikhail Čiaureli)

Paisà (1946, Roberto Rossellini)

Paris nous appartient / *Paris Belongs to Us* (1959/61, Jacques Rivette)

La Passe du diable / *The Devil's Pass* (1958, Jacques Dupont and Pierre Schoendoerffer)

Passe montagne / *Mountain Pass* (1978, Jean-François Stévenin)

La Passion de Jeanne d'Arc / *The Passion of Joan of Arc Orleans* (1928, Carl Theodor Dreyer)

Per qualche ollar in più / *For a Few Dollars More* (1965, Sergio Leone)

A Place in the Sun (1951, George Stevens)

Les Plages d'Agnès / *The Beach of Agnès* (2008, Agnès Varda)

Le Plaisir / *House of Pleasure* (1952, Max Ophüls)

Playtime (1967, Jacques Tati)

Possession (1981, Andrzej Żuławski)

Procès de Jeanne d'Arc / *The Trial of Joan of Arc* (1962, Robert Bresson)

Pulp Fiction (1994, Quentin Tarantino)

Le Quadrille (1950, Jacques Rivette)

Les Quatre cents coups / *The Four Hundred Blows* (1959, François Truffaut)
La Règle du jeu / *The Rules of the Game* (1939, Jean Renoir)
La Religieuse / *The Nun* (1966, Jacques Rivette)
RoGoPaG (1963, Roberto Rossellini, Jean-Luc Godard, Pier Paolo Pasolini, Ugo
    Gregoretti)
Roma, città aperta / *Rome, Open City* (1945, Roberto Rossellini)
Sait-on jamais / *No Sun in Venice* (1957, Roger Vadim)
Schindler's List (1993, Steven Spielberg)
Les Sept Péchés Capitaux / *The Seven Deadly Sins* (1962, Sylvain Dhomme & Max
    Douy, Édouard Molinaro, Jean-Luc Godard, Jacques Demy, Roger Vadim,
    Philippe de Broca, Claude Chabrol)
Sierra de Teruel (Espoir) / *Days of Hope* (1939/45, André Malraux)
Le Signe du lion / *The Sign of Leo* (1959/62, Éric Rohmer)
Soigne ton gauche / *Watch Your Left* (1936, René Clément)
Sous le soleil de Satan / *Under the Sun of Satan* (1987, Maurice Pialat)
Stalingradskaja bitva / *The Battle of Stalingrad* (1949, Vladimir Petrov)
Strangers on a Train (1951, Alfred Hitchcock)
Tagebuch eines Landpfarrers. See *Journal d'un curé de campagne*
Terminator Salvation (2009, McG)
The Third Man (1949, Carol Reed)
Tirez sur le pianiste / *Shoot the Piano Player* (1960, François Truffaut)
Totò contro Maciste (1962, Fernando Cerchio)
Two American Audiences (1968, D. A. Pennebaker & Mark Woodcock)
Ultimo tango a Parigi / *The Last Tango in Paris* (1972, Bernardo Bertolucci)
Viaggio in Italia / *Journey to Italy* (1954, Roberto Rossellini)
Violette Nozière (1978, Claude Chabrol)
Westbound (1959, Budd Boetticher)

Index

Note: Page numbers in italics indicate illustrations.

Fonda, Henry, 90

Fonda, Jane, 87; Godard's open letter
to, 89–90; in *Tout va bien* (film), x,
88

Fondazione Prada, Milan, Godard
exhibition at, 4, 6

"fool"/"idiot" of cinema, Godard as,
130, *130*, 132–33, 134, 140, 141, 162

Fool's Gold (Hitchens), 53

For a Few Dollars More (film), 84

"For a Metahistory of Film" (Frampton), 153

For Ever Mozart (film), 143–44, 145,
162, 200

Forty Guns (film), 61

For Whom the Bell Tolls (film), 31

Foucault, Michel, 62, 100, 108–9

The Four Hundred Blows (film). See
Les Quatre cents coups (film)

Fourier, Charles, 87

Fox, press releases for, 22

fragmentation, techniques of: in *Une
femme est une femme* (film), 42; in
Une femme mariée (film), 57. See
also *décomposer*

Frampton, Hollis, 153, 173

France: cinephilia in, postwar culture
of, 10, 12; film criticism in 1950s,
11–12; liberation of, Godard as child
of, 9, 176; policy of cultural exception in, 118; postwar, anti-American
sentiment in, 16. *See also* Grenoble;
Paris

France, tour, détour, deux enfants
(TV series), x, 101–2, 107–10, 201;
German-language transcription
of, 185n13; and *Je vous salue, Marie*
(film), 122; and *Passion* (film), 118;
at Rotterdam Film Festival, 148

Franco, Francisco, 100

Franju, Georges, 65

French Communist Party (PCF), 72,
99–100

Freud, Sigmund, 122

Die freudlose Gasse (film), 15

Frey, Sami, 54

From the Origin of the 21st Century
(film), 158, 205

Fuller, Samuel, 61–62

Le Gai Savoir (The *Joy of Learning*)
(film), 78–79, 80, 86, 185n19, 197

Galia (film), 74

Gallimard (publishing company), 131,
151

Garaudy, Roger, 156

Gauche-Droite (*Left-Right*) (TV series),
156

Gaumont (media group), 147

Gazette du cinéma (magazine), 14;
Godard's contributions to, 14, 15

Geneva, Lake, Godard's childhood on,
ix, 9–10, 135

Germania, anno zero (film), 11

Germany: Godard's affinity with, 6, 15,
37; Godard's film about, x, 136–38,
139, 200

Germany at Zero (film), 137

Germany Year 90 Nine Zero (film). See
Allemagne neuf zéro (film)

Geva 36, Godard's use of, 30

Ğiaureli, Mikhail, 12

Gilliatt, Penelope, 106

Ginger e Fred (film), 135

Giraudoux, Jean, 137, 141, 152, 159

Giroud, Françoise, 183n14

Giscard D'Estaing, Valéry, 101

Globus, Yoram, 128

Nestroy, Johann, 88
Netherlands, Godard's work in, 148–49
Newman, David, 60
New Yorker (magazine), portrait of
 Godard in, 106
Die Nibelungen (film), 49
Niblo, Fred, 186n13
Niépce, Joseph Nicéphore, x, 175
Nizan, Paul, 72
Nobel Prize, 6
Noël, Bernard, 56
Norris, Chuck, 128
North Vietnam: Godard's desire
 to travel to, 76, 89; Jane Fonda's
 visit to, 89–90. *See also* Vietnam
 War
No Sad Songs for Me (film), 16
Notes from Sarajevo (Goytisolo), 144
Notre musique (*Our Music*) (film),
 163–66, 167, 200
Nous sommes tous encore ici (*We're All
 Still Here*) (film), 127
Nouvelle Vague: *À bout de souffle*
 (film) and, 27, 29, 31, 35, 44; apolitical bend of, *Le Petit Soldat* (film) as
 response to accusations of, 36;
 founding films of, 19, 27–29;
 Godard as member of, 4, 135;
 Godard's films associated with,
 23–24, 27, 29, 184n1; Italian forerunner of, 46; journalistic organ
 of, ix, 15; Mitterand's election and,
 118; and Monogram Pictures (film
 studio), 26; origins of term, 183n14;
 pioneers of, 27, 132; *Les Quatre cents
 coups* (film) and, 22, 64; social
 movement giving rise to, 41; triumph of, 49
Nouvelle vague (film), x, 135–36, 200

nudity, in Godard's films, 83; in *Adieu
 au langage*, 171; in *British Sounds*,
 83; in *Passion*, 117; in *Six fois deux*,
 105
La Nuit américaine (film), 90
Nuit et brouillard (film), 59
Numéro deux (*Number Two*) (film),
 97–99, 198
The Nun (Diderot), 65
"Il nuovo mondo" (episode), 45–46,
 203

Objectif49 (film club), 12, 14
Obsession (White), 61
Odile (Godard), 21
Odile (Queneau), 53
Odyssey (Homer): cinema compared
 to, 5; references to, in Godard's
 films, 47, 48, 49, 50, 51, 61
Oh, Woe Is Me (film). See *Hélas pour
 moi* (film)
The Old Place (film), 158, 202
omnibus films, Godard's contributions
 to, 44–45, 76–77
One Does Not Play with Love (Musset),
 143
One plus One (film). See *Sympathy for
 the Devil* (film)
One P. M. (film), 197
On s'est tous défilé (advertising film),
 204
On the Ground and First Floor
 (Nestroy), 88
Opération "Béton" (film), 19–21, 202
Ophüls, Max, 158, 174
*The Origin of the Family, Private Prop-
 erty and the State* (Engels), 75
Origins of Totalitarianism (Arendt),
 references to, 127

WISCONSIN FILM STUDIES